CW01160944

Man About the House
George and Mildred

The Definitive Companion

Mildred: I went to the beauty parlour this afternoon.
George: Oh yeah, shut were they?

Dedicated to the memory of Yootha, Johnnie, Doug and Roy.

Man About the House George and Mildred

The Definitive Companion

*To Laura
Best wishes
[signature]*

Tex Fisher

Deck Chair Publishing

First published in Great Britain in 2010 by Deck Chair Publishing
www.deckchairpublishing.co.uk

1

Limited Edition Number:

The right of Tex Fisher to be identified as the author of this work has been asserted to him in accordance with the Copyright, Designs and Patents Act 1988.

Text © Tex Fisher

Man About the House © Thames Television
Johnnie Mortimer, Brian Cooke

George and Mildred © Thames Television
Johnnie Mortimer, Brian Cooke

No part of this publication may be reproduced, stored in a retrieval system, or transmitted in any form, or by any means; mechanical, electrical, photocopying, scanning, recording or otherwise, without prior written permission from the copyright owner.

ISBN-13: 978-0956563408

Printed and Bound by CPI Antony Rowe, Chippenham

Every effort has been made to contact all copyright holders. The author and publisher will be glad to rectify any omissions.

Image Credits: Johnnie Mortimer (Estate), Tex Fisher
Back Cover Quote: M Sykes, (Reader)
Cover Design: Tex Fisher

Contents

Introduction i

Getting the Flatmates Assembled 1
Putting the Ropers Centre Stage 6
Behind the Scenes - The Production Process 11
The Writers - Brian Cooke & Johnnie Mortimer 15
Under Direction of - Peter Frazer-Jones 18
Character Profiles 19
Main Cast 23

Man About the House 42
Summary 43
Episode Guide 45
Opening Titles 85
Closing Titles 88
The Film 89
The Film Theme Tune 93

George and Mildred 95
Summary 96
Episode Guide 97
Filming Locations 135
Opening Titles 137
The Film 140
While the Cat's Away - Stage Play 144

Appendix 147
Complete A-Z of Support Cast 148
Going Places - Transportation Used 206
Kensington and Hampton Wick Good Pub Guide 208
Robin's Nest 211
Transatlantic Tributes - Sitcoms Overseas 213
Thinking About Sitcoms 215
Test your Knowledge – A Quiz for the Bog! 217
1970's Phrase Dictionary 220
Acknowledgements 223

Introduction

The word 'comedy' is thrown about far too much these days. Some of the turgid tripe that television production companies have the gall to turn out is beyond summary in terms of it's awfulness. With a Country in such a dire need of a good chortle, Britain finds itself looking back in time for humour, casting an eye back to the supreme comedic days of the 'Golden Age of Television' in the 1960's and 1970's.

The most gleaming of this gold stands out a mile as the excellent series written by Johnnie Mortimer and Brian Cooke, *Man About the House* (1973-1976) and *George and Mildred* (1976-1980). With a mixture of everything, from ripe sexual innuendo to deepest poignancy, these shows weren't just sitcoms, they were an example of society, a piece of a national institutionalism. A snippet of a nostalgic time no longer imaginable, where the Sinclair Pocket Calculator was cutting edge, and a Berni-Inn seemed posh. These gems of British screen history paint a picture of a different world.

The comedy writing is clever and classy, written with a university wit rather than a brash irreverence of social defiance. Completely devoid of expletives, excessive nudity and violence, these series were the very essence of family viewing. Over 20 Million people tuned in weekly. Equal to the population of Australia.

Almost forty years later, these icons have not lost their appeal, and remain hilarious. Still incomparable to twenty-first century viewing, *Man About the House* and *George and Mildred* are still at the top of their game.

In my humble opinion, some of the greatest television ever made.

Tex Fisher, May 2010

Getting the Flatmates Assembled...

Johnnie Mortimer and Brian Cooke were two of the most respected comedy writers of the 1960's and 1970's. Their credits included scripts for Frankie Howerd, Tommy Cooper and Kenneth Williams, and one of their earliest television successes came with the ITV series *Father Dear Father* starring Patrick Cargill. In 1973, an idea for a new programme was sparked. This fresh sitcom would be based around three young adults sharing an upstairs flat in a house run by landlords George and Mildred Roper, at 6 Myddleton Terrace in the trendy borough of South Kensington, London.

This idea formed the base of *Man About the House*, a show that would become one of the most popular series of the 1970's and develop further into two more highly successful programmes; *George and Mildred* and *Robin's Nest*. From the initial episode, *Man About the House* was warmly received by the television public. The show's younger viewers could easily identify with randy Robin and his two adorable flatmates Chrissy and Jo, whilst the older viewers found a familiarity in the discordance of middle-aged landlords, the Ropers. Revelling in unrivalled popularity, *Man About the House* **was** the 1970's.

The Idea
As with any successful sitcom, the comedy behind *Man About the House* reflected the state of society at the time, and can find its inspiration rooted in the similarities to the then culture.

Brian Cooke and Johnnie Mortimer saw the potential to write a sitcom which mirrored the ever increasing trend of mixed-sex flat sharing, gaining stimulus from advertisements in the evening paper which appealed for additional tenants to share a living space. 'We both noticed how many small ads there were for girls sharing with guys', Brian Cooke explained in a 1999 interview. 'We thought there was potential there, certainly for sexual tension in comedy'.

From the initial spark, Johnnie and Brian moved on to consider who should star in their new creation, developing the comedy specifically around it's cast. 'Johnnie and Brian always used to base their shows on it's stars, rather than call on their own experience to write about', explained Johnnie Mortimer's widow, Jytte. 'They used to think who they wanted in the show and then build up the plot around those people'.

'*Father Dear Father* came around in that way. Johnnie and Brian had worked with Patrick Cargill before and were keen to use him again. They always liked to suit the person to the comedy'.

Casting

When it came to suiting actors to their comedy, and casting the parts for *Man About the House*, the writers gained assistance from the director and producer, Peter Frazer-Jones and the executive producer at Thames television, Philip Jones. Correct casting was crucial to allow the characters to develop and blend harmoniously, and true to their previous habit, Johnnie Mortimer and Brian Cooke were keen to use actors they had worked with previously.

Richard O'Sullivan was to be the main star of the show and played cookery student Robin Tripp. 'Richard was the main inspiration for the series', explained Jytte Mortimer, 'It was built around him in the lead. Richard had worked with Johnnie and Brian in a small role in *Father Dear Father* and they wanted to use him again'. Richard had also appeared in Cooke and Mortimer's sitcom *Alcock and Gander* in 1972, and his comedy ridden portrayal of Richard Gander meant that they had no reservations in putting him in the front line of their new invention.

Sally Thomsett was the first choice to play Robin's flatmate Jo, and was chosen by Cooke and Mortimer after they saw her in a memorable 1972 television commercial for Bovril.

Paula Wilcox was chosen as Chrissy by Philip Jones, head of light entertainment at Thames Television. 'After *The Lovers,* which was incredibly popular, Philip Jones asked for a meeting with me', Paula explained. 'We had lunch and he told me about a new series Brian Cooke and Johnnie Mortimer were writing about a young man and a woman who share a flat in a purely platonic way. It seemed a brilliant idea for a show, it didn't seem edgy to me, now that there were two girls in the flat-share, the situation became less threatening'.

With three young single persons living practically out of each other's shoes, the plan for a 'sitcom based around sexual tensions' was steadily building, and was turning into a fairly ground-breaking situation comedy. In order to prevent this formula from turning too promiscuous and sparking controversy among viewers, *Man About the House* needed an additional ingredient to react against the flat-sharers, and brought in landlords, the Ropers. 'It had never been done before', director Peter Frazer-Jones explained in 2001. 'There we had these two girls living with a feller. We had to bring in the landlords downstairs to break things up'.

George and Mildred Roper were the sitting landlords of the house, and became one of the most popular aspects of the show. Brian Murphy and Yootha Joyce were selected for these parts, having worked with each other in the past at the renowned Joan Littlewood's Theatre Workshop,

Getting the Flatmates Assembled...

however their successful reunion in *Man About the House* called for some divine intervention. 'The decision to cast me and Yootha together was serendipity more than anything', Brian Murphy recalled. 'I had worked in an episode of Johnnie and Brian's *Alcock and Gander* with Beryl Reid, Richard O'Sullivan and John Cater. I was cast in a role of a seedy old gent who answers an advert in a window for a masseur and I got the wrong end of the stick with the sexual connotations, it was in fact an advert for a typist and there was much hilarity over the results - it made a very funny scene'.

'Apparently I played the seedy gent so well, that Johnnie and Brian suggested me for the seedy husband in *Man About the House*. Peter Frazer-Jones didn't know me, but he knew Yootha Joyce and suggested her for the wife, a rather glamorous and snobbish wife and me a working class husband. Neither Brian nor Johnnie or even Peter knew we had worked with each other at the Theatre Workshop and a few other television programmes. It was a great joy when I realised that Yootha was going to be the wife, and Yootha said it was a great joy for her when she knew I was to be the husband'.

'We did some very funny scenes together which was a great surprise to everyone, as the chemistry was already there. The others had to work harder to find and develop their characters but we seemed to just drop in like old sinners'.

Costume and Make-Up
The cast were in place, and the fresh challenge for the production team was to turn them into the characters they were playing.

Yootha Joyce had to dampen down her colourful wardrobe and change her style to suit the dowdy chic Mildred in both *Man About the House* and *George and Mildred*. She had a significant influence in what she wore and worked closely with the costume designers to personally chose the material for Mildred. Outside of the studios, Joyce was famed for her vibrant dress, but the downtrodden Mildred called for more bland attire.

Sally Thomsett also looked after her own costume. A self-confessed shopping addict, Thomsett used her production clothing budget to purchase one stunning outfit for each episode from the fashionable shops that lined West London. She personally subsidised her outfits, and at the end of a series, purchased all her outfits off Thames Television at a reduced price so she could keep them for herself.

Hairdressing was the second part of the make-up process. After a few series of going through rigorous hairstyling before each recording, both Paula Wilcox and Yootha Joyce had a selection of 'Chrissy' and 'Mildred' wigs that they used to don over the course of the sitcom. Sally Thomsett had to undergo hair lightening to become the dazzling blonde Jo, and for this, she travelled to fashionable hairstylist Daniel Galvin in Chelsea to suffer hours of blonde highlighting.

The men of the sitcom needed little attention. Away from the studios, Richard O'Sullivan's style remained similar to that of Robin's. Brian Murphy actually had to lose hair to become George Roper. Outside the sitcom he wore a hairpiece, but to prepare as the balding George, this had to be removed.

Music
The man behind the theme tune for *Man About the House* was Johnny Hawksworth. No stranger to composing for Thames television, he had previously been responsible for the music of the opening Thames Skyline ident, 'Salute to Thames'.

Born in 1924, Hawksworth began his musical career as a double bass player in the Ted Heath band and worked his way into television on a commission basis. Throughout the 1960's and the 1970's, he produced countless musical scores for Thames television programmes, including *Roobarb* as well as *And Mother Makes Five*. Hawksworth emigrated to Australia in the late 1980's where he worked as a freelance pianist.

The brassy sounding theme tune to *Man About the House* was not specifically written for the programme, but was instead a piece of library music entitled 'Up to Date', which had been written and composed by Hawksworth for production company De Wolfe Music much earlier. The tune was performed by the Simon Park Orchestra, who had previously enjoyed a lingering twenty-two weeks in the top 40 singles chart with 'Eye Level', the opening theme for Dutch detective show *Van Der Valk*.

The 'Up to Date' theme became a popular track, and remains a sought after tune for television productions, recently finding frequent use as incidental music on Channel 4's *Come Dine With Me*.

Strip Tease
Look-In magazine featured regular comic strip versions of *Man About the House*, drawn by Italian artist Arnaldo Putzu, who was also behind the drawing board for the majority of Hammer Horror film posters. The likeness of the cartoons to the cast was a popular laughing point. 'They were very funny drawings', remarked Sally Thomsett.

Getting the Flatmates Assembled...

Success and End

Man About the House came consistently high in audited viewing figures over it's three year run. The steps Robin took to win over Chrissy, Jo's naivety and questionable intelligence, and the strained relationship of George and Mildred, were of a substance which viewers found hilarious.

'I think we were fairly confident that the series would be successful', explained Paula Wilcox. 'Everybody on the production side had such great credits; they had been working on successful television comedy for a long time, and knew exactly how to produce something that was classy, well shot and fun to do'. But some cast members didn't expect the sudden success the programme achieved. 'I thought it was very funny, but didn't realise it would be so popular', recalled Sally Thomsett. 'It was manic, there were many events, and we usually all went to them together'.

When it was announced in 1976 that *Man About the House* would come to an end, the nation wept. The show was concluded abruptly within it's sixth and final series, seeing Chrissy marrying Robin's brother, Norman. But after thirty-nine episodes, everyone involved felt that it was time to move on to something new. 'I was quite glad when we all called a halt to the series' said Paula Wilcox, 'I felt there was a danger of the ideas running out. It's great that we left the series at a high point, when all the ratings were still enormous'. Sally Thomsett agrees. 'I think we could have had one more series but no more after that', she explained.

Spinning Off

Thankfully for viewers, the end of *Man About the House* would not bring the end of Robin, Mildred, and George. These characters, which had been built up over the run of the series, remained popular with audiences, so the decision to develop them further in their own series seemed an opportunity too good to miss. Brian Cooke told TV Times in 1976 how 'They were so well loved by the public, we couldn't waste characters like that. If we hadn't used them again in something else, then somebody else would have'. Thames television were also keen to repeat the success enjoyed by *Man About the House* and remained on side to develop some fresh situations, sending Richard O'Sullivan to *Robin's Nest,* and posting George and Mildred Roper to aptly named *George and Mildred.*

Putting the Ropers Centre Stage

Five seasons of *George and Mildred* were produced at Teddington Studios between 1976 and 1979. The viewing ratings topped a staggering 20.8 Million individual viewers in it's prime, with even the repeats being in the top five most watched programmes. Ironically it turned out to be the spin-off to *Man About the House* that reigned in the most viewers, and *George and Mildred* was the most watched television programme of 1976.

'Yootha and myself always gelled well and the writers and directors raised their eyebrows and thought of all the mileage they could get from us', Brian Murphy recalled. 'It became obvious as it went along in *Man About the House* that the Ropers were just as popular as the youngsters. We were told that there was a lot of interest in our characters, the feedback was excellent for the whole programme but especially for us two'.

'Philip Jones, who was the head of light entertainment said that "when we finish with *Man About the House*, we're going to run with *George and Mildred*, the writers would love to do that". As old pros, me and Yootha thought to ourselves that it would be nice to do our own series, but we didn't believe it would happen, but then it did.'

'In fact it was confirmed to us at some point when we were getting to the end of *Man About the House*. We found out from the set carpenters and the various backstage workers rather than from the producers. They said to us how "It's a great thing you're going to get your own series". We both said "well, it will be when we do get it", but they replied "What do you mean, we're building the sets for it now!". So they were going ahead with it and we were getting our own series'.

'The audience reacted really well. Over 20 million tuned in to the first episode, it got huge acclaim, great reviews and the audience loved it. Normally only six episodes are made for the first series, but we had made ten episodes and all ten were at number one of the viewing figures, so it's no doubt that we were a success. We had all the same writers and director behind us and it seemed that we were on a winning run. We were wanted everywhere, to open shops and to appear at charity events. It was bigger than us!'.

Casting New Faces
Yootha Joyce and Brian Murphy were the main stars of the new series, but in order to exploit the full humorous potential of the situation, new cast members were drafted in to provide a strong base of sub-plots for the Ropers to interact around. From *Man About the House* came Norman

Putting the Ropers Centre Stage

Eshley, who had previously played Robin's Brother and eventual husband to Chrissy, the irritatingly competitive Norman Tripp. Eshley now played the Roper's snobbish neighbour, Jeffrey Fourmile in the new sitcom. This role was a far cry from his previous character, and required Norman to don glasses and a fake moustache!

Jeffrey's wife in the series, Ann, was played by Sheila Fearn, with the Fourmile's son, Tristram being played by Nicholas Owen. In 1976, both Johnnie Mortimer and Brian Cooke had young children, so sought some inspiration from their own offspring to develop the youngest character of the show. 'I had been offered the part', joked Johnnie Mortimer's son, Roger, 'but I was too shy to take it!'.

The role ended up in the hands of seven-year-old Nicholas Owen, who made his acting debut with *George and Mildred*. 'I was with an agency in Teddington (Magnus Management)', explained Nicholas. 'I was mainly doing modelling work but the producers saw my picture in Spotlight with my glasses on and asked me to come in for an audition, my Mum made sure that I pronounced the lines correctly and the rest was down to luck'. Nicholas had to work around his schooling to rehearse and record the shows. 'I had a private tutor on weekdays' he went on to explain. 'We did most of the rehearsals on Saturday and Sunday mornings (only my scenes)'.

Fresh semi-regular support actors were cast as extended family to George and Mildred, with Mildred's sister, Ethel and her husband Humphrey (Avril Elgar and Reginald Marsh) – and Mildred's mother, played by Gretchen Franklin. Roy Kinnear also reprised his role as Jerry, George's friend and bane of Mildred's life.

Costume and Make-Up

Kathleen Russell was the wardrobe mistress for *George and Mildred*, and recalled the dressing process for the sitcom. 'It was my job to supply the clothes', Russell explained. 'Lyn Harvey, the costume designer, would read through the scripts and decide what was needed and then it was passed on to me and a few other girls to get the stuff together. I worked on the studio floor and liaised with the director in the gallery and the cast on the set.'

George and Mildred worked through many notable costumes; from Jerry's bobble hat, to George's traffic warden outfit and Mildred's banana print trousers, but Kathleen explained how most of these costumes have since disappeared.

'Everything stayed in a *George and Mildred* wardrobe until the series ended. Then they all got moved into the big Thames general wardrobe and would be used for other productions, for the walk-ons and extras to wear. Many items of clothing we used had a liability to 'sprout legs and walk', but it is also possible that the cast took old costumes home with them. Who knows where this stuff could be now!'

Music
George and Mildred managed to use two different theme tunes over the show's run. Following the success of the *Man About the House* title song, Johnny Hawksworth was specifically commissioned to compose a new theme for *George and Mildred*. He didn't disappoint, and dished up another lively melody, which mixed well with the opening titles photo montage.

When the opening titles were changed for the second series, director Peter Frazer-Jones didn't feel that the composer's offering went with the atmosphere and feel that the new titles generated, and the music was replaced by a new version of the *George and Mildred* theme, composed by Roger Webb. This new tune remained as the theme music for the remaining four series of the sitcom.

Success and Merchandising
The popularity of the television series sparked many opportunities for merchandising, most of which were missed, as the only official merchandise to emerge from the series was a board game 'George V Mildred', launched by Denys Fisher in 1976. Apart from an image of the Ropers on the box lid and instructions, the game had little connection to the programme's characters.

Press Reviews
A hat in the air by Alan Coren, The Times - September 7th 1976
'Much was at stake as the 8pm cuckoo whanged back into it's slot last night and the opening credits *George and Mildred* rolled; those who admire good comedy scriptwriting were tense for the pitfalls of Johnnie Mortimer and Brian Cooke and has chosen to ignore in chancing a spin-off from their splendid *Man About the House*; and those who admire brilliant cameo acting chewed a nail for Brian Murphy and Yootha Joyce, nervous that the miniaturised triumph they enjoyed in the sub-plot of their earlier series would wilt under the lights when tested on centre stage.

For there is little enough good serial comedy around, God knows, without our losing these four talents as casualties to opportunism. That we did not, and that the late quartet came out of the test with reputations enhanced is therefore good cause to chuck a hat in the air this morning'.

Putting the Ropers Centre Stage

Viewer Reviews
Mrs L M. Tillyard from Leicester (TV Times 1976)

'Although just out of hospital after
an operation on my writing hand, I
just had to write in and say that
George and Mildred took the pain
away. It's the best half hour on television'.

Farewell to the Ropers...
Concluding a series as popular as *George and Mildred* was never going to be a welcome choice with viewers, but the cast and writers were all in agreement that it had to end somewhere. It was decided that there would be one more series made in 1980, which would be the sixth and final series. However, a sudden and unexpected turn of events put a firm end to the Ropers before they could go any further.

'We all wanted to do other things', explained Brian Murphy. 'I wanted to do some theatre, Yootha wanted to do some Shakespeare and open up a donkey sanctuary. She fancied leading quite a different type of life. So everybody got round a table and decided that we would make one more series and finish on a high, we wanted to go out right at the top of our game rather than fizzle out due to lessened popularity. We had all the scripts for the new series in place, but then Yootha was rushed into hospital'.

Yootha Joyce died just a few days before rehearsals were due to start on series six of *George and Mildred*, she had been sent the scripts in hospital but she was just too ill to even read them. Without the main star, nobody wanted to continue and the show was abruptly wound up at the end of fifth series. The *George and Mildred* film, which had been worked on intermittently over the early half of 1980, was publicly released in cinemas posthumously in Joyce's wake, leaving a sombre end to a classic series.

'It was very sad and took me a long time to get over it', said Brian. 'There was a huge post bag of letters and cards that got sent into the office and the public were very kind. They were genuinely distraught as they actually regarded us as man and wife. Out of all these letters, one of them had the suggestion that I should carry on as George, but as a widow. The writers thought it was too early, and I did as well, but it could have worked in time'. Brian Murphy went on to work again with Roy Kinnear in *The Incredible Mr Tanner*, again written by Johnnie Mortimer and Brian Cooke.

George and Mildred had been firmly finished and the Ropers would no longer be appearing in new misadventures on our screens. Fans adapted to the lack of their beloved series, but still held both *George and Mildred*, and it's predecessor *Man About the House*, with fond nostalgia.

These days, both sitcoms are widely available on DVD across the globe, and are selling incredibly well. Television channels from Spain to Cuba are airing the series in prime time slots, and the viewing figures remain consistently high. Recent British re-runs managed to achieve viewing figures of up to 400,000 people, quite incredible for a daytime slot on a satellite television channel.

It doesn't look like *Man About the House* nor *George and Mildred* will ever fall out of favour. Testament to the sterling writing, incredible acting talent and worldwide fondness for our comedy heritage.

Behind the Scenes
The Production Process

Thames Television

Thames television was responsible for producing and broadcasting some of the most popular light entertainment shows of the 1970's and 1980's. Inaugurated in 1968 after the Independent Television Authority (ITA) merged ABC with Associated Rediffusion to form a new broadcaster responsible for London and the surrounding areas, Thames transmitted programmes from Monday to Friday, handing over at 6pm each Friday to London Weekend Television.

Based originally at Rediffusion's old Television House in Holborn, the administrative division of Thames moved to purpose built Euston Road Studios in 1970, with the main production studios being south of the water at Teddington. Thames used Euston Road Studios for transmitting the news as well as several smaller-scale shows, but the base of the light entertainment sector was firmly entrenched at Teddington.

The Thames trademark 'skyline' ident and end boards quickly became synonymous with quality programmes, and Thames enjoyed over twenty-five years of being at the top of its game in broadcasting, which resulted in the company being the largest independant franchised London broadcaster to date.

In 1992, after screening a politically sensitive documentary which was critical of the then conservative government, the reign of Thames television came to an abrupt end when the franchise for the London region was awarded to Carlton, a result of a secret auction.

'I feel that the demise of Thames itself thanks in full to Margaret Thatcher', explained *Man About the House* actor Mike Savage. 'She had a real hissy fit over the *SAS Death on the Rock* documentary, of which she strongly disapproved. She now had Thames firmly in her gun sights and in effect the documentary actually led to Thames losing their ITV weekday franchise'.

The Thames television brand itself remained as a public limited company but is now owned by Australian group, Fremantle Media, who merged Thames with Talkback Productions to develop 'Talkback Thames' in 2003. Fremantle own the full Thames archive.

Teddington Studios

The majority of Thames' shows, including *Man About the House* and *George and Mildred* were filmed at Teddington Lock Studios, near Richmond-upon-Thames. The studios were established by Henry Chinnery at the turn of the century and were turning out films from as early as 1910.

After years of infrequent use, the site was purchased in 1958 by Associated Rediffusion, before passing into the hands of Thames. Since then, Teddington has played host to numerous shows; most notably *Magpie*, ITV's contender to *Blue Peter*. In recent years BBC shows like *After You've Gone* and *Not Going Out* have utilised the facility, and *Harry Hill's TV Burp* is also recorded on the site. The eight studios within the complex remain a draw for production companies.

The Production Process

The creation of a television show is a lengthy process, with a great deal of work undertaken to create just twenty-five minutes of transmittable programme. Here is the procedure that *Man About the House* and *George and Mildred* had to go through before they hit our screens.

Johnnie Mortimer and Brian Cooke prepared a script a good few weeks before any rehearsals took place. Cooke and Mortimer took equal shares in the writing, working together at their office in Teddington Studios. 'Johnnie did the main structure and Brian did most of the gags' recalled Mortimer's son, Roger. 'When watching the shows back, and a crude joke came on, Johnnie used to lean over and say "that's Brian's bit!".

When a script is completed, it is delivered to the cast to read through and learn the lines, and a copy is also given to the director so he can work out the camera angles, lighting, props and timings, as well as devise a camera script for the crew. A few days before the recording, everyone gets together for a script read-through and the first rehearsal.

Rehearsing

Because Teddington Studios lacked a dedicated rehearsal room, local halls and buildings were utilised by the cast and crew to meet up and rehearse in. *Man About the House* was usually rehearsed at a church hall in Fulwell, with *George and Mildred* being rehearsed in the back room of the Cardinal Wolsey Public House at Hampton Court. To compensate for the lack of props, a great deal of improvising was called for - marking out furniture with bits of tape on the floor and using the odd bit of second hand prop-furniture to simulate the set.

'We always rehearsed *Man About the House* in London, explained Sally Thomsett. 'We worked for about two or three hours on Tuesday and Saturday, and recorded all day Sunday'.

Behind the Scenes - The Production Process

Recording

Programmes were usually recorded on a Sunday evening. 'The cast would do a rehearsal in the morning for the studio crew and a final dress rehearsal before the audience were brought in', recalled actor Mike Savage. 'At 7pm in the evening, the audience would be allowed and be entertained by the warm-up man, usually a retired comedian, before the actual recording commenced at 7.30pm. If all went well, the episode would be in the can by 9pm'. Both shows were filmed inside Studio One, the largest of the complex at Teddington Studios, measuring 8,900 Square feet.

Pre-recorded outside footage was interplayed into the audience recording when necessary. To save a nightmare for the tape technicians, it was usually attempted to record the show all the way through and leave any minor omissions or mistakes in the final edit. An episode of *Man About the House* was once recorded with the cast standing in inches of water on the floor after a plumbing error with simulated rain!

'It is petrifying making a show in front of a live audience.' Explained *George and Mildred* support actor Robert Gillespie. 'The BBC was more civilised as you had two hours per show, but with commercial television it was very stressful, with a lot less time. We improvised on our mistakes, and just left them in the final episode, I worked out that you could get away with up to two and a half mistakes per show!'

Even the main stars had to swallow their nerves for recording to a live audience. 'As actors get older, we don't get less nervous - we get more nervous, as we know all the things that can go wrong', explained Brian Murphy. 'Things went wrong with the sets - like you couldn't get through the door because they had forgotten to un-nail it and we had to come through the fireplace instead, the audience loved that when something goes wrong. Lines could be tricky too. Richard O'Sullivan often tripped himself up verbally in the early stages of recording and that set him at ease for the rest, but it could also be frustrating. The audience relaxed themselves as well after a mistake happened, it was a bit like treading an old tightrope performing a show in front of a live audience'.

Post Production

Once the recording was completed, the post-production aspect of the episode was put together, editing and adjusting the image and sound to create the final tape that would be used for transmission.

The cast and crew were then free for a few days before proceedings for the next episode got underway. They all set off to a local pub together, usually The Three Pigeons in Richmond, where the landlords used to close early to accommodate them, or the Thames bar at Teddington Studios. At the end of a series, it was back to the director's house. Peter Frazer-Jones and Philip Jones, head of light entertainment, all lived nearby the studios, and used to invite the cast for a post-show party.

Public Video and DVD Releases
In accordance with demand, both *Man About the House* and *George and Mildred* have been released globally since being aired on television, with the earliest copies being available from 1981. By the late 1990's, the majority of programmes were widely available on VHS, and most recently, 'Network' have released the full collection of both sitcoms on DVD in the United Kingdom. Umbrella entertainment attained the licence for Australian releases, and some DVDs in this series feature audio commentaries by Brian Murphy and Sally Thomsett.

The Writers
Brian Cooke and Johnnie Mortimer

The idea for the two sitcoms *Man About the House* and *George and Mildred* was the result of a fruitful collaboration between seasoned comedy writers, Johnnie Mortimer and Brian Cooke.

Brian Cooke was born in Liverpool in December 1937. His earliest ambition was to become a cartoonist, and after completing his national service as a tactical sketcher, Brian achieved his desires in the early 1960's when he joined the staff of the Daily Mirror newspaper, contributing a daily strip cartoon.

John Edward Mortimer was born on July 2nd 1930, in Clare, Suffolk, but moved with his family to London at the age of two. With intentions to become an animator, John wrote to Disney studios in Los Angelis, but failed to secure a position, and instead worked at Disney's London Office. Mortimer's career path changed over the ensuing years, and he drew upon his artistry experience to become a cartoonist, contributing works to the Beano and Dandy, as well as illustrating front covers of books at Panther Publishing, usually for children's science fiction titles.

Fate drew together the two future working partners at a cartoonists convention in Butlin's Holiday Camp in Bognor Regis. 'Billy Butlin was chairman of the cartoonists club, and he hosted an event at the camp for all the members', recalled Johnnie's widow, Jytte. 'Brian met Johnnie and they found that they both enjoyed similar things, like playing guitars, they became very good friends'.

A shared sense of humour eventually led to their collaboration in scripting comedy, and their first product, the radio serial, *The Men from the Ministry*. 'They had sent a script to Richard Murdoch at BBC radio, and the script editor Ted Taylor liked it and asked for more for the series', elucidated Jytte Mortimer. 'Then one day, John and Brian went to watch a recording for Marty Feldman and Barry Took's *Round the Horne*. They didn't have literary agents, so asked Marty who he was represented by, and that's how they met Kenneth Ewing'.

Under Ewing's guidance, Cooke and Mortimer's talents were fostered and they took over writing *Round the Horne* when Marty Feldman left the team. The series, starring Kenneth Horne and Kenneth Williams was a huge success, and audiences frequently topped 15 Million as families gathered around the wireless, to listen to the gang unleash the mysterious new language of 'Polari' on the public for the first time.

Johnnie Mortimer and Brian Cooke continued in radio, and produced scripts for their own brainchild, *Stop Messing About*, also with Kenneth Williams. During the mid-sixties, the pair moved into television and, with the assistance of Frank Muir, penned scripts for the BBC. They later worked under contract from ABC, and produced some sparkling material for comedian Tommy Cooper, and later in 1968, episodes for the series *The Ronnie Barker Playhouse*. More writing credits soon followed before work began on the hit sitcom *Father dear Father*, a series that gained great esteem and achieved it's own version in Australia.

Brian Cooke and Johnnie Mortimer's biggest success came in 1973 when *Man About the House* was devised and later spun-off into two further smash series; *George and Mildred* and *Robin's Nest*. The two writers had certainly hit the big time, and their highly successful collaboration with this new series led to the duo becoming light entertainment consultants at Thames Television. Instead of using Brian's house to meet up and write in, the pair got their own office at Teddington Studios, and continued to produce exceptional comedic material. Acting out every scene and 'ticking' through the expectant laughs, was a safe way to ensure a script oozing hilarity.

As well as television, Johnnie and Brian also wrote two theatre productions during their career; a stage version of *George and Mildred* - later entitled *While the Cat's Away*, and *Situation Comedy*, based on the plot of two struggling sitcom writers. Later joint television work included *Let There Be Love*, as well as the screenplay for the film *No Sex Please, We're British*. Brian Cooke also penned some episodes of Vince Powell and Harry Driver's popular series *Love thy Neighbour* and brought out a book teaching budding writers how to script comedy.

In 1980, Brian Cooke and Johnnie Mortimer worked again with Brian Murphy and Roy Kinnear, with the sitcom *The Incredible Mr Tanner*. This new series was based on a sketch previously written for *The Ronnie Barker Playhouse* in 1968. This first version starred Ronnie Barker alongside Richard O'Sullivan, and the idea for the show was also adapted by Cooke and Mortimer under the guise of *Kindly Leave the Kerb* in 1971, a one-off programme starring Peter Butterworth.

In 1981, Johnnie Mortimer created the series *Never the Twain,* which starred Donald Sinden and Windsor Davies. This was one of his only works without Brian Cooke, who was living in Canada at the time. *Never the Twain* became one of Thames Television's longest-running shows, lasting until 1991. Tragically, after thirty years of making people laugh, Johnnie Mortimer died on September 2nd 1992 at his home in East Molesey, Surrey. He was 62.

Brian Cooke's individual writing credits include the hilarious *Keep It in the Family* in the early 1980's, which saw Brian draw upon his own previous work as a cartoonist to create the character Dudley Rush, played by Robert Gillespie. Brian even donated Dudley's lion glove puppet for use on the show. 'It's been in my family for about fifteen years' he told Look-in magazine in 1980. 'It seemed a good prop to use, but we have to guard it jealously in case anyone should stand on it!'

Brian later devised *Tripper's Day* as a vehicle for Leonard Rossiter, which turned out to be Rossiter's last comedy role before his death in 1984, and *Close to Home* with Paul Nicholas. Cooke still writes to this day, with recent credits to his name being the critically acclaimed stage show *Stop Messing About*, based on the 1960's radio show of the same name, and *Round the Horne...Revisited*, another success, based on the original scripts for *Round the Horne*. He also has the esteem of being the only writer to have had a television programme in the number one spot in Britain and America at the same time.

Brian Cooke currently resides in Surrey and recently wrote his autobiography; 'George and Mildred and Me'.

Direction and Production
Peter Frazer-Jones

Man About the House and *George and Mildred* needed an experienced producer and director at the helm, someone to draw all the strings together and make a programme out of the scripts. This job fell to Peter Frazer-Jones.

Born in London in 1930, Frazer-Jones has been responsible for the direction of scores of television and films over the years, working with Brian Cooke and Johnnie Mortimer on a regular basis.

After completing his national service at Ladysmith Barracks in Ashton-Under-Lyme, Frazer-Jones debuted in television with the popular music show *Thank your Lucky Stars* in 1966 and later built on his career working with such talent as Frankie Howerd, Benny Hill and magician David Nixon.

Peter's work with Cooke and Mortimer include *Horne A'Plenty, Man About the House, George and Mildred, Robin's Nest* and Mortimer's creation of the long-running *Never the Twain*. Peter also produced and directed the film adaptation of *George and Mildred* in 1980.

Despite being one of the big guns of the Thames television arsenal, Peter Frazer-Jones ceased directing following the demise of Thames in the early 1990's. His last credit as a producer was in 1992 on *Land Of Hope and Gloria,* and he had previously been nominated for two BAFTA awards for his work on *After Henry*. Peter's last work on television was in 2001, when he appeared in person on *The Unforgettable Yootha Joyce.*

In all the productions he worked on, Peter Frazer-Jones' professionalism shone through to all his colleagues. 'He was a lovely man', recalled *George and Mildred* vision mixer Peter Phillips. 'He was Gentle and a gentleman, totally unflappable, well organised which meant that all the shots worked as he had scripted. Working with Peter meant a stress free day'.

After a few years in quiet retirement, Peter Frazer-Jones died on November 5th 2005 aged 75. His funeral was attended by numerous fellow directors, actors, friends and family, but his passing was not widely reported by media sources, with many of his past colleagues and co-workers left wondering what happened to him. *Man About the House* actor John Colclough explained how; 'Peter sadly seems to have disappeared. I don't even know what happened to Suzie Shields his PA and we were good pals at one time.' Actor George Layton was equally perplexed, stating that he 'lost contact with Peter years ago'.

Peter Frazer-Jones worked his magic on many classic comedies and his charismatic directing style is clearly evident in every episode.

Character Profiles

Richard O'Sullivan (Man About the House)
Robin Oswald Tripp is a son of Southampton and an avid fan of the football team. Tripp is a student at the Euston Road Technical College, where he is learning all there is to know about cooking. Never short of a snappy one-liner, his affable humour and boyish good looks mean he is rarely short of female companions.

Paula Wilcox (Man About the House)
Chrissy Plummer is the spirited but level-headed girl who doesn't give into a boy's advances that easily. She has come a cropper a couple of times, after abandoning her principles, and once went out with a married man. Always ready for a laugh and a good time, but not the sort of person you would want to cross as she is capable of harbouring grudges. Chrissy goes out to work, but we never learn exactly where, only that her place of work is in an office.

Sally Thomsett (Man About the House)
Jo is the archetypal dumb blonde, a scatterbrained wool-head and a rubbish cook, whose feeble attempts at gastronomy make Robin weep culinary tears. Jo will burn anything that moves and garnishes her meals with bits of frazzled saucepan. Her one redeeming feature is her great sex appeal and she is seldom short of male attention. Curiously, Jo never had a surname in the series. 'I don't think it was planned for me to have a surname', explained Sally Thomsett. 'It would have been fun to have something silly like Ramsbottom!'

Brian Murphy (Man About the House / George and Mildred)
George Roland Roper is unemployed. His previous work includes; a retired gas mantle packer and a bus conductor. In *George and Mildred* he finds work as a traffic warden. George is working class and 'bloody proud of it', with friends living in council tower blocks in Hackney and a garden full of weeds. George himself used to live at 27, Lascar Street, Hackney.

George's political views are strong, with him once remarking that Enoch Powell should be prime minister. He is very gullible, often falling for one of his friend Jerry's get-rich-quick-schemes, and wishing to invest money in his ideas - if only he had any money to invest. George takes pride in annoying Mildred, by not eating her cooking and very rarely cooperating with her yearnings for an early night. Never one to have a broad command over the English language, Roper often refers to people and objects as 'wossnames' and unknowingly mixes words together to create his own individual corruptions, well heeled examples being 'Insinuendos' and 'Artificial Insinuation'. His favourite reading material is stated to be 'The Sun' and 'The Beano'.

Yootha Joyce (Man About the House / George and Mildred)
Mildred Dorothy Roper Nee **Asquith** and later **Tremble** is the formidable and nagging wife of George. She desperately wants to fit in socially and integrate into the neighbourhood - with attempts to join flower arranging classes and hosting tea parties. You could zest a lemon on her frown and her stare could frighten you into an involuntary bowel movement, but deep inside, Mrs. Roper only ever wanted a bit of romance and an early night. Mildred's shoe size is stated to be seven and a half.

Mildred's maiden name changes between *Man About the House* and *George and Mildred*. In the 1974 *Man About the House* film, it is stated to be Asquith, but in *George and Mildred*, this is changed to Tremble (be it only to support the joke; 'Mildred Roper, Nee Tremble!').

Doug Fisher (Man About the House)
Larry Simmonds lives on the top floor in a converted attic room and is constantly popping down to his 'friends', though the welcome he receives is seldom a warm one. Larry is the ubiquitous pest who always overstays his welcome, a great one for borrowing things and never returning them. Never short of a tarty girl on his arm, Larry's companions are not the type you would dream of introducing to your mother.

Roy Kinnear (Man About the House / George and Mildred)
Jerry is the useless handyman who occasionally turns up to ruin something. Frequently taking advantage of George's gullible nature, and fondly referring to Mildred as 'Mildew', Jerry is an odd job man who tries his hand at everything, failing miserably at most. The lardy nuisance always has a 'get poor quick scheme' on the go, from Kentucky Fried Pigeon to repairing gearboxes and installing showers. Suffice to say, Mildred doesn't really like him. Jerry is a single father with one grown up daughter, Vera. He has a cousin called Kevin.

Oscar (Man About the House / George and Mildred)
Oscar the Budgie is George's beloved pet, caged in the corner but usually given more attention than Mildred. The budgie is by no means an es-

Character Profiles

sential character, and is more of a stage prop more than anything else. It is, however, worth drawing attention to how the creature changes colour over the course of the series. Originally green, he morphs into snow white, green-pied, and canary yellow. George is bereft when Oscar dies of old age in the *George and Mildred* episode 'Jumble Pie'.

Norman Eshley (George and Mildred)
Jeffrey Fourmile is the Roper's neighbour in Hampton Wick - a prosperous estate agent and proud conservative supporter. He drives an estate car, and later in the series also purchases a sports car. Jeffrey gets outraged at more or less everything, especially the Labour party and the lower classes.

Sheila Fearn (George and Mildred)
Ann Fourmile is Jeffrey's wife. A significantly middle class trophy wife who is somewhat under used in the sitcom, seemingly only there to look pretty, cook dinner and look after the children.

Nicholas Bond-Owen (George and Mildred)
Tristram Fourmile is their precocious son, who is constantly pressured by his father to succeed with his education. Sadly, the only thing he comes top of the class in is detention. Tristram aspires to the trends and fashions of his school friends, but his requests for skateboards and posters depicting 'The Stranglers' are never met by his father.

Avril Elgar (George and Mildred)
Ethel Pomphrey is Mildred's sister, an agonisingly posh being whose success falls solely on the income from her husband. Ethel has a fleet of executive cars, an Italian housekeeper, and lives in a large country house. Ethel takes holidays in Barbados and has a wardrobe brimming with fur coats.

Reginald Marsh (George and Mildred)
Humphrey Pomphrey is Ethel's husband. He is a big player in the meat trade and attends sausage conventions across Europe, leading to his nickname as 'the offal king of Oxshott'. Humphrey is a rogue at heart, on one occasion having a fling with his office secretary and planning secret getaways with her to Jersey.

Pussy Galore (George and Mildred)
Truffles Debourbon Fitzwilliam III or **'Truffles'** for short, is Mildred's

Yorkshire Terrier dog. George purchases the dog for his wife in place of an adopted child in the episode 'Baby Talk', but starts to regret his decision when Mildred spends an inordinate amount of time looking after it. He delights in calling Truffles a 'mobile dish mop'. Truffles is registered with the Kennel Club.

Moby the Goldfish (George and Mildred)
Moby is another family pet - George's prized goldfish whom he adores. Roper takes an unhealthy interest in the creature, offering it cups of tea, playing scrabble with it and refusing to undress in front of him. George is heartbroken when Moby is accidentally dispensed down the waste disposal unit by Mildred in the episode 'Fishy Business'. Moby, is however, replaced by a new goldfish - Moby II.

Main Cast

Richard O'Sullivan

Richard O'Sullivan was born in Chiswick, London to Irish parents on May 7th, 1944. 'I'm still trying to work out how I got into acting' he explained in the first chapter of his book, 'Man About the Kitchen'. 'My grandfather played the bagpipes, but that's the nearest our family ever got to show business'. But wherever the initial spark of talent materialised from, O'Sullivan became one of the most prominent stars of the 1970's and 1980's.

Educated at the St. John the Evangelist's Roman Catholic primary school in Brentford, Richard attended the Corona stage Academy, apparently being sent there to remove an accent picked up whilst on a family holiday in Ireland.

'I was a close friend of Richard's as we both attended Corona' recalls actor David Barry. 'It is highly unlikely he attended just to get rid of his dialect, but having said that, when I first went to the school I had a welsh dialect and we were all given elocution lessons and learnt to speak RP. In those days actors didn't have regional accents.'

A promising young actor, O'Sullivan made his debut in the 1953 film *The Yellow Balloon*, where he appeared as a boy in a Sunday school choir. More parts followed, several with the Children's Film Association, and in 1956 Richard's blossoming career received a major boost when he secured a part in *It's Great to be Young* - starring opposite screen legend John Mills. O'Sullivan also appeared in *Great Expectations*, but broke both legs during production, forcing him to appear seated in most of his scenes.

'I'd always admired Richard since I'd seen him play a schoolboy in a film where he played in an orchestra', *Man About the House* actor John Colclough recalled. 'At the age of 13, me and my pal Jonny Woods rather envied this actor getting his hands on an expensive French Horn!'

For the next three years, O'Sullivan's work rate was reliably steady, and the critical acclaim which had so far eluded him finally arrived after playing Robin Stevens in one of the earliest films of the *Carry On* series, *Carry On Teacher*. Most of the children from the Corona academy were brought in to play 'the saboteurs' in the popular film, and Richard was cast as the lead. Subsequent film parts came courtesy of Cliff Richard's pop music vehicles; *The Young Ones* and *Wonderful Life*, both of which did a roaring trade at the box office.

Richard also jetted off to Italy for a few months to film the epic *Cleopatra* with Elizabeth Taylor and Richard Burton. 'I was only 18 at the time' he later told press. 'It was a wide-screen film, and the main reason I was cast was to replace another boy whose head appeared egg-shaped with the broad cameras. I got the nickname Spaghetti O'Sullivan, as I learnt a lot about the food when waiting to film my scenes. I was there for nine months but only filmed for eight days. When I got back home to England, a cable arrived from Liz Taylor inviting me to a party she was holding for Richard Burton, but it said "black tie". I didn't have one, so didn't go, but looking back on that I'm kicking myself for being so naive as it turned out to be one of the best Hollywood parties'.

Following further film work, Richard took a step into television and his first series. In 1971, Richard was offered the part of snivelling creep Dr Lawrence Bingham, in the London Weekend Television sitcom, *Doctor at Large* and also *Doctor in Charge*. The series proved an immense hit with viewers, catapulting him into the top echelon of TV personalities. The year of 1971 also saw Richard enter into a short-lived marriage with Diana Terry, but they divorced soon afterwards.

Barely twelve months later, O'Sullivan was appearing in Brian Cooke and Johnnie Mortimer's comedy show, *Alcock and Gander*, his casting the result of a brief appearance in their earlier sitcom *Father Dear Father* in 1968. It was mainly due to O'Sullivan's accomplished portrayal of Richard Gander that led him to being offered the lead role of Robin Tripp in *Man About the House*.

This new sitcom achieved an instant rapport with television viewers, and was O'Sullivan's strongest role yet, winning him the 1979 Spanish 'TP de Oro' award for Best Foreign Actor. The roguish charm of Robin Tripp endeared Richard to legions of female fans, a lop sided grin suggesting the character could at once be an out and out charmer, or a wolf in sheep's clothing. When questioned about his smile by TV Times in 1975, who enquired as to why he seemed to have a permanent smirk on his face, he replied 'A dentist did a mucky job on a tooth and I tried smiling sideways to hide it, then I caught a cricket ball in the mouth, which seems to have fixed it for good!'

One of the key elements to *Man About the House* was Robin's smouldering passion for Chrissy, but away from the cameras, reality took a different course of events. Working closely together on set, and as the only single members of the cast, Richard and co-star Sally Thomsett entered into a relationship, remaining an item until the series concluded in 1976. In a recent newspaper interview, Sally explained how contrary to common belief, 'there was never any candlelight dinners in posh restaurants' and 'it was quite a simple life, just often eating a meal together in front of the television. When the series ended, the relationship gently fizzled out and we went our separate ways'.

With the conclusion of *Man About the House* in 1976, Richard reprised his role as Robin Tripp in the new series *Robin's Nest*, receiving a Look-In star award in 1977 for his part. Whilst in this sitcom, Richard again settled in a relationship with a co-star, this time Tessa Wyatt, who went through a very public break up with Radio DJ Tony Blackburn to be with him. Wyatt and O'Sullivan had a son together, called Jamie, but the partnership dissolved. They remained friends after the split.

Off-screen, Richard O'Sullivan capitalised on his television role as a chef to publish a cookery book in 1980 entitled, 'Man About the Kitchen - the book for people who can't cook...much'. He was himself a very good cook, and greatly enjoyed gastronomy, explaining in his book how 'I can do roasts, I don't make sauces and stuff like that. I enjoy simple tasty foods the best and I love to cook for others - I'm quite a pig really and I can easily do a whole roast for myself. Robin is more into sauces but I prefer the traditional English bit because I like to taste the meat'.

'It all started when I was younger and my mum had several spells in hospital', Richard went on to discuss. 'Dad wasn't a very good cook, so I said one day how I'd cook dinner instead. I don't think he ever got over the fact that I boy, he was ready to christen me as Maureen after the hospital accidentally told him I was a girl. My cooking started from there onwards, I had to work around the larder to make my meals. As a young actor in rep, there isn't that much money to eat out, so from a one-ring gas burner in a bed-sitter in Worthing where I was appearing at the Connaught Theatre, to a flat of my own in *Man About the House*, I learnt as I went along'.

When *Robin's Nest* drew to a close after six series in 1981, O'Sullivan focussed on his title role in the children's drama, *Dick Turpin*. He later embarked on a new project, starring in *Me and My Girl* alongside one third of *The Goodies* - Tim Brooke-Taylor. Around this time, O'Sullivan took to the stage to appear in various pantomimes including the Shaftesbury Avenue Theatre production of *Aladdin* with Roy Kinnear, Jill Gascoigne and Tudor Davies.

'Richard was very pleasant and he was very much the star of *Man About the House*', remembers co-star Mike Savage. 'He was riding on a huge wave of popularity at the time. He was certainly the most popular of the Thames sitcom stars'.

In the late 1980's, Richard took on several smaller parts including; *Mr H is Late* and *The Giftie*, whilst making a gradual retreat from acting roles. In 1994 it emerged how he was suffering as a 'hard-drinking depressive' and his divorce from second wife Christine Smart had 'pushed him over the edge', he booked himself into a Berkshire clinic to recuperate.

A mere handful of subsequent minor screen appearances followed. Richard was a guest chef on a 1997 programme of *Light Lunch* and also appeared on the 1997 clip show *Has Anyone Seen My Pussy?*, with Sally Thomsett, to look back at British sitcoms with host Julian Clary. O'Sullivan retired from the limelight to live a private life. In a 2001 exclusive, the Daily Mail reported him to be a 'virtual recluse', proclaiming how he 'lives alone with his 21-year-old son Jamie in their small, two-bedroom flat in West London.'

In 2003, he suffered a stroke and chose to move into Brinsworth house in Twickenham, a home for retired actors where he still lives today. Only recently, a mainstream newspaper published a photograph of Richard walking to the shops, remarking how 'worryingly frail' he looked. The story concerned many of his fans, as O'Sullivan's appearance has certainly changed, but Richard's old friends and co-stars who still visit him frequently have the general consensus amongst them is that he isn't nearly as poorly as the media makes out.

Despite the tabloid tarnishing Richard O'Sullivan's name has taken in recent years, his fans are still loyal to him and have fond memories of his time on *Man About the House*. Sally Thomsett recently remarked how she 'doesn't have one bad memory of Richard'.

Titbits... At the age of nineteen, Richard bought an MG TF car for £470, but had to give it up less than a year later after a collision with a bubble car!

Paula Wilcox

Paula Wilcox was born on December 13th 1949 in Manchester and took a broad interest in performing whilst in her early teens.

'I auditioned for a television series, *The Lovers*, written by Jack Rosenthal, during the school holidays when I was a member of the National Youth Theatre. Whilst in this series I got lots of other work and the first of these was a comedy series called *On Her Majesty's Pleasure*'.

Wilcox later made a couple of appearances in Granada's short-lived comedy series *The Dustbinmen*, also scripted by Rosenthal, but it was her work in *The Lovers* which gained Paula the most acclaim. The series focussed upon the sexual innocence and inexperience of a young courting couple. Paula's character, Beryl Battersby, was the lustily desired object of fumbling boyfriend Geoffrey Scrimgeor, played to perfection by a prosper-

Main Cast

ing new talent - Richard Beckinsale. Running to a total of thirteen episodes over two series, *The Lovers* was a huge success, turning both of it's young stars into household names.

Wilcox took subsequent comedy roles in *The Benny Hill Show* and *The Liver Birds* before stepping into *Man About the House,* in the part of Chrissy Plummer, a character not too dissimilar to Beryl Battersby with her personal tenets but equally capricious attitudes to life. Suffice to say that Paula's wide brown eyes and her character's flirtatious attitudes secured many a male viewer, and led to the running success *Man About the House* achieved. When the series was broadcast in Spain, it also led Wilcox to be awarded the 1979 'TP de Oro' prize for Best Foreign Actress.

'We all became the best of friends working on the sitcom. We had been chosen for our ability and we each respected the other's talents. We knew that we were very lucky to have a brilliant team working behind the scenes'.

'All the work on the scripts had been done long before we walked into the rehearsals room, so our work was very easy. The scripts arrived a few weeks before rehearsals started, by which time we were all quite familiar with our lines. All this meant that we were incredibly relaxed during the production period, and there was plenty of time to lark about and have fun. We went out together a lot and knew each other's families. It was a very happy time'.

When the show concluded, Wilcox moved on to star in the leading role of *Miss Jones and Son*, playing Elizabeth Jones. 'This series was considered very edgy at the time. It was about an unmarried mother and was a lovely sitcom written by Richard Waring. *Miss Jones and Son* went straight to number one in the ratings for a couple of seasons before I started to become more committed to theatre work'.

In the late 1980's, Wilcox returned to her classical stage training to appear in London's West End in *The Queen and I* and later *Anyone can Whistle*. Latterly, she performed Shakespeare in Regent's Park Open Air Theatre, and in 2009, her theatre work extended to the acclaimed *Dreams of Violence* at the Soho Theatre, later going on national tour.

'I was in *Z Cars* with Paula', recalled *Man About the House* actor John Colclough. 'Paula lived in Twickenham so we were almost neighbours at one time. I saw her recently at a book launch which was a nice reunion'.

Paula recently told press how if she hadn't been an actress, she would 'have enjoyed being an interpreter', being fluent in both French and Spanish and 'loving the study of languages whilst at school, even Latin and Greek'. She went on to elucidate that her greatest extravagance is 'clothes and lovely face creams'.

During a holiday at the Kahala Hilton Hotel near Honolulu, Hawaii in 1992, Wilcox met her future husband, American businessman Nelson Skip Riddle, son of Frank Sinatra's band leader, Nelson Riddle. The pair returned to England together and married the next year. Paula's first husband, the actor Derek Seaton, died in 1979.

In recent years, Wilcox has made television appearances in *Smokescreen* and children's drama *The Queen's Nose* - based on the books by Dick King Smith. Wilcox made further guest appearances and one-off roles in the popular hospital drama, *Holby City*, and worked on seventeen episodes of *The Smoking Room*. In 2007, she took on the part of Hilary Potts - Laurel Thomas's mother-in-law - in the soap *Emmerdale*, a role she kept for a run of thirty-nine episodes.

Despite her extensive resume of television and stage work, Paula Wilcox will always be best remembered for her role of Chrissy Plummer in *Man About the House*. She provided some brilliant moments in the sitcom, with her gift for comedy timing and delivery of lines providing the very essence of enjoyable viewing.

Titbits... During the 1970's, Wilcox stayed at the infamous Torquay Gleneagles hotel, the inspiration for John Cleese to devise *Fawlty Towers*.

Titbits... Paula Wilcox gets mentioned in the Belle & Sebastian song 'Photo Jenny'. The lyrics contain the phrase; 'What's on the box? - *Man About the House* with Paula Wilcox!'.

Sally Thomsett

Born on April 3rd 1950, Thomsett knew she wanted to enter showbusiness after taking singing lessons at school, and competing in various local competitions. She made her screen debut at the age of fourteen in the 1964 production, *Seventy deadly Pills*.

Following a six episode stint in *Dead End Creek* the next year, Thomsett won her big break in the 1970 feature film, *The Railway Children*, playing the eleven-year-old Phyllis Waterbury, despite being twenty at the time. The film was warmly received, and the role gained her a BAFTA nomination for Most Promising Newcomer.

Looking like the beacon of eternal youth, Thomsett found it very difficult to land parts that reflected her real age. 'I started acting when I was about twelve, so I never had a different job', recalled Sally. 'I didn't really get to play my own age until *Man About the House*'. Off-screen, she had the

Main Cast

same trouble with her personal relationships. In a 2006 newspaper interview she explained; 'when I was a teenager, I never dated many men, they said I looked like their little sister'. Thomsett did however find a partner in Nigel Newman, son of a transportation mogul, and the pair soon wed. However a turbulent relationship made it dawn on Sally she had made a mistake and they divorced soon after.

In 1973, Thomsett was offered the part of Jo in *Man About the House*, a role she was delighted to take as she 'didn't have to prepare much for the character', as 'Jo was fairly similar to myself'. There was also the added bonus of working with Richard O'Sullivan, and before the first series had been completed for transmission, Thomsett and O'Sullivan had become entwined in a relationship, one which was kept secret from the public and press. 'No-one outside the studio knew anything about it', Sally explained. 'That's something that would probably be impossible now'.

Whilst with Richard, Thomsett shared a Queensgate flat with school friend and actress Sally Harrision. 'I went to school with Sally Thomsett in Hove' explained Harrison. 'I also shared a flat with her whilst she was having a relationship with Richard O'Sullivan. It was much more like *Man About the House* in our flat in Queensgate than on the telly. Richard was a great cook in real life as well!'

As *Man About the House* came to it's natural conclusion, Sally all but disappeared from television, with her last role arriving in BBC's *Wodehouse Playhouse* in 1978. 'When the series ended I went travelling and had a marvelous time, I got married and also went over to LA to make a series over there'.

Sally dated Dai Llewellyn and David Lee, before marrying telecoms manager Claus Nielsen. It was another mistake and the partnership dissolved in 1982, Nielsen later slandering Sally by putting it to a National newspaper that she was a lesbian, and allowing her to sue them for libel.

Plagued by a run of tempestuous relationships, Sally finally found happiness with landscape gardener Paul Agnew, and she has a thirteen-year-old daughter, Charlotte, who she described to the Daily Mail as 'the best thing that's ever happened to me'.

It's been a long time since Sally took to our screens in a dramatic role, a great shame as she was a clearly a very talented actress, with the origins of her successful career rooted firmly to *Man About the House*. Is there any particular role that Thomsett would return to the acting business to play? - 'A dotty old aunt in a comedy', she explained. 'I'd like that!'

Doug Fisher

A classically trained actor, Douglas Fisher was born in 1941 and started his acting vocation whilst performing on stage at the theatre in Oxford University. Fisher was studying French and Russian alongside future *Monty Pythons* Terry Jones and Michael Palin. Doug appeared in several productions in Oxford before making a television debut in 1965 with *The Illustrated Weekly Hudd*. Subsequent parts came in 1969's *World in Ferment*, and Fisher later became a regular fixture in *All our Saturdays*.

Fisher took on numerous comedy roles throughout the early 1970's, including *Comedy Playhouse* and *The Importance of Being Hairy*. He also appeared in an episode of Cooke and Mortimer's *Father Dear Father*, which influenced his casting as Larry in *Man About the House* three years later. Doug subsequently took his character of Larry to the big-screen in the 1974 film adaptation. Fisher turned back to theatre in 1975, when he went on tour with co-stars; Richard O'Sullivan and Sally Thomsett, in Marc Camoletti's stage show, *Boeing Boeing*. Joined intermittently by Yootha Joyce and Paula Wilcox, the show opened in London's West End and later toured the country and also Australia, performing to rave reviews. Fisher also tread the boards alongside Richard O'Sullivan and Cheryl Hall in the 1980 production of *Never Say No*.

Whilst filming *Man About the House*, Fisher lived in Chelsea, London. 'I live alone as a bachelor', he explained to TV Times magazine in 1975, 'I've got no choice but to be a housewife. I often head over to Richard O'Sullivan's place, he's a great friend and we've known each other for about 10 years'.

'I think I'm the better cook!', he went on to discuss. 'I'm rather good in the kitchen if I say so myself. Roast beef is a speciality, I do it just like mother used to make. I sometimes give Richard a cookery lesson at his house, but he would wrap one of his dumplings round me if I ever strayed into the studio kitchen!'.

In 1979, Douglas appeared in Gerry O'Hara's film, *The Bitch* with Joan Collins and also featured in an episode in 1982 of Antony Jay and Jonathan Lynn's *Yes Minister*. Fisher continued his career with numerous more credits to his name, notably playing Stanley in *Goodnight Sweetheart* and Jim Medhurst in *London's Burning*. His last role was as a clergyman in a 1999 episode of *Oliver Twist*.

Douglas Fisher died from a heart attack on July 9th 2000. He was 59.

Titbits... Doug Fisher had an affair with actress Susan Penhaligon, a relationship which caused the eventual break-up of her marriage.

Main Cast

Yootha Joyce

Yootha Joyce was born in Wandsworth, London on August 20th 1927. An only child, her father was the singer, Hurst Needham and her mother was a pianist for concert theatre shows. The unusual name of Yootha derives from the Maori word for Joy, but Joyce herself detested the name.

At the age of fifteen, Joyce left school to follow her dream of becoming an actress. She later joined up at RADA, and subsequently the Croydon Grand Repertory Theatre as a theatre manager. Yootha later worked with BBC Radio, but it wasn't until the late 1950's that things started to happen for her. She went to an audition with theatrical producer, Glynn Edwards, who was seeking a young lady to play the part of 'a naughty prostitute' on tour with him. Yootha was chosen, and the pair hit the road together and then entered into a relationship, marrying in 1958.

Glynn Edwards and Yootha Joyce later enrolled at the prestigious Joan Littlewood Theatre Workshop together, where Joyce met Brian Murphy for the first time.

'Joan took her on for an extra actress in *The Gold Soldier Schweik*' Brian Murphy explained. 'The show was going to Paris for a festival and Yootha was brought along. Joan thought she was a great comedienne, as indeed she was. I was bit in awe of her really because she had a car, and none of us had cars. Yootha and Glynn only had one of those converted aeroplane cockpits, a bubble car, but it seemed grand to us. They used to go abroad in it for their holidays. So I was a bit in awe of her at first, but later got to like her and enjoyed working with her, little knowing that in the future we would be bonded together as on-screen husband and wife'.

After appearing in several plays at the workshop, Yootha made her name starring in *Fings Ain't what they used t'Be*, with Glynn Edwards and Miriam Karlin. Her performance in this show was sighted by audience member, Frank Muir, the assistant controller of Light Entertainment at the BBC, who offered Yootha her first television appearance - *Brothers in Law*, in 1962.

After making her television debut, Yootha extended her talents to other popular series including *Steptoe and Son* as well as an episode of kitsch drama, *The Avengers*. She gained further recognition from her part in *Me Mammy* with Milo Shea. In 1968, Joyce divorced from Glynn Edwards, but the pair remained great friends afterwards, even appearing as on-screen husband and wife in *Burke and Hare.*

In 1973, Yootha Joyce received her big break, being cast as Mildred Roper in *Man About the House*. Yootha achieved an instant rapport with audiences at home. Sally Thomsett remarked how 'She had loads of admirers, to think she had much more fan mail than the rest of us put together!'

Throughout 1976, Joyce continued in character for the spin-off series *George and Mildred*. With the spotlights pointed directly at her, this new series allowed Yootha to shine, and her portrayal of the put-upon Mildred won her the nation's affections. Joyce had become a huge celebrity and was in constant demand for public appearances, one notable example being the opening of a new Wickes DIY store in London Road, Slough.

But behind the seemingly strong and domineering character she portrayed, Yootha was 'desperately frightened' about performing in front of a live audience.

'Yootha blatantly signalled how scared and frightened she was in the live shows', *George and Mildred* actor Robert Gillespie recalled. 'The director didn't see how petrified she was, she showed absolute terror. Joyce used to fluff a line in rehearsals and instantly shout "another retake". She came clean to me at the end of a rehearsal, saying "It doesn't get any better" and she explained her fears to me. I was touched that this national star was talking to me openly about what a horrible task a live audience recording was, I was very moved to share those few moments with her'.

Brian Murphy explained how nerves can build when waiting to perform. 'We used to wait backstage together before going on, and we paced up and down behind the set prior to the recording' he recalled. 'I used to smoke then, and Yootha smoked like an old trooper. Despite our years of experience, it was still very nerve racking. We paced about so much that I swear that we dug a trench in one of the studios with all our walking. She is used to say to me, "what are we doing this for, Brian?", I used to reply with "Erm, money?", and she said that was a good excuse. But once we were out there, we did enjoy it'.

In 1980, the *George and Mildred* feature film was made, but tragically this was to be Yootha's final project. She was admitted to hospital in mid-August, but after ten days of treatment she died from liver failure on August 24th 1980. Just four days earlier, she had celebrated her 53rd birthday.

Brian Murphy sat at her bedside when Yootha Joyce took her last bow. He remembers the day vividly. 'I went over to the hospital one Sunday. I'd gone to visit my own dear mum and I was on the way back home when I decided to pay Yootha a visit instead. She went into a coma as I was there. It was a great shock, as only two days earlier she was sitting up in bed surrounded by hundreds of flowers and cards from fans and the press and it looked like she was improving. But she had a relapse and slipped away literarily while I was sitting there. It was so very sad'.

Despite immense public popularity, in her private life Yootha Joyce was

Main Cast

very much alone. She had many friends and co-workers who cared for her, but no proper relationship that lasted. In her final years Joyce lived on her own in a basement flat in West London and turned to drink. It had come to the attention of a few of her friends that she was drinking a bit too much, but she always denied it most categorically from herself and others. As ex-husband Glynn Edwards remarked in an interview, 'how can you solve a problem you don't feel exists yourself'.

Yootha died before the *George and Mildred* film had it's general release to the public, and the movie has since been dedicated to her memory. Her funeral was on the same day that the cast were due to start rehearsals for a new series of *George and Mildred*, she had been sent the scripts for the new series whilst in hospital, but she had been too ill to even read them.

Her sudden passing was a great shock to all that knew her, but it was revealed at the inquest to her death that she had been drinking heavily for the last ten years – consuming over a litre of brandy every day. Her lawyer, Mario Uziell-Hamilton stated how he was 'absolutely shattered' when the news came out, later explaining how Joyce 'had become a victim of her own success', drinking herself into depression at the fear of being typecast as a nagging old woman.

Despite her battles with alcohol, Yootha remained the consummate professional.

'She was always very professional and never appeared drunk to me', recalled Nicholas Owen, who played Tristram in *George and Mildred*. 'I think it got worse towards the end when her relationship ended but I didn't know a thing about it until we were due to start rehearsing for the next series and then suddenly we were told that Yootha had died, it was a terrible shock to us all'.

David Barry, who played Elvis in the *George and Mildred* film, explained; 'I have some fond memories of working with Yootha, she was so professional and nice. I don't know how others received news of her death, filming was long over so everyone had gone their separate ways, but I was very upset to hear the news'.

The suggestion that Joyce successfully hid her addiction from friends and colleagues, however, remains open to question. A source close to *George and Mildred* explained how; 'She used to stagger in at 8 O'clock in the morning legless. It was very sad to think how she could have got so drunk by that time in the morning, but she picked herself up and got on with the show, she was a total professional'.

It is a sad thought that the accomplished work Yootha Joyce produced was also a catalyst to her own internal upset – but despite her own thoughts of herself, she will never be forgotten by the thousands of fans that still hold her dear to their hearts.

Miss Yootha Joyce Dies, Obituary August 25th 1980

Miss Yootha Joyce, the actress, died on August 24th in a London hospital at the age of 53. She had been currently starring in the part of Mildred in the highly successful ITV comedy series, *George and Mildred*, with Brian Murphy as George. The series sprang from an earlier popular series, *Man About the House* in which the characters of George and Mildred as landlord and landlord's wife, acting as foils to the younger players, Richard O'Sullivan, Paula Wilcox and Sally Thomsett as the occupants of the flat above.

It is often said that there is far too few good women comedians in Britain but if true, Yootha Joyce was one of the few; caustic but warm-hearted she knew how to make the most of an ironic line; this was abundantly plain when she played Mildred, the frustrated, childless wife of the ineffectual George, skillfully played by Murphy.

An only child born in South London of musical parents, she confessed in later life that she could neither sing nor dance and had a disappointing period at RADA but managed none the less to build a career in entertainment appearing in radio, in repertory and touring. Her big break came from a chance given to her by Miss Joan Littlewood in *Fings Ain't Wot They Used t'Be* put on at the Theatre Royal, Stratford East and subsequently transferred to the West End.

The Ghost of Yootha Joyce

It could be argued that Yootha Joyce always held an incredible stage presence around her, but the aura that surrounded the late actress could sometimes become quite apparent when being photographed and interviewed. Brian Murphy recalled the curious occurrences that sometimes brought to light, quite literally, the ghost of Yootha Joyce...

'Whenever we had to be photographed for continuity and have press stills produced, there would be an appearance of a sudden flash of what I can only describe as lightning, above our heads. When being interviewed and having the discussions recorded on magnetic tape, they would play the tape back and it would be blank. Then they'd play it back later on and the conversation would be there, it was weird'.

'No one could understand where this light was coming from but it happened quite often, we used to have to warn the studios in advance but they always dismissed it, until it actually happened'.

Main Cast

'When Yootha sadly died, I was invited to ITN news to talk about her and discuss my feelings. It would be pre-recorded in the afternoon and played that evening on television. This interview would also spare me all newspaper interviews afterwards, as the press would be given a transcript of what I said on the news. The recording went fine but then when it was broadcast that evening the weirdest thing happened. They led up to the interview, saying "we have Brian Murphy in the studio to discuss the sad demise of Yootha Joyce", but after the link when my interview was played, it all went quiet'.

'We had lost sound, nationwide. Everybody had lost sound on their televisions all across the country for my interview, but afterwards the rest of the news went without a hitch. When my bit was replayed later on in the evening, it was perfect. The sound was restored and was clear as a bell. It was so odd. There were no known technical problems and we could only assume that it was Yootha's influence, looking down on us. To this day I still think that'.

Could it have been just temporary static on the magnetic tapes preventing sound being transmitted, or could Yootha Joyce really be having her final laugh from the great studio in the sky, the mystery remains!

Brian Murphy

Brian Trevor Murphy was born on 25th September 1933, in Ventnor, Isle of Wight, moving with his parents to London as a child.

'I left school about 15 and did various jobs before I got into acting. I was an electrical assistant for Sainsbury's at their main factory in Blackfriars and I moved on to become a wireless mechanics assistant and TV repairs assistant. It was always as an assistant, I never got much further than that!'

'My parents adored the theatre and I was taken to see variety shows at the theatres and sometimes up to the West End. Theatre was expensive but we saw lots of things, and that's where I got my first whiff of greasepaint and desire to be upon the stage. I used to love watching the contortionists, musicians and great bands and magicians'.

'As I got older I saw the wonderful power of these fine actors, like Ralph Richardson and Lawrence Oliver. I thought then that this is what I wanted to be, and maybe I could go to the Royal Academy of Dramatic Art'.

Brain soon started working on his ambitions, putting on performances on his own home-made stage in the basement of his parent's house and charging his friends halfpence admission to watch.

'I was attending evening classes and I got a bursary to go to RADA, but I was too young and had national service coming up shortly. When I left that they weren't doing the bursary any more and couldn't have it awarded retrospectively. So I struggled with what savings I had, got an audition at RADA and I was there for the first year before having to go out and look for some odd jobs to pay the rent. I used to save money by walking to work, which was about five miles from my digs at the time, such was my driving ambition'.

In 1955, Murphy secured an audition for Joan Littlewood's Theatre Workshop, a position that would change his life. 'I got it through my teacher at the evening classes, he said it was a wonderful company and was quite different to everything else which exists up the West End. So I went along to a show and I was wildly excited by what I saw, and I auditioned to join the company. Joan was very kind and sweet, she said "you're young, and you're not up to it yet - get some more life experience and come back later". I regarded that as the big elbow, but that Saturday I received a telegram from her saying "you can start Monday". I was so very excited. I don't know to this day whether someone dropped dead or whatever, but I was suddenly at Joan Littlewood's. I had a wonderful learning experience there, it was marvellous'.

Following a few years on the stage with the workshop and parts in productions like; *Every Man in His Humour* in 1960, co-starring Roy Kinnear, Bob Grant and Victor Spinetti, Brian made his television debut, as an uncredited extra in the show *Probation Officer*.

'It wasn't such a huge difference moving from theatre to television. The main thing was that the acting had to be scaled down and you weren't projecting as you were on the stage. Thoughts could be transferred in the flick of an eyebrow or just the look in your eye and you had to get used to that sort of technique, which was great as it helped you develop as an actor'.

Brian Murphy continued his work on television, starring in an episode of *The Avengers*, with Patrick McNee, and small parts in various programmes, including *Z Cars* and *The Plane Makers*. After several more years in theatre including *Sweeney Todd, the Demon Barber of Fleet Street*, Murphy stepped into the television limelight in 1973, when he was cast in *Man About the House* as George Roper, a character that would secure his fame forever more.

'I spent seventeen weeks at Joan Littlewood's at Stratford East' recalled actor Robert Gillespie. 'It was there that I fell over Brian Murphy. I did a few shows with him, and it was quite a reunion for us with *George and Mildred*, I enjoyed working with him. Joan used to laugh the way we both signed on the dole before going to rehearsals!'

Main Cast

In 1974, Murphy played Archie Rice in *The Entertainer* at the Northcott Theatre in Exeter, later creating and playing the part of Pal in *Glorious Miles* at the Crucible Theatre, Sheffield. Back on-screen, Brian continued his part of George Roper in *George and Mildred*, until the series was discontinued following the death of Yootha Joyce.

'I had various theatre offers afterwards. Television was a bit tricky as they often wanted me for a similar type of role, always as George. After a few suggestions, I had a read through the scripts for *The Incredible Mr Tanner* with Roy Kinnear. Whereas before I was contracted to do *George and Mildred,* we now had an empty space because the final planned series had been cancelled. We didn't have to do anything we didn't want to, but we thought it would be a good idea to tackle this new show and the series was made. Roy and I had got on very well in the past when he had scenes in *George and Mildred*, there was an obvious partnership there, so we went for it. But it seemed to me that it was all too soon, perhaps we should have waited longer to allow the viewers to see us in different characters'.

Brian Murphy later took the starring role as driving instructor Lester Small in the short-lived *L for Lester*. 'I hadn't worked with the BBC for some time so I was quite flattered when they offered me the new series. It was a lovely character to play and it was received well - there was about five or six million watching on BBC 2, which was great. Sadly the writer, Dougie Lock, prematurely died not long after so there would never be a chance to do a new series, which was a shame'.

'I did various other television parts after that, things came my way and I did a few guest appearances, sometimes as me and sometimes as George. I was very careful to limit what I did, I didn't want to do any pale imitations of George. I did a lot more theatre which I loved, I could have gone on and on and on'.

In recent years, Brian has had many memorable roles, such as Mr Foskett in *One foot in the Grave*, Stan the shopkeeper in the children's show *Wizadora* and Ansell in *Lame Ducks*. In 2003, Brian was cast as Alvin Smedley in Roy Clarke's *Last of the Summer Wine*, still starring in the popular sitcom to this day. 'Alvin is fun to do. He can be quite sly and witty in his own way, a gentler soul in comparison to George, he deals with women better than George every did!'.

Brian has also appeared on the *Catherine Tate Show*, in addition making a cameo appearance as useless ventriloquist in the children's variety show, *The Slammer*. 'I'm happy to plod along and just turn up where people need me. The only role that I would have loved to play but I am too old now would be Cyrano De Bergerac, a mixture of being a romantic and a clown which I think lays upon my own description. There is a lot of fencing in it, and I'd loved doing all that physical stuff, but sadly I'm too old now. I've just done some more *Summer Wine* and also an episode of *Hustle*'.

'*Man About the House* and *George and Mildred* is always what I am remembered for. I still get called George in the streets. It was an extremely happy and rewarding time in my career. I realise the interest these series promoted and it is very flattering that there is still a lot of nostalgia for the programmes'.

Brian is married to actress and novelist, Linda Regan, his second wife. They met in 1988 whilst playing a couple in the play *Wife begins at forty*. Linda invited Brian round for coffee sometime and he turned up that same afternoon - 'He's been here ever since', she explained. They both currently live in Kent.

A truly underrated actor, Brian Murphy has been bringing talent to television for over fifty years, and in every role he has undertaken, pure professionalism, commitment and competence clearly show through his performances.

Sheila Fearn

Sheila Fearn was born on October 3rd 1940 in Leicester.

After making a television debut at the age of seventeen in the TV series, *Emergency Ward 10*, Fearn's next part came six years later in the acclaimed film, *Billy Liar,* in which she played an uncredited telephonist.

Sheila Fearn's big break came after she accepted the role of Audrey Collier in *The Likely Lads* in 1964, working again with Rodney Bewes, who had also appeared in *Billy Liar*. Fearn reprised her character of Audrey in 1973 with the reprisal series *Whatever happened to the Likely Lads.*

Sheila took on numerous smaller roles during the 1960's and early 1970's, making appearances in; *Thriller*, *The Avengers* and *The Beverly Hillbillies.* Fearn also used her friendship with Beatle John Lennon to secure a brief background part in the film *A Hard Day's Night.*

After a run in *Z cars* playing Josie Benson, Fearn was cast as Ann Fourmile in *George and Mildred,* a role she described as 'a super, witty part' to TV Times magazine. 'At last I'm middle class' she went on to describe, 'I've been twelve years doing northern sluts and kitchen sink drudges. It's real progress - by the time I'm 40 I might get a few well-heeled, wealthy upper-crust parts!'.

But this career target never materialised for Fearn. After taking the part of Kathy Carter in *The Flockton Flyer*, and later working on *Time Bandits* and *Sorry,* Sheila took her last role in *News at Twelve* in 1988, at the age of forty eight.

Despite becoming such a familiar face on our screens, Fearn has since disappeared from the public spotlight and her current whereabouts remain uncertain. There are sources suggesting that she has moved to America, but these reports remain unconfirmed.

'I lost touch with Sheila Fearn a good few years ago', explains Brian Murphy. 'It's a shame as I'd like to see her again. I think she has moved off to the United States now, I recall she married and was a film producer for a little while, but I don't see or hear of anything at all at the moment'.

Fearn's sudden departure from acting is the subject of much conjecture, and there are a few sparked rumours as to what may have happened to her after 1988. One story suggests that she sustained a leg injury whilst mountain climbing, and quit acting as a result. Another tale follows the line that Sheila opened a guesthouse in the early 1970's and retired from the acting business to work there full-time. Reports have also emerged that she now runs a pet-care business.

After her sterling work on *George and Mildred*, it is disappointing that Fearn ceased to act. Until any confirmed information on the current whereabouts of Sheila Fearn surface, we will be guessing for many years to come.

Titbits... Sheila Fearn had problems taming her Siamese cat, Claude. 'The neighbours have christened him 'Kamikaze', she told press in 1978. 'He fights with everything and it's costing me a fortune in vet's bills getting him patched up!'

Norman Eshley

Norman Eshley was born on May 30th 1945 in Bristol and after attending Bristol Grammar School, worked as a clerk in a local bank. But it was the acting profession that had the largest appeal to Eshley, and he later joined up at the Bristol Old Vic Theatre School. After many theatre shows, mainly Shakespeare, Eshley made his television debut in 1968, in the film *The Immortal Story*, directed by Orson wells.

Building upon an impressive debut, Eshley appeared in other roles throughout the late 1960's and early 1970's, frequently popping up in series like; *Department S, Crossplot, Randal and Hopkirk Deceased* and *Thriller*. Norman secured his first full-series role in the 1973 Action Drama, *Warship*, where he played Lieutenant Last for 17 episodes over the show's two year run. He also acted in Pete Walker's Golden Scroll nominated horror film, *The House of Mortal Sin* in 1976.

Later in 1976, Eshley worked on *Man About the House*, in which he starred as Norman Tripp, Robin's brother and the eventual husband to Chrissy. Eshley had previously appeared in an earlier episode of the sitcom as Ian Cross in 1974. His work on the series clearly left a lasting impression on the production team, as Eshley was given a leading role in *George and Mildred* just a few months later in 1976. However, this new part may have come too soon after his work on *Man About the House*, as some viewers found the transition between the characters of Norman Tripp and Jeffrey Fourmile confusing. One writer in a 1976 television magazine's correspondence section jokingly questioned; 'Why is Robin's brother now living next door to George and Mildred?!'

Eshley's role of Jeffrey Fourmile had an unexpected effect on audiences, and in some parts of the world secured cult status. In Spain, the comedy show *Aplauso* held a search for his exact double in a segment of their programme; *El Doble De Los Famosos* (The double of the famous ones). The competition was won by stout chap from Barcelona.

Following the end of *George and Mildred*, Eshley took on more one-off parts in popular dramas like *The Professionals* and *Minder,* as well as six episodes of *The Outsider* in 1983. Norman returned to television, appearing in a 1986 episode of *Brookside*.

From then, Norman took bit parts in *Taggart, Cadfael, One foot in the Grave, Harbour Lights* and *Goodnight Sweetheart*. He appeared in four episodes of *The Bill* in 1999 and then took his last television role in an episode of *New Tricks* in 2007. Eshley still works as an actor, but mainly in theatre.

Nicholas Bond-Owen

Born in Middlesex on November 13th 1968, Owen lived in Kenilworth Road, Ashford and attended Ashford high school. He never meant to get into the acting business, describing the fact that he did as 'pure luck'.

Joining a modelling agency on the back of his older brother, Matthew, Owen was spotted by the *George and Mildred* production team and went along to an interview, securing the part of Tristram Fourmile.

This series was Owen's first work as an actor, and he appeared in every episode of the sitcom. As the show progressed, it became apparent that he needed to distinguish himself from the other similar names on the acting directories. From the second series onwards, he starts to be credited as Nicholas Bond-Owen, a name chosen by himself because he was a big James Bond fan. Owen describes this action to have 'haunted me ever since!'.

Main Cast

After starring in the *George and Mildred* Movie in 1980, Nicholas took his talents to *Rhubarb Rhubarb* and later *The Coral Island* in 1983. Owen mastered the character of Charley Bates in several episodes of *Oliver Twist*, other credits running to *Dramarama* and *David Copperfield*.

Owen's acting career was a fairly short one, ending in 1988 when he faded out of the business to concentrate on his A-levels at college.

After a final stage role in 1993, Nicholas moved into the press industry, working with Penguin Publishing. He currently works as the distribution manager for London's City AM financial newspaper.

Nicholas had some cracking lines, and showed off the scripting of Cooke and Mortimer with excellence, setting up some of the very best scenes. Whereas many child actors seem flustered in front of the camera, Owen always seemed totally competent with his work and acted, in some cases, better than his co-star peers. A true professional from an early age.

'There are so many special memories that I have of working with *George and Mildred*, I just couldn't put them all into words. It was an absolute pleasure to work with all the cast, Norman Eshley was a top bloke and he really looked after me. My whole family was treated like royalty and came to watch every live show with our friends and family, we were all part of something really special'.

Man About The House

Summary.. 43
Episode Guide... 45
Opening Titles.. 85
Closing Titles... 88
The Film.. 89
The Film Theme Tune.......................... 93

Man About the House - Episode Guide

Summary

Man About the House follows the lives of Chrissy, Jo and Robin sharing a house run by landlords George and Mildred Roper, who are actually sub-letting landlords placed by the Church Commission. Robin is a master chef and is eager to jump into bed with any bright-eyed girl, but his flatmates are strong-willed and difficult to win over. Landlord George is a weak, bumbling and gullible man, endlessly frustrating his man-hungry wife - who spends a fair deal of her time flirting with Robin, a waste of effort, as Robin is after Jo and Chrissy.

Originally, this formula caused a few raised eyebrows at the time, but looking back from a modern day attitude, the permissiveness the series portrayed seems tame. 'It was deemed to be risqué and all saucy, but if you look at what we have got now, its so tame and cute in comparison', remembered Sally Thomsett in a 2004 interview. 'Even though sometimes it looked a bit saucy, we knew that nothing untoward was ever going to happen, Robin would never get his wicked way!'.

The first episode of *Man About the House* aired on 19th August 1973 and set the scene for the audience at home. Current tenants Chrissy Plummer (Paula Wilcox) and Jo (Sally Thomsett) have just held a farewell party for their flatmate Eleanor, who has upped sticks and left the house to get married. The next morning, they find a complete stranger, student Robin Tripp (Richard O'Sullivan) asleep in the bath. Robin is a trainee chef who attended the party the previous night, and was swiftly put to sleep by Chrissy's strong punch concoction. He has just left home in Southampton is at present without any fixed abode, living at the YMCA.

After he shows off his cookery skills to the girls, they agree that Robin can take the place of Eleanor and move into the house. Jo and Chrissy are more than happy with this, favouring him over a girl (Helen Fraser) who comes around to view the place. But landlord George Roper (Brian Murphy) needs some convincing that there won't be any 'carrying on' with the females in what he asserts is a respectable household.

Chrissy informs the Ropers that Robin is homosexual, so will not try anything on – and it is decided he can stay, but as soon as the doors close Robin tries to seduce the girls. George swallows the charade, but Mildred (Yootha Joyce) can see through the act and realises that Robin isn't gay - and that she may be in with her chances.

The scene is then set for a hilarious line of thirty-nine episodes following a similar story, with Robin after the girls – and Mildred after him. The six series from 1973 to 1976 drew in exceptional viewing figures, with millions eagerly tuning in each week to see if the three young, single stars ever actually got together - but they never did!

Episode Guide

It was once said by eminent sitcom writer and producer David Croft that; 'Comedy's unwillingly tire after forty episodes'. This may be the reason why Johnnie Mortimer and Brian Cooke chose to end *Man About the House* swiftly after episode thirty-nine!

Here is a closer look at all those episodes in their full glory, providing; an episode synopsis, details of the guest stars, original transmission dates and times as well as VTR (Video Tape Recording) numbers where issued. My own personal 'chortle rating' for each episode are also listed.

Additionally, there are a few 'Titbits', explaining a curious back-stage story or interesting fact, as well as 'Recollections' from the stars.

Cast and Crew

Unless otherwise stated, all episodes feature:

Richard O'Sullivan as Robin Tripp
Paula Wilcox as Chrissy Plummer
Sally Thomsett as Jo
Yootha Joyce as Mildred Roper
Brian Murphy as George Roper

Full series scripts by: Johnnie Mortimer and Brian Cooke
Full series production and direction by: Peter Frazer-Jones

Series 1 - Designed by: Gordon Toms, John Wood
Series 2 - Designed by: Alex Clarke
Series 3 - Designed by: Peter Elliott
Series 4 - Designed by: John Plant
Series 5 - Designed by: Alex Macintyre
Series 6 - Designed by: Robin Parker

Head of Light Entertainment: Phillip Jones

Man About the House - Episode Guide

Three's a Crowd - Series 1, Episode 1
Broadcast: Wednesday August 15th 1973 at 20:30
VTR: 7187A

Chrissy Plummer staggers out of bed with a grim hangover, the very mention of food driving her to retch and the noise of Jo's vacuuming interfering with her head. It's all because of the wild wedding reception party the night before for previous flatmate Eleanor. Chrissy goes to drown herself in the bath, but upon drawing back the shower curtain, finds a man sleeping in it. Robin Tripp. He had been at the party, coming along with a fellow gate-crasher and practically passing out after sampling some of the intoxicating punch.

The girls get to know their interloper. Having a chat over one of Jo's typical breakfasts, a disgusting concoction of scrambled egg garnished with slivers of supposedly non-stick frying pan, served on a bed of cremated toast. It's an inedible serving and all agree that Eleanor's cooking is missed, Jo is clearly no Fanny Craddock. Fortunately, Robin happens to be a cookery student at the technical college, and after a rapid inventory of the cupboard's contents, he serves up the best he can muster from limited supplies, a great meal. It seems to be match made in heaven. Robin is a great cook and needs somewhere to stay. Jo and Chrissy need a man about the house and, best of all, have a recently vacated room.

But before Robin can move in, there are is a slight problem that has to be addressed. The main issue lies with his gender. Despite this being the swinging 70's, landlord George Roper objects most strongly to a man sharing with a couple of girls, convinced there would be endless carrying-on. Mildred disagrees. Jo and Chrissy want Robin to stay as well, but how to change George's mind?

Chortle Rating: A firm, funny introduction - 9/10

Guest stars: Helen Fraser

And Mother Makes Four - Series 1, Episode 2
Broadcast: Wednesday August 22nd 1973 at 20:30
VTR: 7951

A visit from Chrissy's mother coincides with the day that new tenant, Robin Tripp, is moving his belongings in from the YMCA to his new lodgings at Myddleton Terrance. If Chrissy's mum sees a man in her daughter's flat, she will instantly expect that she is a frolicking female philanderer, so Robin and Jo are despatched to The Mucky Duck pub to keep them out of the way. Chrissy's mother soon arrives, and when she hears that Eleanor has left the flat, she is quick to stake her claim to the spare room for the night.

To save Robin walking the streets in atrocious weather conditions, Chrissy and Jo reluctantly agree to let him stay in their room for the night, smuggling him in past Chrissy's mother and then sticking him to an armchair to prevent any randy sleepwalking. Robin is relishing in the arrangement, but when a sudden gust of wind causes the lounge window to crash wide open, Tripp has to go and sort it out, meeting mother on the way and running into trouble.

Titbits... Keep an eye on the floor towards the end of this episode to witness some splashing. Director and producer Peter Frazer-Jones explained the reasons for this in a 1974 interview for Look-in magazine: 'The episode required continual rainfall outside the flat, and so we had plumbers in to lay special pipes and drains in order to get rid of the water from the special effects. But the drains blocked, and the show was put on with everyone wading around in three inches of water. The cameramen made sure that Richard O'Sulivan and co. were only shown from the waist upwards throughout the whole programme!'

Chortle Rating: Strong guest star and entertaining plot-line. 8/10

Guest Stars: Daphne Oxenford

Some Enchanted Evening - Series 1, Episode 3
Broadcast: Wednesday August 29th 1973 at 20:30
VTR: 7952

Jo needs some help with a boyfriend who is acting too shy towards her, preferring to shake her hand in favour of a canoodle, and ballroom dancing instead of the disco. Robin offers some advice in the form of Jo hosting a romantic evening, with some ambient lighting, sultry music, and fantastic cooking. Whereas Jo can muster the first two, the food bit will be a complete mess, unless the chef of the house can be persuaded to offer his help...

Robin reluctantly agrees, and after preparing a culinary feast, leaves Jo to take the credit and goes downstairs with Chrissy to spend some time with the Ropers, playing monopoly and talking about George and Mildred's honeymoon in Dunkirk. Whilst chatting to Mildred about Jo's boyfriend, it emerges his surname is Bloomstein. David is Jewish. Ham and Bacon Pate with Roast Pork may not go down so well for dinner then...

Titbits... Notice how the sound of the television continues for a few seconds after Chrissy pulls the plug out of the wall.

Chortle Rating: Excellent, simple story line. 9/10

Guest Stars: Steve Patterson

And Then There Were Two - Series 1, Episode 4
Broadcast: Wednesday September 5th 1973 at 20:30
VTR: 7955

Something's not right. It's only Wednesday, but already Robin has had several baths. Chrissy is convinced that a woman is the reason behind his sudden interest in male grooming, and that she will become the target of his pent-up desires. When Robin starts reading 'Quorum' - the journal of personal relationships, her mind is made up. The problems really start to arise when Jo announces she will be away for a few days, staying at her sisters, and leaving Chrissy alone with a lounge lothario and nobody to defend her honour!

That evening, Robin makes a move on his flatmate, slithering down to her end of the sofa and mouthing suggestions of his lusty intentions. Chrissy manages to remain aloof and succeeds in fielding his amorous advances. Accepting defeat, Robin joins Larry at the Mucky Duck pub, where he meets Liz - an old flame.

Robin suggests to Liz that they go back to his place, and she waits outside while Robin tells Chrissy of his plans for a wild night of passion. Totally unaware that Liz is standing outside, Chrissy gets the wrong end of the stick, and is under the belief that Robin wants to spend the night with her. When he explains that it's not her he wants to spend the night with, she retires to her room.

After an hour of solitary confinement, Chrissy emerges and enters the lounge to find Robin and Liz in a passionate embrace. The romance of the moment is well and truly killed when she turns off the music, turns up the lights, and settles into an armchair with a ball of knitting. When Chrissy talks about 'going to the clinic', Liz leaves instantly. Robin is peeved by his flatmate's scheming behaviour, but at least they are alone once more, and Robin is determined to get something out the evening...

Titbits... Although this episode was aired fourth in series one, it was actually sixth to be recorded. 'Match of the Day' was the fourth to be recorded, yet the sixth to be aired.

Chortle Rating: Favourable use of double entendre. 9/10

Guest Stars: Doug Fisher, Janine Drzewicki, Jenny Hanley

Man About the House - Episode Guide

It's Only Money - Series 1, Episode 5
Broadcast: Wednesday September 12th 1973 at 20:30
VTR: 7954
Viewing households - 7.6 Million
National television chart position - 1

Chrissy and Robin return home to find their front door ajar. With Jo out until later that evening, it strikes them that after a recent spate of break-ins, there may be a burglar in their flat. Chrissy nudges Robin inside, and after gingerly skulking around, he draws the conclusion that all appears fine. Except for the rent - £80 has mysteriously vanished. The tenants are already one month behind on the payments, and quickly set about trying to re-muster the money.

When George brings up the topic of the rent in the pub that evening, Robin, Chrissy and Jo are quick to run away from the discussion, and end up avoiding Roper for days whilst they attempt to gain some cash. George continues to pursue them, determined to discuss the rent, but the tenants don't stay around long enough to listen. If only they did, they may learn the true whereabouts of some money...

Chortle Rating: An entertaining farce. 9/10

Guest Stars: Michael Segal, Ken Watson, Derek Seaton, Colin McCormack, Raymond Farrell

Match of the Day - Series 1, Episode 6
Broadcast: Wednesday September 19th 1973 at 20:30
VTR: 7953

When Robin is asked to replace an injured player on the technical college football team, he is ecstatic, that is until he catches Roper's cold and it looks like his chances at sporting glory may be over. Desperate to recover in time for the game, Robin tries every remedy in the book; from lemon juice to Old Mother Asquith's goose fat concoction rubbed on his chest.

After a visit from the cantankerous Doctor Macleod and being prescribed a high potency vitamin injection, Robin returns to his usual form and is once again match fit. However, he receives a disappointing phone call; Barry, the player he is replacing, has recovered from his toe injury, pushing Robin out of the team once again.

Robin, Chrissy and Jo go along to the match anyway, borrowing the Roper's car to get to the away game in Catford. When parking up at the pitch, Robin makes a hash of the manoeuvre and manages to drive over Barry's foot - rendering him match useless again. Robin is back in the game, but now facing a new dilemma. It turns out that he has made a slight mistake with the sport he is playing - namely with the shape of the ball...

Chortle Rating: Perfect punch line and ending. 8/10

Guest Stars: Duncan Lamont, Michael Redfern, Michael J. Jackson

Man About the House - Episode Guide

No Children, No Dogs - Series 1, Episode 7
Broadcast: Wednesday September 26th 1973 at 20:30
VTR: 7956

Larry's dog has had puppies and he is having a difficult time trying to find a suitable home for them. Robin mentions that Jim, the barman at The Mucky Duck is looking for a dog, and he reluctantly agrees to deliver one of the puppies to him later that evening. When Robin arrives at the pub, he is aghast to discover that Larry has beaten him to it. Jim is the proud owner of a new pet. Robin has been diddled and left with a dog he cannot keep, with the lease at the flat firmly stating 'No children, No Dogs'. With the only other home being the pound, Robin and the girls decide to give the dog some temporary accommodation. But how to keep it out of George's sight?

The puppy whimpers all through the night, disturbing everybody's sleep, and it falls to Robin to take it for a stroll. Whilst perambulating around the block, he bumps into barman Jim, who is also having to tire out his pup to get a decent night's sleep. Despite it being after hours, Jim suggests a nightcap at the pub to relieve the tired dog-walkers.

Robin staggers home bleary-eyed at 3 O'clock in the morning. Any more nights like this would be intolerable, and it is agreed that the dog has to go. The problems are solved by Jo, who accidentally leaves the front door open when collecting the paper, and provides the perfect escape route. Mildred gets a surprise when she finds the dog on the doorstep and assumes it's a stray, taking it into her home and heart. Just as it seems that life can return to normal, Jim comes round to explain that there has been a 'mutty' mix-up!

Titbits ... The statement Robin makes in this episode, about bread 'belonging to Cyril from Hounslow', is a direct reference to a television advertisement of 1971. The advert for Wonderloaf, a long since defunct brand of white sliced-bread, incorporated a catch phrase 'nice one Cyril'. The catchphrase caught on and entered the national vocabulary practically overnight. The squad of Tottenham Hotspur Football club also got in on the act, releasing a record under the collective name of 'The Cockerel Chorus', celebrating their star left-back Cyril Knowles in 1972.

Chortle Rating: Compelling ad-lib from Richard O'Sullivan dealing with his unravelling finger bandage. 8/10

Guest Stars: Doug Fisher, Michael Segal, Emmett Hennessy

1973 All Star Comedy Carnival Special Short
Broadcast: December 25th 1973 at 18:30

The last edition of a yearly comedy bonanza, the first being in 1969, *The All Star Comedy Carnival* celebrated Christmas with barrels of ITV fun, comprising of specially created bite-sized editions of the nation's favourite shows with surprise celebrity guests.

This 1973 edition was broadcast on Christmas day at 18:30, hosted by 'the old J.T. himself' - Jimmy Tarbuck. Running for 90 minutes, this programme featured festive editions of; *Man About the House, My Good Woman, Sez Lez, Billy Liar, Spring and Autumn* and *Doctor in Charge*.

The condensed programmes ran to about seven minutes each, and were little more than extended sketches, interspersed by a host of festive frolics and specially invited guests. Artistes appearing in the 1973 *All Star Comedy Carnival* included: Henry Cooper, Val Doonican, Kenny Lynch, Hugh Paddick, Fyfe Robertson, Rachel Stuart, Josephine Tewson, Bobby Moore, May Warden and Frank Williams.

The *Man About the House* festive short revolves around Mildred inviting the tenants down to her flat to celebrate Christmas. George is busy pinching all the gifts from inside the crackers when the guests arrive, causing him to cease his 'Humbug' activities to be social for a few moments. After a boring discussion about the berries falling off the Roper's mistletoe, George offers to show everyone a card trick - yet this too is stymied when Robin shuffles the deck!

The evening drags by painfully slowly, with the tenants thoughts preoccupied with missing out on the party next door. In a last-ditch attempt to lighten the atmosphere, Robin has a tinkle on the piano, but when George joins in singing 'The road the Mandalay', everyone agrees to call it a night. Robin leaves with Chrissy and Jo, and out of the sight of the Ropers, they sneak out to the party.

George and Mildred are relieved to be rid of the guests, as they have plans themselves. Poking their heads out the door to see if the coast is clear, they too head off to the party next door!

Chortle Rating: Filled with festive fun. 9/10

Man About the House - Episode Guide

While the Cat's Away - Series 2, Episode 1
Broadcast: Wednesday January 9th 1974 at 20:00
VTR: 8594A

To break the monotony of a routine weekend, the tenants decide to have a party. When the Ropers announce they are going off to Mildred's sisters for a couple of days, it seems an opportunity too good to miss, and the arrangements for the party are quickly in place. Robin invites his girlfriend, and gets the booze from the pub in preparation. Chrissy invites boyfriend Mark, an actor most famous for his exemplary deodorant commercial.

The party gets in full swing and Liz arrives to join the fun. Entering the room she is immediately transfixed by Chrissy's boyfriend, Mark, who is soon regaling her with anecdotes about Michael Caine in the Pinewood Canteen. It is an obvious case of lust at first site, which has the unfortunate result of leaving both Chrissy and Robin partner-less. In an effort to console each other, they go downstairs to the Roper's empty flat where they can be alone and enjoy some privacy. Chrissy and Robin discuss the situation of their relationship over a glass of wine, and the platonic relationship they have always abided to looks about to be broken. Just as a spark is about to ignite between the pair, the Ropers make an unexpected return...

Titbits... When Mark runs off with Liz, Jo says to Chrissy; 'He had big ears anyway!'. This was a catchphrase Thomsett used in a 1972 television advertisement for Bovril.

Chortle Rating: Sparkling humour with a hint of broken heartedness 9/10

Guest Stars: Ian Lavender, Jenny Hanley, Jeffrey Gardiner, Michael Segal, Colin McCormack

Colour Me Yellow - Series 2, Episode 2
Broadcast: Wednesday January 16th 1974 at 20:00
VTR: 8595

The girls are busy redecorating the flat when Robin struts in. He has just returned from a Judo lesson and is keen to show off his new found skills. Suppressing their laughter at Robin's antics, Chrissy and Jo are clearly unimpressed and get on with the refurbishments. When they tire of wallpapering, they go to the pub instead.

Robin and the girls take their seats at a table, and with drinks placed before them start a quiet conversation about nothing in particular. So far, no-one has noticed a well built bruiser who is propping the bar and drinking heavily. The leering nuisance has certainly noticed Chrissy and Jo, and approaches their table with a string of suggestive chat-up lines. The girls ignore the comments but Robin feels it his moral duty to see off the intruder and defend the honour of his flatmates. After all, he is almost an expert in self defence.

Robin's reproach of 'now look here...' gets stuck in his throat. The nuisance is huge, and could most likely flatten him with a cold stare. Heroic intentions quickly evaporate. The following morning, all Robin can think about is his cowardly actions of the previous night, and is set on returning to the Mucky Duck later that evening to have it out with his lumbering adversary. A High Noon showdown looks set to take place, but when the bruiser walks in, it's Chrissy, not Robin who is first on the draw.

Titbits... In the final scene of this episode, keep watch on the area behind the bar. In some of the shots looking from Robin's table to the back of the set, a camera and operator can be seen getting into position to capture the discussions between the Jim and Chrissy. The black camera hood can be seen fleetingly above Richard O'Sullivan's right shoulder.

Chortle Rating: Interesting work from Paul Angelis. 9/10

Guest Stars: Paul Angelis, Michael Segal, Eamonn Boyce

Man About the House - Episode Guide

In Praise of Older Men - Series 2, Episode 3
Broadcast: Wednesday January 23rd 1974 at 20:00
VTR: 8596

Chrissy has been going steady with her latest boyfriend, Ian Cross, who according to Robin and Jo is little more than an 'ancient' 30-year-old. Their opinions of Miss Plummer's new boyfriend are far from high and they are convinced there is something fishy about him. They are proved correct when Mildred mentions in the pub that he is married. Chrissy is shattered to learn the news, and confronts Ian over dinner later that evening. Ian denies the allegation and assures her he is divorced.

The following evening at the Mucky Duck, Robin tells Mildred her assumptions were false, but Mrs. Roper is sticking to her guns and is adamant her facts have a solid foundation. Ian Cross is most definitely married. It's clear that Chrissy is being led down the garden path, but how can Robin convince her?

A plan of action seems the obvious course, and the following day, borrowing the Ropers car, Robin and Chrissy set out for a drive. They stop outside a house that is up for sale and go inside for a viewing. Chrissy has no idea what is going on until she is introduced to the owner, Mrs Cross - Mrs Ian Cross. It then dawns on her that Robin was right all along, and she now has the evidence that her suitor is a two-timing rat.

Recollections... My agent got the call and asked me if I was available to play Mrs. Cross, all the cast were pleasant and we just got on with rehearsing and recording the show. I think it was Teddington Studios - Audrey Nicholson

Titbits... Robin makes a remark about Ian's 'old' age, but in reality, it's interesting to note how Richard O'Sullivan (Robin) was actually older than Norman Eshley (Ian). In 1974, Richard was 30 and Norman was only 29!

Chortle Rating: Did Norman Eshley get danger-money for all that tea and sherry being poured over him? 9/10

Guest Stars: Norman Eshley, Audrey Nicholson, Michael Segal, Chet Townsend

Did You Ever Meet Rommel? - Series 2, Episode 4
Broadcast: Wednesday January 30th 1974 at 20:00
VTR: 8597

It's the Roper's wedding anniversary and Mildred is certain that once again, George has forgotten. Prompting her husband with suggestive hints, she stresses the point that today has a special significance, and challenges him to recall what it is. 'Arsenal versus Chelsea' is all he sees worthy of remembering.

Feeling sorry for the crestfallen Mildred, Chrissy invites the Ropers for a celebration dinner upstairs, the only satisfaction Mildred is likely to receive that evening. When Robin is told of the new dinner guests, he is not in the least bit happy, having already invited a friend from college, Franz Wasserman, a German. Sadly, George and Germans don't really mix. He still hasn't forgiven them for blowing him out of the bath with a buzz bomb.

As feared, Roper drones on throughout the dinner, doing his Nazi salutes and making repeated references to England's 1966 world cup victory over the Germans. Giblet and Pork Stew being dished up as the main meal irritates him further. Could this evening have a happy ending or is there another blitz around the corner?

Titbits... The bra and suspenders kitchen apron that Richard O'Sullivan wears over the run of the series, seen most clearly in this episode, was exceptionally popular with viewers. Thames television received so many enquires about it, that they licensed the design to a manufacturer to create them for retail!

Chortle Rating: Superb example of comedy stereotyping. 10/10

Guest Stars: Dennis Waterman

Two Foot Two, Eyes of Blue - Series 2, Episode 5
Broadcast: Wednesday February 6th 1974 at 20:00

When Jo organises a night out on the same day she has promised to baby-sit for the Randall's, it falls to Robin and Chrissy to take her place and look after the infant for the night. Neither of them are too happy about the set-up, but agree regardless, with the lure of 40p an hour proving the biggest draw for the flat-broke flatmates.

It's a long night for the pair, with the baby constantly crying and the key to the drinks cabinet hidden away. Under different circumstances, this would be an ideal opportunity for Robin to get closer to Chrissy, but with a tot bawling in the background, even a cuddle seems out of the question. With mounting desperation, a phone call is placed to Mildred, to draw upon her experience of infant welfare. She used to work in a maternity hospital, be it only in the laundry room, and has a smattering of knowledge on how to deal with babies.

After endless hours of hard work, Chrissy and Robin get the baby to sleep, just in time for Jo to return after a miserable night out with boyfriend Philip. Her arrival coincides with that of the baby's grandmother, a matriarchal battleaxe who is quick to bark orders and has Jo running ragged in double quick time. Due comeuppance!

Recollections... I had great fun in *Man About the House*. I had done a lot with Peter Frazer-Jones and he asked me up for the job. Everyone was so very professional, but Yootha Joyce was ultra-professional. She really knew what she was doing and she was a wonderful actress. - Bella Emberg

Chortle Rating: Firm cameos make interesting viewing. 7/10

Guest Stars: Richard Fraser, Jo Kendall, Karl Howman, Bella Emberg

Carry Me Back To Old Southampton - Series 2, Episode 6
Broadcast: Wednesday February 13th 1974 at 20:00
VTR: 8599
Viewing households - 8.2 Million
National television chart position - 1

When Robin fails his catering exams at the technical college, he is distinctly downcast. Chrissy and Jo can't see how he could possibly have failed, being a wonderful cook, but when Robin explains how nerves got the better of him and he put curry powder in his custard, the reasons are apparent.

Robin's father had always wanted his son to enter the family business 'Tripp's Extruded Tubing', and now that Robin is qualification-free, it looks like he is destined for a career in plumbing. Larry's notion of all that crumpet falling for 'the boss's son' improves Robin's attitude towards the situation, and he agrees to up sticks and go home to Southampton. Chrissy and Jo are upset at the prospect of losing their flatmate and even more disappointed with the suggestion that Larry becomes his replacement.

With tearful goodbyes from the girls and the Ropers, it looks like Robin is going for good. That is until his father turns up at the flat and explains how the business would be better without his influence, insisting instead that he goes back to school and this time 'passes the bloody exams'. Everything is sorted out and Robin is staying. One small problem remains though. Larry has just left his digs to take Robin's place, and having unleashed a torrent of critical insults on his landlord, there is no going back!

Chortle Rating: Emotional with a happy ending. 8/10

Guest Stars: Doug Fisher, Leslie Sands, John Carlin

Man About the House - Episode Guide

Cuckoo in the Nest - Series 3, Episode 1
Broadcast: Wednesday October 9th 1974 at 20:00
VTR: 9675

The tenants are in a state of near mutiny. For the past few weeks, Larry has been sleeping on their sofa after Robin promised him a non-existent room and made him leave his digs. The temporary guest is costing them a fortune, pinching their food, nicking all the milk and draining the larder dry. Robin, Chrissy and Jo are unanimous in their decision that he has to vacate, but with Larry's capacity for ceaseless consumption, who would have him and where can he go?

As luck would have it, there is an empty attic space at the top of the house, where George occasionally retreats to escape Mildred's nagging. It's a complete mess up there, littered with the detritus of brown ale bottles and Roper's supply of smutty 'reading' material, but with a bit of work it could soon become habitable for a certain cadging lodger.

When George is informed about the decision to put Larry in the attic, he is unhappy with the prospect of losing his private den. However, faced with an ultimatum - to bring in some more rent or get a job - he chooses the least punishing option. Determined to see the back of their freeloader; Robin, Chrissy and Jo set to work clearing the attic. It's an arduous task, until they discover some hilarious reading material - George's old love-letters!

Chortle Rating: My favourite episode. 10/10

Guest Stars: Doug Fisher, Norman Chappell

Come Into My Parlour - Series 3, Episode 2
Broadcast: Wednesday October 16th 1974 at 20:00
VTR: 9676

Robin's girlfriend is coming to the flat, and he is busily hatching a fiendish plan. If he gets her drunk, she'll drop her defences and hopefully a few other things too. Chrissy doesn't agree with his methods, especially this time when he is dating Angie, an old school friend of hers. Chrissy feels responsible for Angie's welfare with the sex starved Robin ready to strike - after all she used to be her milk monitor.

When Angie arrives and commences taking a lengthy trip down memory lane with Chrissy, Robin retreats to bed early. For him the evening is ruined and the blame lies solely at his flatmate's door. Determined for another chance with Angie, he sets aside a future evening to demonstrate his passion, this time planning in advance and preparing the scene by booting the troublesome Chrissy downstairs to look at George's soul-destroying holiday snaps of Benidorm.

When Angie arrives, Robin feels gratified to have his clutches on her, but upon being asked if he is serious about his intentions, he realises that he is only after a quick fumble and couldn't possibly commit for life. Robin feels guilty at the fact that Angie has been saving herself until her soul-mate arrives, does he really have the selflessness to not exploit this opportunity?

Chortle Rating: Favourable comedy with decent sub-plot. 8/10

Guest Stars: Doug Fisher, Caroline Dowdeswell, Hilda Kriseman

Man About the House - Episode Guide

I Won't Dance, Don't Ask Me - Series 3, Episode 3
Broadcast: Wednesday October 23rd 1974 at 20:00
VTR: 9677

With the annual office party just one day away, Chrissy is still without a partner to go with. Worse still, there is nobody in the office who would make a suitable escort, as everyone is paired, including the office boy. In desperation, she approaches Robin, who is happy to help with her obvious dilemma and agrees to go with her. If he plays his cards right, he can build up a bit of future canoodle credit at the same time.

There is, however, a fly in the ointment to what would otherwise be the perfect evening. It involves ballroom dancing, a skill at which Robin is woefully inept. With no other option, Robin and Chrissy approach the Ropers, and ask for assistance with the forthcoming function; Mildred is only too happy to oblige, and adopts the mantle of a domineering dance tutor, prancing about to an ancient melodies including Guy Lombardo's Royal Canadians. George also gets in on the act and tries to flog Robin his moth-eaten dinner jacket.

On the night of the party, Robin's nerves are beginning to show, and his confidence is further eroded when Chrissy forbids him to divulge his student status. Most of the guests have professional backgrounds, and Robin is eager to create an impression. However, after putting it about that he is a Jesuit priest, a brain surgeon and a member of parliament, Robin falls foul of his concoction of lies when an attractive young cookery student catches his eye...

Recollections... I remember having to wear a huge moustache in this episode, so not to be recognised for later casting when I appeared in the episode 'The Tender Trap'. It was quite the fashion then! - John Colclough

Recollections... I turned up to an audition for *Man About the House* and got the role in this episode. The cast were very nice and friendly and I later worked again with Brian Murphy in the play *Shut Your Eyes and Think of England* when it went on tour. - Sally Harrison

Chortle Rating: Nice dance moves from Brian and Yootha! 9/10

Guest Stars: John Colclough, Gareth Johnson, Frances Jeater, Sally Harrison, Peggyann Clifford, Alison Hughes, Robert Swales, The Ambrose Quilby Four

Of Mice and Women - Series 3, Episode 4
Broadcast: Wednesday October 30th 1974 at 20:00
VTR: 9678

Jo is terrified when a brown mouse scuttles across her feet in the morning. Larry has chased it down from upstairs with an egg whisk. Jo refuses to sleep in the same room as the rodent, so Robin agrees to swap beds with her, meaning he will be in the same room as Chrissy. Two of the three flatmates are happy with the arrangement, and with Chrissy fretting at the thought of her bedroom being violated by randy Robin, she and insists he spends the night on the sofa instead.

The next morning, it is clear that Robin has had a rough night, and looks worse for wear after sleeping in the lounge. After some gentle persuasion, Chrissy relents and agrees he can spent that night in her room. Robin is quietly delighted, but when Larry comes down to cadge some coffee and tells anyone who will listen how he killed the mouse by chucking a radio at it, the mood changes. Robin is swift to silence Larry and insists he keeps his trap shut about the incident. If truth became known, it would scupper his plans of sharing with Chrissy. When George also hears the mouse is dead, he too persuades Larry to keep quiet, having managed to use the rodent as an excuse to cancel a visit from Mildred's mother.

The men of the house are delighted with the situation. The mouse has scored them unrivalled victory over the females. It's just a pity when Larry lets the truth slip...

Chortle Rating: Excellent nose-tapping work from Doug Fisher. 8/10

Guest Stars: Doug Fisher, Annie Hayes

Man About the House - Episode Guide

Somebody Out There Likes Me - Series 3, Episode 5
Broadcast: Wednesday November 6th 1974 at 20:00
VTR: 9673

Chrissy is receiving gifts from a secret admirer, but finds the prospect of being pursued from a distance unnerving, especially when Robin starts doing 'Quasimodo' impressions. Rather than keep her flowers and chocolates, she passes the gifts to a grateful Mildred. not the best idea, as it convinces George that his wife is having an affair!

Mildred delights in baiting George, fuelling his jealousy with hints and suggestions of a secret lover. Convinced the milkman is to blame, George is pacing the lounge, determined to uncover the identity of Mildred's suitor. Upstairs, and Chrissy is also wracking her brains as to who would be sending her gifts, and has been phoning around a few old boyfriends. When one of them turns up on her doorstep the next day, he is greeted by George who assumes the caller is Mildred's lover. When Roper confronts the visitor, it prompts Chrissy to tell him the truth about the presents, enlightening him that Mildred doesn't have a lusting fan after all.

Later that evening, Robin answers the phone to a mysterious stranger who is enquiring after Chrissy. Her secret admirer is finally revealed and he soon comes around to see her in person and make sure that she received the presents. He seems a nice bloke and it looks like Miss Plummer may have found a suitable partner, until her dreams get crushed when it turns out that Alan thinks that Chrissy is actually Jo!

Titbits... We hear the radio announcer at the start of the episode explain how 'up next is *The Men from the Ministry*'. Johnnie Mortimer and Brian Cooke wrote some episodes of this series.

Chortle Rating: Some more excellent work from Brian and Yootha. 9/10

Guest Stars: Christopher Chittell, Colin McCormack

We Shall Not Be Moved - Series 3, Episode 6
Broadcast: Wednesday November 13th 1974 at 20:00
VTR: 9674

When Mildred goes away for a week, George and useless friend Jerry set about making their plans for turning the flat upstairs into 'smaller dwelling units' a reality, a simple way to rake in some more cash. Using the expired lease as an excuse, Roper presents Robin, Chrissy and Jo with an ultimatum. Leave before the end of the week.

But Roper is fighting against canny flatmates, and they are quick to get on to the citizen's advice bureau where it's confirmed that George has to give at least three months notice, and then apply for a possession order before they legally have to leave. Jerry issues a counter argument laden with emotional blackmail, saying that George's frail mother wants to move in upstairs. The fact she has been dead eleven years doesn't seem to put a stop to the plans, but the revelation that the flatmates may be preventing an old woman from having a home prompts them into packing their bags.

As the moments before eviction slowly count down, Robin, Chrissy and Jo spend an emotional few minutes to say their farewells. Robin is off to the YMCA, Chrissy to the YWCA and Jo is destined to stay at a friend's house. Thankfully, Mildred returns in the nick of time, and when she discovers the nefarious deeds George has been planning, she starts to tackle her tactless husband. If anyone is leaving, it is likely to be him...

Chortle Rating: Entertaining with pathos. 8/10

Guest Stars: Roy Kinnear, Michael Redfern, Ian Sharp, Derek Seaton

Man About the House - Episode Guide

Three of a Kind - Series 3, Episode 7
Broadcast: Wednesday November 20th 1974 at 20:00
VTR: 9679

Robin has a raging sore throat but would rather ignore it to concentrate on his poker game than get medical attention. Fortunately one of his friends, Derek, is a trainee doctor, and after an impromptu examination, Robin is diagnosed with inflamed tonsils. He will have to go into hospital for an operation to have them removed.

Derek pulls some strings and fixes it up for his friend to get an appointment the next day, and when Robin turns up at the infirmary and has last night's diagnosis confirmed, he is whisked into theatre for the surgical procedure. But it's not going under the knife which is the most pressing on his mind. Robin has another poker game in a matter of days, and with the star player laid up in a hospital bed, it falls to Chrissy to take his place. It's just a shame she has never played in her life and doesn't have a clue how to!

The night of the big game arrives and even George turns up for a piece of the action, clutching a small wad of notes he has pinched from Mildred's savings jug. With Chrissy's maximum penny bet in place it's not a very exciting evening, but to prevent everyone from going home the game is soon set to no limits. Chrissy is flustered by a confusing hand she gets dealt and has to telephone Robin in hospital for assistance. She has King High, one of the worst possible hands in Poker, and winning seems unlikely. Unless Robin can get her to do a bit of involuntary bluffing...

Recollections... I was a good poker player, so perhaps I was cast for that, but I think it was more likely to be from my agent. Teddington studios used to put on loads of different series and we got known by the directors for our comedy work. I went up for the interview and got the job. We were all young, it was nice to be working. We all got on very well with one another. We filmed in front of an audience, but when you are younger you have very little fear and get on with it. - Jeremy Bulloch

Chortle Rating: Witty with a funny hint of light sexism. 9/10

Guest Stars: Doug Fisher, Duncan Lamont, Jeremy Bulloch, Louisa Martin

Home and Away - Series 4, Episode 1
Broadcast: Thursday March 6th 1975 at 20:00

Robin is in an unusually good mood, he has managed to wrangle a couple of tickets to the Southampton Vs Arsenal match, and when he finds out that Chrissy is an Arsenal fan and she agrees to go with him, his mood gets even better. The problem of how to get down to Southampton arises, with Chrissy not over-enthralled at getting the train and then spending the night in a hotel, it's decided that they will try and borrow the Roper's car.

Meanwhile, George is eagerly expected the postman to deliver a parcel for him - containing a toupee to render his sex-appeal forever potent. He looks a complete moron in the new hairpiece, but he is convinced that his new rug looks undetectable. Mildred on the other hand, doesn't.

Robin and Chrissy hit the road in the Roper's car, which breaks down on the way and ends up having to be pushed. They eventually give up all hope and stop by a telephone box to call George and ask for help, who is hardly any help at all. After spending hours at the roadside, a troupe of motorcyclists pull over to see if they can be of assistance help and eventually get the rotten old banger going again.

Back home, and George has been drying his hairpiece in the oven after spilling beer on it, but it shrinks and becomes useless. George is narked at the loss of his £12, but Mildred is pleased to get her bald, ratty old husband back again.

Chortle Rating: Fantastic Roper wig-work! 10/10

Titbits... As with the next episode, Brain Cooke was solely responsible for the scripting of 'Home and Away'. Johnnie Mortimer suffered a short spell of illness in 1975, meaning he was absent from co-writing these episodes. Mortimer, however, still receives a credit for series co-conception.

Guest Stars: Doug Fisher, John Carlin, Michael Redfern, Hilary Minster, Drew Wood

Written by: Brian Cooke
Series Created and Devised by: Johnnie Mortimer, Brian Cooke

Man About the House - Episode Guide

One for the Road - Series 4, Episode 2
Broadcast: Thursday March 13th 1975 at 19:55

Chrissy is brushing up on her highway code, preparing for her practical driving exam in ten days time. Robin helps her with it, laying out tins on the floor to simulate the pedals; Beans - clutch, Tuna Fish - brake, Chunky Chicken - Gas. Jo also helps out by handing them a toilet brush for a gear stick.

Meanwhile, George is becoming the 'Home beer King' and brewing his own snifter, determined not to pay the extra penny that the British Legion has added to the price of their booze. After hours of work, and straining the liquid through Mildred's tights, the brew is ready. George reluctantly takes a sip. Incredibly, his creation isn't that bad at all and even Robin samples the concoction before taking Chrissy out on her driving lesson.

Whilst out on the road, it becomes clear that Plummer isn't a fantastic driver and she crushes a bicycle whilst reversing around a corner. Robin has to move the car off the wreckage, but when the police spot him driving the car whilst under the influence of alcohol, he gets himself into trouble.

After being taken down to the police station, he is summoned to the local magistrates court. Robin pleads guilty and is fined £25 and disqualified from driving for twelve months. When the court adjourns, Robin and George accompany Chrissy down to her driving test centre for her practical examination. When they see a familar face in the examiner, namely as the owner of the crushed bike, there is very little hope of Chrissy getting her full licence any time soon. Especially as she starts naming the peddles after canned food...

Recollections... I can't remember any episodes I'd call my favourite. After all this time I don't recall much about the series at all (I never even seem to catch the repeats), but out of all of the episodes, people often tell me how they love this one - where Robin teaches me to drive, using various cans of food as the pedals in the car. This is the one that has been mentioned to me a lot, this is only one I can remember! - Paula Wilcox

Chortle Rating: A host of guest stars make enjoyable viewing. 9/10

Guest Stars: Ken Watson, Harry Littlewood, Frank Lester, Alister Williamson, Erik Chitty, Marc Boyle

Written by: Brian Cooke
Series Created and Devised by: Johnnie Mortimer, Brian Cooke

All in the Game - Series 4, Episode 3
Broadcast: Thursday March 20th 1975 at 20:00

George has noticed an influx of wood worm in the flat upstairs (in truth the tenant's dart holes) and calls in useless Odd-job man, Jerry, to carry out maintenance and spray the rooms. The poisonous fumes the wood preserver gives off mean that Robin, Chrissy and Jo have to camp downstairs with the Ropers for the night to avoid asphyxiation.

Whilst Chrissy and Robin are being bored senseless with George's prisoner of war escape game, Jo is down the pub with her new boyfriend, Colin, a policeman. The pair head back to Jo's flat and are met by Jerry and workmate Tom, treating the floorboards. The copper seems to recognise the 'wood preserver' as a consignment of stolen antifreeze, nicked from a local warehouse. Jerry is dragged of to the station to assist in some enquiries, but at least Robin and the girls won't have any trouble in starting up the floorboards in the morning!

Chortle Rating: Entertaining. 9/10

Guest Stars: Roy Kinnear, Doug Fisher, Hessel Saks, Jo Garrity, Ian Sharp, John Carlin

Never Give Your Real Name - Series 4, Episode 4
Broadcast: Thursday March 27th 1975 at 20:00

Larry has been dating different girls almost daily, using a variety of aliases so he can 'love 'em and leave 'em'. When he gets stuck for an idea one day, he passes himself off as a certain Robin Tripp. When a girl called Sandra starts asking around for him, in fear that she is pregnant, she calls up the first and only Robin Tripp in the phone book, the real one.

Sandra calls round later in the day, but enquiring after Robin she is directed to the wrong flat and talks to Chrissy and Jo about her predicament. When Robin returns from a football match, he is told that his girlfriend has come round saying she is pregnant. Robin thinks that they are talking about his real girlfriend, Linda, and decides he has to do the honourable thing and ask her to marry him.

Larry's tangled web of deceit is eventually rumbled and Robin has to pick up the pieces of what his worthless friend has done, the burning problem being how to un-propose to non-pregnant Linda...

Chortle Rating: Robin's shallowness makes uncomfortable viewing. 7/10

Guest Stars: Doug Fisher, Alison Hughes, Suzanne Moore, John Carlin, Mostyn Evans

The Tender Trap - Series 4, Episode 5
Broadcast: Thursday April 3rd 1975 at 20:00

George is rehearsing for the British Legion concert, where he has been chosen to sing a medley of wartime songs. He has also been given twenty tickets to sell, but it appears that everyone has heard him sing once before, and all are steering clear of a repeat performance. Chrissy and Jo have ready excuses and manage to escape the threat of the concert, but caught unawares, Robin is nabbed and roped into going.

Meanwhile, Chrissy's Mum has come up from Sussex, bringing news of an invitation to a family Christening. The announcement provides Robin with a perfect escape clause, and will protect his eardrums from Roper's caterwauling.

Mrs Plummer is an over-persuasive woman, and one who is obsessed with marrying off her daughters. Since arriving in London, and throughout the Christening, she has been appraising the attributes of Chrissy's flatmate, and sees Mr Tripp as the perfect husband. After putting up with her mother's hinting throughout the ceremony in the Countryside, Chrissy has had enough. Using a telephone call from Jo as cover, she pretends there is an emergency back at the flat. They will have to leave for London immediately. It gets Robin and Chrissy out of one problem but back into another, the British Legion beckons...

Filming Locations: The railway station depicted in this episode was actually Teddington railway station. Dudley's car is parked directly in front of the main station building.

Chortle Rating: Sitcom on top form. 9/10

Guest Stars: Glynn Edwards, Daphne Oxenford, John Colclough, Sheila D'Union

My Son, My Son - Series 4, Episode 6
Broadcast: Thursday April 10th 1975 at 20:00

Jo is preparing another disgusting breakfast for her flatmates, discovering in the process that there is a distinct lack of shopping in the cupboard. After the revelation that there wasn't enough spare cash to indulge in such luxuries as food, it prompts Robin to have a look in the rent book to see exactly how much in funds they actually possess to pay the next month's rent - the findings are grim, they are short of £68!

    Downstairs, George is going through his post and comes to a shocking letter. The Inland revenue are looking to question him about his tax returns. Mildred doesn't see anything unusual in the situation, until she learns that her penny-pinching husband has been claiming tax relief on an imaginary son, Leslie, for the last nineteen years!

    Meanwhile; Robin, Chrissy and Jo are still desperately trying to muster the necessary funds to pay their way. They come up with the precarious decision to bet it on a horse called 'Front Page', a supposed dead-cert, which comes last. Losing both the race, and their remaining rent money, it falls to Robin to go downstairs to enlighten Roper to the bad news, but before he can explain that the bookie's are now in possession of the rent money, George offers a proposal to him. The Inland Revenue are coming round that afternoon to talk to Roper and his 'son', but Leslie needs to be present, surely Robin could pass for a 19-year-old in a good light?

Titbits... Larry is frequently seen sporting a yellow 'Oxford University' sweater, seen most prominently in this episode. This was Doug Fisher's own jumper from his time at Oxford.

Chortle Rating: A thoroughly enjoyable tangled web. 10/10

Guest Stars: Doug Fisher, Anthony Sharp, John Carlin

The Last Picture Show - Series 5, Episode 1
Broadcast: Thursday, September 4th 1975 at 20:30

Chrissy is dating a new man, a frightfully boring film fanatic called Neil. Determined to succeed with her new boyfriend, she too takes an absorbing interest in film, and is presented with a cine-camera for a birthday gift. Chrissy uses the camera to make her own film, capturing the dramatic environment of Myddleton Terrace.

In order to display her freshly filmed motion picture, Neil lends her an expensive projector so everyone can gather in the flat for the grand premiere. It's not the best film in the world, but Larry has spotted potential in the projector. He has obtained a black market 'blue movie' from some bloke in the pub, and is eager to watch it.

Larry is threading the movie onto the projector when Chrissy returns home early from her date with Neil. Initially surprised at the projector being turned on, her mind is settled when Larry explains how he is actually threading her film tape through the machine so they can watch it again. Delighted that someone has finally taken interest in her masterpiece, she sets up the projector screen, and allows George, Mildred and Jo in to see the picture as well. Larry and Robin cringe at the thought of smut being aired to a broad audience, but it appears however, that Larry has been diddled. *Red Hot and Randy* is in reality...*The Nearsighted Mr. Magoo!*

Chortle Rating: Another favourite. 10/10

Guest Stars: Doug Fisher, Peter Greene, Catherine Riding

Man About the House - Episode Guide

Right Said George - Series 5, Episode 2
Broadcast: Thursday September 11th 1975 at 20:30

Robin's attempts at playing guitar leaves much to be desired, leading Chrissy to suggest something easier on the ear. A dab hand herself at tinkling the ivories, she suggests that Robin takes up the piano. The lack of an instrument is no deterrent, and they pop downstairs to borrow the Roper's Upright and give Robin a few lessons. Tripp however is more interested at getting to Chrissy's soft pedal rather than the Piano's and makes a mockery of her tutoring, causing the lesson to be abandoned.

George's car is due for its annual MOT, and unsurprisingly the wreck fails dismally. The main problem is the dodgy brakes, but when Jerry suggests that his brother fixes it on the cheap, the setback may be solved. Funding, however, remains problematic, so George attempts to flog some of Mildred's possessions to the tenants to gather some cash. When she objects, George tries to sell their piano instead. Robin is taken at the idea of having the instrument upstairs and he settles down to give the piano a tinkle, performing Edvard Grieg's 'Wedding Day at Troldhaugen' with perfect harmony - he could play all along!

Later that day, and the arduous task of moving the piano up the stairs is undertaken by George and Robin. After getting stuck halfway and crushing Roper's foot in the process, Jerry comes to the rescue with a foolhardy plan of lifting the piano through the patio doors upstairs using a large crane. True to his promise, he arrives with the hoist later in the day, borrowing it from a friend at a building site, and commences the difficult manoeuvre, attempting to swing the Piano in through the patio doors. It seems to be going well, until predictably Jerry makes a mistake of pulling the 'drop' handle, landing the piano squarely onto George's car, squashing it to bits. At least he won't have to fix the brakes!

Chortle Rating: Superb slap-stick. 9/10

Guest Stars: Roy Kinnear

A Little Knowledge - Series 5, Episode 3
Broadcast: Thursday September 18th 1975 at 20:30

Robin's cooking is proving to be an expensive pursuit, costing the household a substantial sum in the weekly shopping bills with Tripp insisting on pricey ingredients in his concoctions. It is decided that if Robin wants to continue with his culinary creations, he will have to help fund them. With his student grant all but depleted, there is no other option but to go out to work.

After reading an engaging newspaper advertisement, Robin goes for an interview at 'International Educational Services'. They are offering a good salary for a representative to 'ensure the educational needs of children are covered by disseminating knowledge among households', or in simplified terms, someone to 'flog encyclopaedias door to door'.

Back home, and George is convinced that he is going to win a holiday in Barbados, collecting labels off numerous Carter's Baked Beans tins to enter the competition. Amassing the labels is the simple part (Roper peeled them off the tins in Tesco), but when it comes to the general knowledge quiz, he is stumped. George needs help, and it just so happens that Robin has some encyclopaedias for sale...

Titbits... Notice how Mr Morris asks for seven sugar cubes in his tea, but only puts in five.

Filming Locations... The tower block that Robin mistakenly walks into in search of International Educational Services was located on Triton Square, just off Euston Road, London, positioned directly opposite the Thames television building.

Chortle Rating: An enjoyable Peter Jones cameo. 9/10

Guest Stars: Peter Jones

Man About the House - Episode Guide

Love and Let Love - Series 5, Episode 4
Broadcast: Thursday September 25th 1975 at 20:30

When Chrissy brings home a new boyfriend, Desmond, and finds Robin relaxing on the sofa with a sandwich, she is eager to usher her flatmate off to the pub to enjoy some privacy. Robin leaves, but gets bored and decides to go home early. Chrissy is livid, and over breakfast the next morning, a new house rule is introduced; Everyone has to give twenty-four hours notice before taking an acquaintance home.

Robin is quick to reserve Monday night so he can bring his girlfriend back, but when he meets Susan in the pub later that evening and learns she can't make Monday but is free that night, he hastily agrees to the change of plan. Chrissy, however, remains bitter from the night before and refuses to vacate. Robin has to think on his feet in order to keep his arrangement and instead borrows Larry's flat upstairs - he is going round to a girlfriend's house and his gaff will be empty...or at least it should be!

Downstairs, Mildred is stewing with frustration over George. He has been avoiding his demanding wife by not going to bed at the same time as her for weeks, instead favouring odd jobs and sharpening his pencil collection. George also has to fix a leaky cistern upstairs, but Mildred is adamant that he spends the night with her instead. Something just has to give, and it does. It's just a pity that it's the ceiling!

Recollections... I had a great time on this episode, and I really loved my character. We rehearsed this somewhere in Fulwell and when we had finished we all jumped in the cars and went back to the Thames bar. They were a lovely cast to work with, and so very kind, especially Yootha. The visiting artists weren't allowed to buy a drink, only the regulars - so we were treated to a smashing time on the cast! - Veronica Doran.

Recollections... The cast were a fabulous group. I was friends with Richard, so had been to see some studio recordings of the show already, and I was invited to be in the episode from there. When we had to redo a take, Richard would always get the audience on his side, and laugh would be so much bigger the second time around! - Wendy Allnutt.

Chortle Rating: Funny scripting and brilliant acting. 9/10

Guest Stars: Doug Fisher, Wendy Allnutt , Veronica Doran, Mark Cooper

How Does Your Garden Grow - Series 5, Episode 5
Broadcast: Thursday October 2nd 1975 at 20:30

Mildred is climbing the social ladder by entering a flower arranging competition. George offers his input on how to improve her arrangement, suggesting a mouldy Wellington boot when Mildred asks for 'something tall and green at the back'. Whilst the couple bicker about horticulture, the topic slides to the Roper's back garden, which is riddled with weeds and has not been cut for at least twenty years. At the risk of having to pay for a professional gardener to come in to fix it up, George asks the tenants to take it to task, with the threat of the rent tardiness spurring them on.

The next morning, Robin and Chrissy have cleared the back yard, extracting a few interesting specimens from it to decorate the flat, and add a splash of green to Mildred's flower arrangement. Their chosen leaves seem a harmless enough bunch, until Larry identifies them Cannabis plants. Flustered as to what they can do to be legally rid of it, Chrissy and Robin wrap up the plant and take it to the Police station, but when the vice squad starts to ask leading questions, they take the only way out - running away when the officer isn't looking.

Heading for home, Robin and Chrissy spy a bin-lorry and ask the dustmen if they can take away the disguised bush for them. They agree, and the tenants are safely shot of the incriminating plant, until Chrissy remembers that she gave the other stalk to Mildred, who at this very minute is standing proudly alongside it at the town hall!

Titbits... Because of the references to Cannabis in this episode, the British Video Standards Agency have deemed all VHS and DVD releases of this episode as certificate 12.

Titbits... Look at the swinging doors after Robin and Chrissy flee the police station. A line of fishing wire tied to the handle is being used to provide this effect, and can be seen glistening under the studio lights.

Chortle Rating: Excellent stuff. 9/10

Guest Stars: Doug Fisher, Charles Morgan, Ken Watson, John Lyons, Mike Savage

Man About the House - Episode Guide

Come Fly with Me - Series 5, Episode 6
Broadcast: Thursday October 9th 1975 at 20:30

Chrissy returns home from work with two tickets to a Frank Sinatra concert which her boss had spare and has given to her. Unfortunately the aging crooner does nothing for her, but to Robin and Jo the tickets are gold-dust, and the pair begin squabbling as to who should have them. Robin is dating a Swedish bird, Inga, and front row seats at the Albert Hall would make for an excellent night out. Inga would be delighted with a ticket, and Robin really wants to give her one!

Meanwhile, Mildred is nagging George regarding their forthcoming wedding anniversary, pestering him about the present he is planning to buy her. True to form, George neglects traditional jewellery, bunches of flowers or boxes of chocolates, and instead buys a budgie. Partly because its 'cheep', but mainly because Oscar could do with some company in his cage. Roper gets the tenants to look after his feathered wedding anniversary gift, so Mildred doesn't become suspicious if she hears the wardrobe chirping. They are happy to oblige and keep the pet in the bathroom, but when Jo leaves the window open its cheerio to Mildred's present.

Desperate to find a replacement gift, and to prevent a murder (his own!), George is compensated with a pair of tickets to see Frank Sinatra. The Ropers are set for the Albert Hall, until Mildred spots something yellow on the front lawn...

Titbits... Notice how the dress Mildred is wearing in the last scene changes colour between the studio shots and when she is standing next to the tree in the location shots. It morphs from purple to pink, and Yootha's hairstyle is also noticeably different.

Chortle Rating: An exceptional story line with very clever writing. 9/10

Guest Stars: Doug Fisher

The Party's Over - Series 6, Episode 1
Broadcast: Wednesday February 25th 1976 at 20:00

Robin, Chrissy and Larry are sneakily organising a party, but landlord George is on to their plan when he sees the boxes of booze arriving at the foot of the stairs. When he spies the masses of sandwiches and sausages the tenants are preparing, it confirms to him that there is a party on the cards, and he puts his foot down. Chrissy appeals to a higher authority, the true head of the household - Mildred, who allows the shindig to go ahead, especially as she has been invited to join the fun. George still objects to the plans, and is determined to rain on Mildred's parade, by deviously pinning a 'Party has been cancelled' notice on the front door and disconnecting the doorbell.

After a few hours without guests, Robin heads downstairs to see what is going on, sighting George's conniving sign. Mildred is following close behind, and when she sees the notice, she is furious. After putting up with George for years, this is the straw that broke the camel's back - she finally ups sticks and flees to stay with her sister.

After days of solitary living, Roper is desperate for some company, and starts pestering Robin, Chrissy and Larry. Every night, George intrudes on their dinner by dropping broad hints of his hunger - the knife and fork in the pocket being a suitable heart-string puller. Sick of his whining, Chrissy eventually talks to him and persuades George to do something about his broken relationship. It gives him the motivation to clean himself up and go and drag Mildred back...

Titbits... Notice how the 'party has been cancelled' sign Brian writes in the living room is different to the one seen on the door later.

Recollections... I had suspected appendicitis on the day of recording this episode, so I was written out of it at the last minute. - Sally Thomsett

Chortle Rating: An excellent guest appearance from Hilda Braid. 9/10

Guest Stars: John Carlin, Hilda Braid
Sally Thomsett Does Not Feature

Man About the House - Episode Guide

One More for the Pot - Series 6, Episode 2
Broadcast: Wednesday March 3rd 1976 at 20:00

When George shows his greedy side again and hikes up the tenant's rent behind Mildred's back, it leads Robin, Chrissy and Jo to consider how they are going to pay the additional £25 per month. They eventually decide on getting another lodger in to spread the cost of living between four.

Chrissy and Jo phone up an old friend, James, who is looking for somewhere to stay and he pops round later to have a look at the place. Meanwhile, Robin is at the pub persuading his girlfriend to move in with him, asking her come round later in the day and have a look at the flat. He also encourages her to keep quiet about their relationship, so Jo and Chrissy don't get wind of his intentions, but when Linda turns up, Jo is quick to recognise her as the same person Robin was smooching at the back row of the Odeon a few nights before, and rumbles his plan.

Whilst Robin, Chrissy and Jo bicker about which new lodger they are going to choose, Linda and James are talking about other flats they've seen around London, eventually agreeing that because they are causing so many ructions between the present flatmates, neither of them should move in. They instead go and live a platonic life together in a flat in Gloucester Terrace.

Downstairs, George is feeling self-conscious about the decision he has made to increase the rent, dreading the fact that Mildred may find out about his money-grabbing activities any minute and make his life a misery. After sweetening his wife with flowers and chocolates, he eventually summons the courage to tell her what he has done. She is not pleased. Just as the tenants are thinking about who else they could invite to share the flat, Roper turns up at the door with his toothbrush and budgie!

Chortle Rating: More superb Brian and Yootha collaboration. 10/10

Guest Stars: Alison Hughes, John Flanagan, John Carlin

The Generation Game - Series 6, Episode 3
Broadcast: Wednesday March 10th 1976 at 20:00

Robin and Chrissy return home from seeing an x-rated movie at the cinema and are feeling amorous, but when Jo enters the lounge with a bowl of cornflakes, the romance of the moment is immediately lost. However as Jo will be out the following evening, there may yet be a chance for lost opportunity...

Meanwhile, Mildred is excited about her invitation to attend a boat party, but when George refuses to go and locks himself in the bathroom, it looks like her dream night out will never materialise. Desperate for a male escort, Mildred approaches Robin to take her to the dinner dance. He is far from keen on the idea. For the first time in years, Robin has Chrissy virtually melting in his hands, and he is determined not to sacrifice the rare opportunity, but Mildred has been looking forward to this dinner dance for weeks.

After a significant amount of gentle persuasion from his flatmates, Robin eventually gives in and accompanies Mrs. Roper to the dance, with George being left alone at home to take Robin's place at dinner with Chrissy. As the pair discuss the soiree, it suddenly occurs to Roper that Robin may be taking gross advantage of his wife whilst out together. After a moment to consider what may be going on, he sets out in hot pursuit of the merry couple. George arrives at the boat and tries to reclaim his wife, but as he quarrels with Mildred out on deck, he suddenly gets a sinking feeling...

Chortle Rating: George finally gets his just deserves! 8/10

Guest Stars: Mike Savage

The Sunshine Boys - Series 6, Episode 4
Broadcast: Wednesday March 17th 1976 at 20:00

The tenants are planning their summer escape, leafing their way through a large pile of holiday brochures. Chrissy and Jo quite fancy Spain, but Robin is set on an Alpine location. Larry has the casting decision and goes along with the girl's choice - mainly because of the prospect of continental crumpet - the beaches are bursting with bronzed Senioretas. Now, if only they can get a suntan in advance, they will be able to compete with the local Lotharios...

Their problems could be solved by George downstairs, who is once again hard up for cash and trying to flog his wife's possessions. He drags Larry into the flat to see what he would be interested in purchasing. An old wireless and a sewing machine don't prove much of a draw, but when Roper offers a sun ray lamp for sale, Larry decides to buy it off him for £5, and promptly sells it to Robin for twice the price.

When Mildred sees the tenants enjoying the artificial sun later that day, she is quick to offer the services of her lamp as well so they can bronze both sides at once. After a fruitless search for it, she comes to the conclusion that someone has walked in to her flat and taken it. After taking a closer look at Robin's lamp, Mildred notices the same scratches on the back and is convinced it has been stolen from her. She is fuming. Until Larry spills the beans that George has been hawking the furniture again...

Chortle Rating: Fast-paced plot with classic scenes. 8/10

Guest Stars: Doug Fisher

Mum Always Liked You Best - Series 6, Episode 5
Broadcast: Wednesday March 24th 1976 at 20:00

Robin isn't looking forward to his taller, more attractive brother, Norman, arriving in London for a visit. He has excelled Robin in everything he has ever done, and is always keen to outdo his brother at any given opportunity. True to form, Norman is after Chrissy from the moment he arrives, inviting her out to a dinner dance that evening. They are strongly attracted to each other and when Norman proposes another night out with Miss Plummer, Robin is stewing. He has competition for the girl he has been after for years, and he doesn't like it.

Meanwhile, Mildred is pestering George to take her out for a meal, having only been frequenting plastic-fork fish and chip shops for a dinner-a-deux in the past. George bemoans that fact that if they do go out, he will miss the banjo-playing dog on *Opportunity Knocks*, but Roper reluctantly relents and takes Mildred out to a local French Bistro. Sadly, George has left his wallet in his other suit, and instead of a night cap, they are left with having to do the washing up...

Back home, Chrissy has fallen head over heels for her new admirer. Norman is fluent in French, drives a white Morgan sports car and is splashing his money on her like water. He seems to have everything that Robin doesn't, and when Norman decides to stay for another week, it looks like Chrissy may have found her soul mate.

Chortle Rating: Norman's competitiveness is frustrating. 8/10

Guest Stars: Norman Eshley, Steve Plytas, Lawrence Davidson, John Harvey

Man About the House - Episode Guide

Fire Down Below - Series 6, Episode 6
Broadcast: Wednesday March 31st 1976 at 20:00

Chrissy has been going steady with Robin's brother, Norman, for months. He writes sloppy sentimental letters daily and oozes suaveness in every aspect, her kind of man. Soon enough, Norman drives up from Southampton for another visit, landing on Chrissy's doorstep to take up her offer of a tour of London. Robin is distraught as he watches his girl fall for another man. He still has affectionate feelings for Chrissy but just can't summon the confidence to tell her how he really feels.

Attempting to forget his true love, Robin spends a night with one of Larry's acquaintances, but soon realises that his flatmate is the only woman for him. After some gentle persuasion, he finally gathers the courage to explain his desires to the girl he is infatuated with, hoping that he is not too late to save her from the clutches of his brother. But he is. Chrissy is getting married to Norman. Robin congratulates his brother. The best man won, but Robin is quietly heartbroken.

Recollections... Although this was the penultimate episode to be aired, it was the last one ever to be rehearsed and recorded, so the atmosphere on set was very jolly and fun. Yootha brought champagne which I indulged in, and it was all very good fun. The cast were all lovely to work with, especially Richard. There was a certain line I was concerned about and I was talking it over with Sally Thomsett. Richard walked over to me and could see that I was a bit worried about it, but he was really calming and helped me out a lot.

'I haven't actually seen my episode of the series since it was broadcast so I can't recall too much about it. The controversy surrounding the show was all very over-hyped and my one abiding memory is how tatty the flat set looked in real life. On camera it appeared quite nice but that wasn't the impression they intended to give'. - Frankie Jordan

Chortle Rating: Desperately poignant. 9/10

Guest Stars: Norman Eshley, Doug Fisher, Frankie Jordan, Cecily Hobbs

Another Bride, Another Groom? - Series 6, Episode 7

Broadcast: Wednesday April 7th 1976 at 20:00
Viewing households - 9.2
National television chart position - 1

The wedding is imminent and everyone is looking forward to seeing Chrissy and Norman tie the knot, except Robin who is still upset at losing out to his brother. In good spirit, he still makes a masterpiece of a wedding cake, but even that turns out to be a disappointment. After giving Norman a decent stag night, Larry and Robin stagger back to flat pie-eyed and jointly ruin it within a few minutes. Jam sponge all round for the reception...

The big day looms and the extended family from the Tripp and Plummer tribes arrive for the ceremony. After taking the vows, Chrissy and Norman are man and wife. Everyone wishes the newlyweds good luck for the future at the reception, and Robin finally manages a passionate embrace. But it is too little, too late. He never got his girl. But at least their relationship will end with a laugh, Larry and Robin have one last surprise for the wedding car...

Chortle Rating: Emotional comedy. A touching end to the series, with a nice send off from a host of guest stars. 8/10

Guest Stars: Doug Fisher, Norman Eshley, Glynn Edwards, Daphne Oxenford, Leslie Sands, Hilda Kriseman, Dennis Ramsden

Opening Titles

With Johnnie Mortimer and Brian Cooke's previous hit, *Father Dear Father*, using a different opening title sequence for every single episode, the *Man About the House* titles being changed just five times over the six series seemed a fairly tame alteration. However, this was an important factor to the success of the programme.

Firstly, by updating the opening sequence, the series could maintain a vitality and freshness reflecting upon the youthfulness of the programme's characters and, without the risk of alienating it's core audience, increase it's appeal to new viewers.

Secondly, fiddling about with the various title effects available was a useful way for the production crew to experiment with new technology (at a time when a simple fade-in transition was considered advanced). Programme titles were frequently used as a drawing board to try out new ideas and techniques with the format, fonts and title board graphics.

Here is a closer look at the opening sequences of each series of *Man About the House*.

Series 1 & 2 - 'Going Home' Opening Titles:
The opening titles to *Man About the House* remained the same for the first two series, showing our three main characters going home from college and work respectively. We start by seeing the 'Euston Road Polytechnic' ending classes for the day, and most of the students departing on motorbikes, leaving Robin behind on his unreliable moped. The theme music strikes up, and after a close up shot of a wry smiling Robin, we cut to Chrissy who is boarding a bus, losing her shoe in the stampede of commuters and not having a chance to reclaim it.

The shot then cuts to Jo, who we see leaving an office building. She walks past a busking ex-serviceman who, while ostensibly blind, raises his tinted glasses for a lecherous leer at Jo's posterior before she disappears into an underground station. Then its Back to Robin, who's bike has broken down right in the middle of Piccadilly circus, the scene juxtaposing to Chrissy getting off the bus - her odd shoe wedged in the used ticket bin.

Jo leaves the Underground and meets up outside the house with a shoeless Chrissy to witness a haggard Robin pushing his bike up to the kerb. The *Man About the House* title flashes up and we launch into the episode.

Recollections... I was in the these titles. I was standing in front of Paula Wilcox at the bus stop, wearing the white cardigan. I was also with Richard O'Sullivan in the motorbike scene, which was filmed at a school behind Euston Road. Sally Thomsett coming out of the revolving doors was filmed at Thames television building. - Melinda Tracey

Filming Locations... The Underground Station that Sally Thomsett struts into was the York Road entrance to Waterloo. The sequence was filmed by a camera placed on the top of the Shell centre footbridge.

Paula Wilcox's bus-boarding scene was filmed just across the road. She jumps on a London Transport AEC Regent III RT bus which sets off towards Lambeth.

Series 3 - 'Day Out at the Zoo' Opening Titles

Following the Thames ident, we see our stars driving across a bridge in a classic black vintage car, before pulling up outside the Zoological gardens.

We then see the gang inside the zoo. Chrissy is offering a banana to a monkey, but when she receives a ticking off from a keeper, Robin scoffs it instead. The scene then cuts to Chrissy taking a thirst quencher from a drinking tap, causing an ornamental fountain to dry up behind her, only to resume when she has finished drinking. A quick zoom in on her puzzled expression, leads us on to the next segment. Jo is blowing her noise in a rackety manner, causing an elephant to reciprocate with a loud trumpet.

The three main characters settle down for a refreshing beer, each of them gaining a well styled frothy moustache from the head on the pint. The *Man About the House* title appears with a new 'pinwheel' animation, and fades to the episode.

Filming Locations... The bridge at the beginning of the sequence was Westminster Bridge in London, with Big Ben and the Houses of Parliament visible in the background. Later we see the gang walking around London Zoo.

Series 4 - 'Day Out at the Zoo' Version 2 - Opening Titles

A variation on the titles from the previous season, this fourth series opens in the same way, with the gang driving across Westminster Bridge in their Austin car. They arrive at London Zoo, but encounter some problems with a lady traffic warden who is on the prowl. Robin hatches a cunning plan

Man About the House - Opening Titles

and parks the car in the same parking place as a visiting Fiat 500, causing considerable confusion to the warden.

We then cut to the gang walking through the Zoo. They make a stop for lunch, and with some snappy editing, their eating habits are likened to that of animals. Robin's consumption of a hamburger being matched to a lion with a chunk of red meat, Chrissy's lettuce chomping being not too dissimilar to a giraffe licking it's lips, and Jo throwing a grape then catching it in her mouth being likened to a seal catching a fish.

Robin takes another bite of the burger, and after a close up of his ketchup-ringed mouth, the *Man About the House* title pinwheels in and cuts to the episode.

Titbits... This is the first series we have a guest star in the titles. Bella Emberg plays the uncredited frumpy female traffic warden.

Recollections... I remember doing these titles, I was paid double time because they told me it was only for the trailers. I got about £40 for doing them, but I didn't realise they would be at the start of every single episode. Nobody told me that bit! - Bella Emberg

Series 5 - 'Boat Charter on the Thames' Opening Titles

Opening with a speedboat rushing under Tower Bridge, we see Robin, Chrissy and Jo on a boat on the Thames. Chrissy is trying to get the motor started on their chartered craft but Robin is not bothering to help, sipping champagne with Jo out on deck.

They cruise past the Houses of Parliament, accidentally knocking off a scuba diver's snorkel as they float down the river. Jo is sunbathing on the deck but when the boat drifts a too close to a fisherman on the riverbank, she ends up losing her bikini top to the end of his rod!

Richard and Paula entertain the camera with a few shots of them playing directly to the viewers, and a new design of the *Man About the House* logo boxes in to the screen and then cuts to the episode.

Series 6 - 'Chartered boat on the Thames' Version 2 - Opening Titles

The second version of the Series 5 opening credits sees the team still out on the Thames in a chartered boat, the good ship 'Dudeen', enjoying a drop of champagne. Chrissy is at the helm, and rests her glass of bubbly on a ledge to steer, but Jo knocks a bottle of suntan lotion into it, and when

Chrissy takes her next sip it seems that sea-sickness has kicked in early!

Jo throws an empty can overboard and hits a diver on the head as he surfaces for air, and a fisherman chucks his cigarette butt into the river, missing completely and sending the hot ember right into Robin's shirt!

New fonts and logos appear for the first time in this last series, and then the episode commences.

Titbits... Observe the boat closely after the cigarette butt falls down Robin's shirt, and a stage hand can be seen through the back window. This is most likely to be the director's assistant who passes on instructions to the cast. He ducks down out of sight when he sees the camera!

Closing Titles

What better way to end an episode of a sitcom than with a set of double entendre visually humour-intensive titles. Throughout the six series of *Man About the House*, the closing titles are also worthy of note.

Produced using still photographs of household objects, the combination of items cleverly reflect the relationship between the main characters of the show, and also offer a bit of subtle saucy humour in places along the way.

Alas, nobody receives a credit for the inspired closing titles, which is a shame as they evidently ooze creativity.

The most hilarious frame in these credits is that of a photograph depicting two china cats and a cockerel in the middle. On initial inspection this seems harmless enough, but delve into the world of innuendo, and the significance of 'a cock between two pussies' becomes noticeably amusing.

We also see a pair of Y-fronts hanging on a washing line between two frilly pairs of knickers, a teddy bear between two dolls, a football boot next to a platform shoe, aftershave between two perfume bottles, a pair of football socks between two bras on a washing line, and a pint of beer between two glasses of wine.

These credits can all too easily drift over the subconscious viewer without being deemed thought-worthy, but delve a little deeper and its interesting to note exactly what is going on.

The Man About the House Film

Cast
Richard O'Sullivan - Robin Tripp
Paula Wilcox - Chrissy Plummer
Sally Thomsett - Jo
Yootha Joyce - Mildred Roper
Brian Murphy - George Roper
Peter Cellier - Morris Pluthero
Doug Fisher - Larry Simmonds
Jack Smethurst - Himself
Rudolph Walker - Himself
Arthur Lowe - Spiros
Bill Maynard - Chef
Spike Milligan - Himself
Aimi McDonald - Hazel Lovett
Patrick Newell - Sir Edmund Weir
Michael Robbins - Second Doorman
Michael Ward - Mr. Gideon
Bill Grundy - Interviewer
Norman Mitchell - Doorman
Andria Lawrence - Miss Bird
Julian Orchard - Producer
Aubrey Morris - Lecturer
Bill Pertwee - Postman
Johnnie Briggs - Milkman
Melvyn Hayes - Nigel
Berry Cornish - PA
Bill Sawyer - Chauffeur
Pauline Peart - Secretary
Arthur Hewlett - Elderly man
Annie Leake - Tweedy Lady
Corinne Skinner - Housewife
Mark Rogers - Boy Scout

Crew
Written by - Johnnie Mortimer and Brian Cooke
Produced by - Roy Skeggs
Directed by - John Robins
Director of Photography - Jimmy Allen BSC

Production Manager - Dennis Hall
Film Editor - Archie Ludski GBFE
Art Director - Don Picton
Assistant Director - Derek Whitehurst
Sound Recordist - Claude Hitchcock
Sound Editor - Roy Hyde
Boom Operator - Keith Batten
Camera Operator - Rodney Anstiss
Continuity - Renee Glynne
Make-Up Supervisor - Eddie Knight
Wardrobe Supervisor - Laura Nightingale
Hairdressing Supervisor - Betty Sherriff
Construction Manager - Jock Lyall
Recording Director - Tony Lumkin
Dubbing Mixer - Dennis Whitlock
Gaffer - Ted Hallows
Music Composed by - Christopher Gunning
Musical Supervisor - Philip Martell
Lyrics - Annie Farrow
Title Song Performed By - Jane Christie (Uncredited)

Copyright MCMLXXIV Hammer Film Productions Limited
Produced in Technicolor

Released on December 22nd 1974 with the tag line; 'The hilarious adventures of two girls with...a man about the house', the Hammer produced spin-off film rode on the back of the success of the first two television series. Written by Johnnie Mortimer and Brian Cooke and directed by John Robins, the eighty-five minute movie followed our stars on the big screen with the regular sitcom cast joined by an extensive line up of comedy cameos. Rudolph Walker and Jack Smethurst of *Love Thy Neighbour* fame made appearances, as did Spike Milligan. Arthur Lowe plays property magnate Spiros and Bill Pertwee makes a brief appearance as a postman. Director John Robins was responsible for casting the support roles, and subsequently chose to re-use many actors who had worked under his direction in the film adaptation of *Love thy Neighbour* earlier in 1974.

Plot
The plot follows events at Myddleton Terrace and the battle to save the Roper's home from being demolished. Local property developers are look-

ing to flatten the entire street and have offered to purchase the house, but while Mildred is in staunch opposition, George is liable to persuasion of selling up.

Morris Pluthero, leading property buyer to the ruthless Spiros' empire, is responsible for purchasing the properties on Myddleton Terrace and is gradually increasing his portfolio of houses in the line, using his ingenuity to secure the tightest of deals. Robin, Chrissy and Jo swiftly organise a petition to campaign against the demolition of their homes, and with over 1000 signatures, take it to their MP, Sir Edmund Weir. Thinking of all the positive publicity the campaign will create, the vain Weir is spurred into action, yet when it threatens to emerge that his mistress is occupying a house in the Terrace, he steps down and leaves Mildred and the tenants to fight on their own.

After days of cunning plans, all of which fail, Pluthero has run out of ways to gain the Roper's property, even failing to win over Chrissy with a meal out. In a last ditch attempt, Spiros despatches him off to appear on *The Today Programme* at Thames television to participate in a public argument. With a final effort to have 6 Myddleton Terrance signed over to him, he first visits George alone, knowing he is liable to cave in without Mildred present. True to form, Roper is about to sign, but Mildred interrupts him.

Kicked out of the house, Pluthero sets off to attend his interview, leaving George behind at home. Convinced that selling up is the best option, Roper sneaks out of the house when his wife is out of the room, and drives to the studios in hot pursuit with the purchase agreement. Mildred and the tenants see him leave and chase after him in Larry's car.

The film cumulates with a hectic chase around Thames television, with George desperate to deliver the purchase agreement, but Pluthero on the brink of cancelling the whole scheme.

From Small Screen to Big Screen

The *Man About the House* movie took six weeks to film and was fairly successful in the box office. It's first television airing was on January 2nd 1981 to 15.2 million viewers. Despite being an enjoyable production to watch, the cast of *Man About the House* didn't feel that the film was a particular success. 'I don't think the series did transfer particularly well to the big screen' Paula Wilcox explained. 'We were all of course very excited to be making a movie, but I remember being a little disappointed when I read the script; because I didn't think it was quite as original and witty as the series'. Sally Thomsett concurs. 'I wasn't a great fan of the movie, but it was fun to make', she recalled.

Filming Locations
The exterior location for the fictitious 6, Myddleton Terrace in the film was actually 40, Hamilton Gardens, Paddington, NW8. In the opening titles we see a long shot looking down on the street. This sequence was filmed from the top of a crane at the far end of Alma Square looking south down Hamilton Gardens. We then cut to a close up on a slightly rudimentary 'Myddleton Terrace' street sign which on closer inspection, can be identified as a simple piece of card stuck over the top of the real street sign.

Later in the film, we see Larry swerving around the streets in a yellow Volkswagen Beetle, this was filmed around the streets of St. Johns Wood, with the roundabout being located at the junction of Fairfax Road and Belsize Road. Other locations nearby to the film studios (including Swiss Cottage and Maida Vale underground station) were also utilised.

Recollections... When we were making the film, there is a scene where Robin plays strip poker with Chrissy. He things his ship has come in because I agree to play. Of course, it turns out that I am a bit of a card sharp, so he ends up in his knickers while I am fully clothed. Well, in order to prove how accomplished a poker player I am, there had to be a close up of me doing amazing things with a pack of cards. I am not that good at card tricks, so a hand artist was brought in and he did several extremely deft passes, shuffling the cards like a professional. In the close-up of 'my' hands, you may see, if you look very closely, that I appear to have rather a lot of red hair around my fingers and knuckles. Maybe I'm the only one who noticed that! - Paula Wilcox

Titbits... Jack Smethurst and Rudolph Walker appear in the film, and Nina Baden-Semper appears in an episode of *George and Mildred*. This means that Kate Williams is the only actress from the television sitcom *Love thy Neighbour* not to appear in either *Man About the House* or *George and Mildred*. Kate did however, train as an actress at the E15 theatre school, an off-shoot from Joan Littlewood's workshop where Yootha Joyce and Brian Murphy performed.

Titbits... Spike Milligan never behaved on set. On one take, he came out of dressing room with newspaper stuffed under his coat, pretending to be the hunchback of Notre Dam. Several re-takes followed, but director John Robins failed to see the funny side!

The Man About the House Theme Tune

The placid theme music for *Man About the House* film theme was not, contrary to popular belief, sung by main star Paula Wilcox, but instead performed by 19-year-old jazz singer, Jane Christie. Virtually unknown on musical circles when she was invited to perform the mellow classic, here Christie explains the story behind the short easygoing track that warms the soul of all who hear it.

'At the time of my being asked to the sing the song I was nineteen and singing regularly in a hotel restaurant with a resident band in my hometown of Bristol. *Man About the House* was my first gig, as previously all I had ever done was record demos of my father's songs in his home studio - he was a musician and song writer. Roy Skeggs happened to visit Bristol from London and was dining in the restaurant one evening. He was very impressed and asked me if I would join him and his partner for a drink, he explained that he had just finished filming *Man About the House* and that he wasn't too happy with the final rendering of the title song - it had already been sung by a session singer. Roy said that he would send me a copy of both the song and the backing track for me to sing and send back to him to see what he thought of my version'.

Virtually everything about the film was complete, apart from the soundtrack. The opening and closing titles had been prepared already, meaning that Jane wouldn't get a mention for her rendition of the track in the credits.

'The tape arrived 3 days later, and I was able to use my father's small home studio to record my version very quickly, having learnt the lyrics from the session singer's tape. It was posted back to Roy the next day, and I think within a two week time span I found myself at Elstree Studios recording it for real. What a wonderful experience that was for a very naive nineteen year old who had only a few months previously started singing professionally, I was paid £60 including expenses!'

'I remember feeling very excited about the whole thing and became a bit of a local celebrity at the time, being invited to the premier showing of the film in Bristol and being interviewed for Bristol Radio. Sadly I didn't get to meet any of the cast of the film. I did however watch the sitcom often and used to enjoy it immensely. I even have to admit to having a soft spot for Richard O'Sullivan at the time!'

George and Mildred

Summary.. 96
Episode Guide... 97
Filming Locations................................. 135
Opening Titles...................................... 137
The Film.. 140
While the Cat's Away - Stage Play......... 144

Chrissy and Jo are looking for a third girl to share their flat. But a good girl nowadays is hard to find.

So when Robin comes along, he looks like the answer to all their problems. He takes the spare bedroom.

But then Chrissy's mother turns up unexpectedly. And the girls realise their problems are only just beginning.

MAN ABOUT THE HOUSE

a new seven-part comedy series from Thames Television starring Richard O'Sullivan, Paula Wilcox, Sally Thomsett 8.30 pm Weds from 15 August.

THAMES
Thames Television
306-316 Euston Road
London NW1 3BB
01-387 9494

Above: Original Thames press material to publicise *Man About the House*

Above: Press flyer to advertise the first series of *Man About the House*
Opposite Top: Mass confusion in 'The Last Picture Show'
Opposite Bottom: Locked out of their new house - the Ropers hit Hampton!

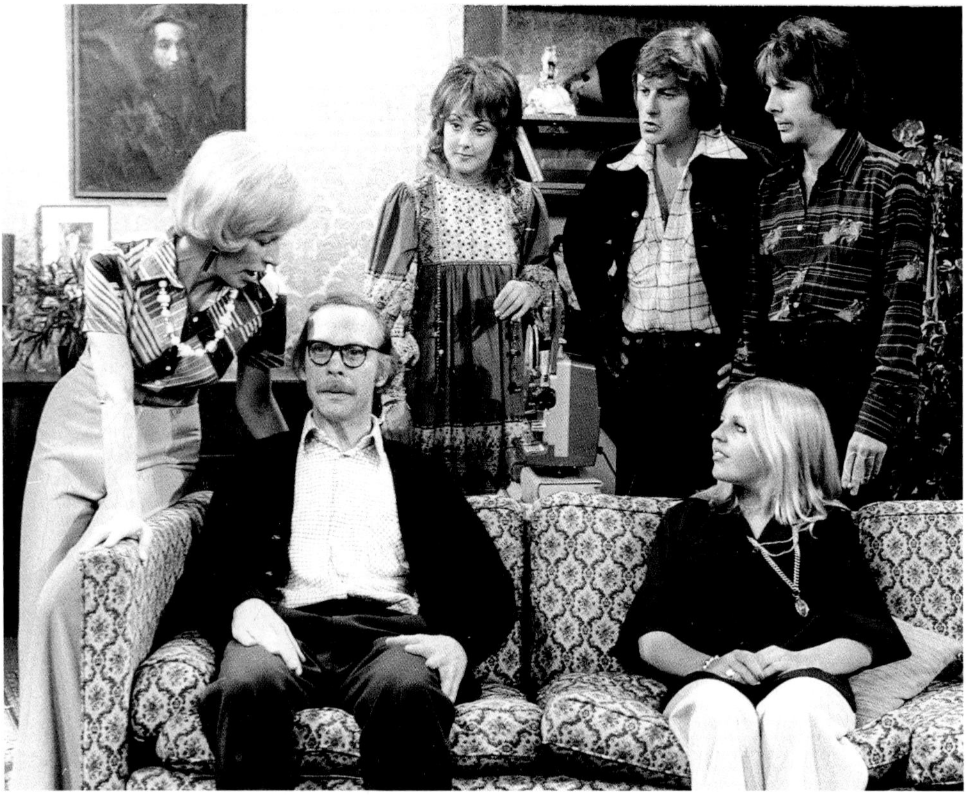

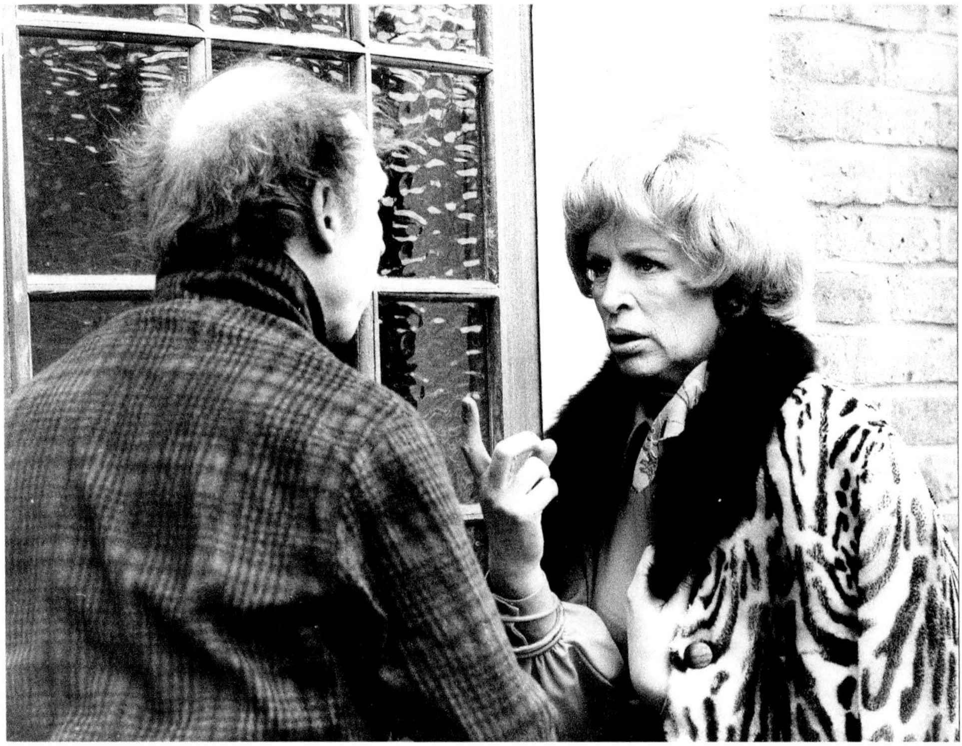

THAMES IS THE CHANNEL THAT MADE HAPPY HALF HOUR SHOWS LIKE BLESS THIS HOUSE, FATHER, DEAR FATHER, FOR THE LOVE OF ADA, THIRTY MINUTES WORTH, ALCOCK & GANDER, LOVE THY NEIGHBOUR. THEY ALL REACHED NUMBER ONE IN THE LONDON TOP TEN. AND NOW, THAMES HAS MORE LAUGHS IN STORE. TURN OVER FOR THE SHAPE OF GRINS TO COME....

Source: ACB/JICTAR

Above: Laughs all the way with Thames Television

Below: Robin never got his girl. Norman Tripp weds Chrissy in 'Another Bride, Another Groom', the last episode of *Man About the House.*

Above: Decorating the Christmas Tree at 46, Peacock Crescent
Below: George tries to reclaim his 'Gardening' Magazines from Jeffrey

Above: Nicholas Owen played Tristram Fourmile
Below: Mildred seldom got her 'early night'!

Programmes from the *George and Mildred* Theatre tour

Above: Richmond-Upon-Thames
Below Centre: Australia

Below Left: Bournemouth
Below Right: Edinburgh

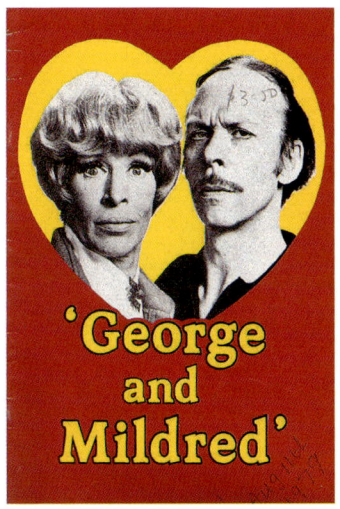

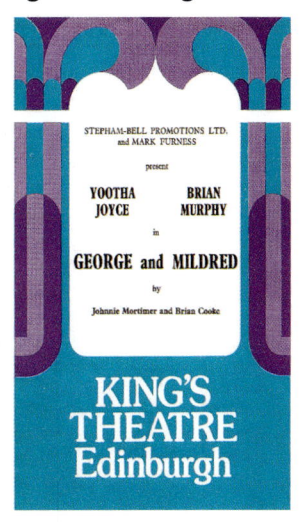

Filming locations for *George and Mildred*

Above: The Roper's House in Manor Road, Teddington as it looks today. Below: Brian Murphy walks down The Causeway, Teddington, in the episode 'Just the Job'. Fourmile's estate agency was the shop in the foreground.

George and Mildred - Episode Guide

Summary

The first episode of *George and Mildred* introduced us to how the Ropers came to leave their home in South Kensington. The council have placed a compulsory purchase order on their house, and the pair are going to view a new property in Hampton Wick. George hates the prospect of going up in the world, but Mildred is keen to improve her social status by relocating to the classy suburb.

The Roper's potential new neighbour, Jeffrey Fourmile, isn't too keen on having the class-less George and Mildred next door, and in his capacity as the estate agent selling the house, puts several obstacles in the Roper's way to stop them moving in. However his plans are foiled by his son, Tristram, and Mildred manages to put down a deposit on the house and move in shortly afterwards. George isn't happy.

Episode Guide

A guide to every *George and Mildred* episode, together with original transmission dates and times, repeats dates and times, VTR numbers (where stated) and all the credited guest stars. Also included are 'Titbits' which explain an interesting fact or backstage story, as well as 'Recollections' from main cast and support cast. Individual 'chortle ratings' are also featured.

Cast and Crew

Unless otherwise stated, all episodes feature:

Yootha Joyce as Mildred Roper
Brian Murphy as George Roper
Norman Eshley as Jeffrey Fourmile
Sheila Fearn as Ann Fourmile
Nicholas Bond-Owen as Tristram Fourmile

Full series scripting credits: Johnnie Mortimer and Brian Cooke
Full series production and direction: Peter Frazer-Jones

Series 1: Theme Music - Johnny Hawksworth
Series 2-5: Theme Music - Roger Webb

Series 1: Designed by - Michael Minas
Series 2: Designed by - David Richens

Series 3: Designed by - Colin Andrews
Series 4: Designed by - David Ferris
Series 5: Designed by - Allan Cameron, Anthony Cartledge

Operational Supervisor: Del Randall, Peter Sampson, John Eveleigh, John White-Jones.
Studio Supervisor: Bruce Englefield, Dave Sparks, Fred Cope, Dick Hibberd, Peter Groome.
Lighting Director: Keith Reed, Bob Simmons, Richie Richards, Ken Tester-Brown, Bill Lee, Malcolm Harrison, Andy Andrews, Luigi Bottone, Allen Harradine.
Video Tape Editor: Fred Turner, Dave Lewinton, Campbell Keenan, Colin Bocking, Campbell Keenan, Colin Bocking, Mike Sage, Camilla Keenan.
Senior Cameraman: Peter Howell, Roy Easton, Peter Coombes, Mike Baldock. Albert Almond, Michael Baldock, Chas Watts, John Darnell, Adrian Fearnley.
Sound Supervisor: Mike Westlake, Brian Moray, Mike Pontin, Peter Willcocks, Julian Ford, Brian Hibbert, Dick Hibberd, Peter Stoddart, Bill Rawcliffe, Stan Lee, Dick Bradford, Richard Churchill.
Vision Controller: Bill Marley, Brian Kerr, Alan Fowler, Allan James, Ian Jones, Paul Stripp, Bob Mason
Vision Mixer: Martin Perrett, Peter Boffin, Peter Phillips, Nick Bigsby
Graphics: John Stamp, Ruth Bribham
Film Editor: Tony O'Toole, John Wright, Peter Barton
Film Cameraman: Andrikos Kikos-Adonis, Simon Kossoff, Mike Rhode
Film Sound: Dennis Whitlock, John Pearce
Location Manager: Eric Pavitt, Peter Crowhurst
Rostrum Camera: Peter Goodwin
Casting: Iris Frederick, David Asche, James Liggatt
Costume: Lyn Harvey, Maureen Booth, Ray Cooper, Kathleen Russell
Make-Up: Pauline Saunders, Gillian Wakeford, Christine Morrell, Joan Hills, Cherry West, Anne Edwards, Angela Seyfang
Floor Manager: Peter Errington, John Lynton, Phill Hill
Stage Manager: Nora Stapleton, Mary Douglass
Production Assistant: Susie Shields, Angela Carter, Janet Mullins

George and Mildred - Episode Guide

Moving On - Series 1, Episode 1
VTR: 13635
Broadcast: Monday September 6th 1976 at 20:00
Repeated on ITV, September 1986 at 19:30

The Roper's house is being requisitioned by the council with a compulsory purchase order - it is due to be bulldozed and replaced by a fly-over. They have received compensation and the hunt is now on for a change of address. George would be happy in a council flat, but Mildred has her heart set on higher things - a lovely semi-detached townhouse in Peacock Crescent, Hampton Wick. A viewing has been arranged.

The Roper's arrive in Jerry's truck, making a poor impression on estate agent and future neighbour Jeffrey Fourmile, to begin their tour of the upmarket property. Mildred loves it, and delights in the prospect of moving up in the world. George, on the other hand, dislikes it intensely, mocking its features of bidets and an Adam (or as he calls it 'a damn') fireplace.

Nevertheless, The Ropers put down a deposit on the house - after considerable attempts by Fourmile to prevent it - and George and Mildred plan the big move. As the Fourmiles bid farewell to their future neighbours, they receive a taste of what they have let themselves in for. The gears slip in George's car and instead of driving forwards, he reverses back through the Fourmile's garden fence; ploughing the lawn and killing several defenceless pansies. Life with the Roper's next door will take some getting used to!

Titbits... It's rather humorous to see that the 'Sharkman' comic being read to Tristram is actually an edition of 'Aquaman', with a canny prop department title being blatantly pasted over the front!

Chortle Rating: An excellent transition between shows and firm introduction to the new cast. 10/10

Guest Stars: Roy Kinnear, Jeannette Farrier, Margaret Lacey

Baby Talk - Series 1, Episode 4
Broadcast: Monday September 27th 1976 at 20:00
VTR: 13638

Mildred has offered her services as baby-sitter while the Fourmiles go to see Tom Stoppard's *Jumpers*. After spending time with Tristram, she soon realises that her maternal yearnings have never been fulfilled by her reticent husband. Feeling broody, she is convinced that a child would be at home in her life.

After all these years, George is unlikely to provide her with offspring, so Mildred decides that adoption is the only answer. Desperate to get her husband to agree, she pesters George with unsubtle hints and a ceremonial feast of his favourite supper. George soon gives in for a peaceful life.

A few days later, the Roper's are visited by a representative from the adoption society, who will vet their qualities as prospective parents. After quizzing the Roper's, it is clear they are unsuited to coping with children. Mildred is distraught at the fact that she is unlikely to hear the pitter-patter of tiny feet on the linoleum, but later that day, George springs an uncharacteristically pleasant surprise on his wife, returning from the pet-shop with a Yorkshire Terrier dog that she can love instead.

Titbits... Playwright Tom Stoppard is mentioned in this episode. His work was represented by literary agent Kenneth Ewing, who also fostered the talents of Johnnie Mortimer and Brian Cooke.

Chortle Rating: 'You're talking about Artificial Insinuation by wossname!' - A classic line! 8/10

Guest Stars: Anthony Sharp, Veida Draisey, Pussy Galore

Your Money or Your Life - Series 1, Episode 5

Broadcast: Monday October 4th 1976 at 20:00
Repeated on ITV: October 14th 1986 at 19:30
VTR: 13644

George's uncle Nathaniel has died and the Ropers attend his funeral. As usual George makes a nuisance of himself, with his stomach rumbling in the church and dropping 50p into the grave when he gets a hanky out for Mildred wipe away her tears. At the wake, Mildred is speaking to Nathaniel's widower Kate, and whilst discussing death, realises to her horror that George does not have life insurance. Mildred would have nothing if he suddenly died, and would have to pay for the funeral herself.

'I have got a small endowment' George announces back home, but on checking his policy, it is discovered that he has not paid the premiums since 1952 and his life cover is void. Mildred is determined to get her husband properly insured, allowing her to celebrate his departure with champagne and a band, but until he gets a policy sorted out he would have to be sent off in a cardboard box. The next day they go to a funeral directors to get some advice on the cost of a decent service, and when they realise exactly how much it costs to die these days, it is confirmed more than ever that they need to get some compensation sorted out.

It so happens that Jeffrey Fourmile deals in the insurance field, and he comes round later in the day to fill out a form with the Roper's, eager to imagine that George is dead. However there is a slight problem with insurance, as George needs to get a doctor's certificate first before any policy can be arranged.

Roper is despatched for an examination, which amazingly he passes, and once the medical certificate is attained, the cheque for the first premium is sent off. It is swiftly returned - George has dated the cheque wrong. It's the perfect excuse Roper needs to forget the whole thing, and he delights in ripping up the payment. Mildred is planning a world cruise when she learns what George has been up to, and she is distinctly disheartened when she learns he will be living for a good few years to come.

Chortle Rating: I particularly like the funeral director's scene. 9/10

Guest Stars: Stella Moray, Michael Ripper, John Carlin, Rafiq Anwar, Arthur Howard

Where My Caravan has Rested - Series 1, Episode 6

Broadcast: Monday October 11th 1976 at 20:00
Repeated on ITV: September 30th 1986 at 19:30
VTR: 13639

Mildred is sick and tired of George's rotten old wreck of a car outside the house and so is Jeffrey next door, who thinks that is spoils the view of the crescent and significantly lowers the tone of the neighbourhood. Mildred wants it shifted before her sister Ethel pops round for tea that afternoon, and George reluctantly agrees to push the car down to the local garage to see if he can get anything with part exchange. Without Mildred there to stop him, he returns home the proud owner of an even rustier caravan!

The grotty piece of junk is ten times more unsightly than the car, and Mildred is very much underwhelmed at the thought of caravan holidays in the country. Jeffrey too dislikes the sight of the mobile home, and swiftly organises a local neighbourhood committee to appeal to George's better nature in removing the caravan, but the suggestion is shunned. Roper's ears soon prick up, however, when he is offered £25 by the committee, who will buy the caravan and have it destroyed.

That afternoon, Ethel and Humphrey arrive for refreshments, staying over at the Roper's house until the next morning. Determined not to undergo her sister's snubs, Mildred gives them the master bedroom to sleep in, leaving herself and George in a single bed in the spare room. Roper is having none of this, and rather than get static shocks all night rubbing up against Mildred's nylon nightie, he decides to sneak out and sleep in the caravan.

As morning breaks, Jeffrey is delighted to see the caravan being towed away to the breaker's yard, but when Mildred pops out to collect the milk off the doorstep, and sees the lawn empty, she is quick to question Jeffrey regarding its whereabouts. When it is known that it's gone to the breakers yard with George still asleep inside, they set off in hot pursuit.

George wakes up in time and vacates the caravan, but as Mildred and Jeffrey arrive they see it being flattened by a solid concrete block. When George staggers out of the breaker's yard office very much alive, Mildred is disappointed...

Chortle Rating: Good, honest comedy. 8/10

Guest Stars: Michael Redfern, Alister Williamson, Pamela Watling, Ralph Ball, Eamonn Boyce, Margaret Lacey

George and Mildred - Episode Guide

The Little Dog Laughed - Series 1, Episode 7
Broadcast: Monday October 18th 1976 at 20:00
Repeated on ITV: October 28th 1986 at 19:30
VTR: 13641

Mildred is getting to know her new pet dog, who she has lovingly named Truffles. George is regretting ever purchasing his wife the dog, especially when he is lumbered with taking it for walks down to the park.

En-route to the recreation ground, Roper gets conveniently lost and ends up in the pub. Sadly, it appears Truffles is not house trained, and after piddling on a patron, is constrained to the lamp-post outside to keep her out of harms way. George's knot-tying skills are grossly under par, and Truffles soon pulls free from the leash and goes on the run around Hampton Wick. If George doesn't find it before Mildred, his life will not be worth living!

After a failed search for the dog, Roper plods home to ask Mildred exactly what will happen to him if her beloved pet accidentally went missing. He doesn't approve of her reply, and runs out to the pet shop to replace it with another similar dog. Mildred will never know.

The plan is almost perfect apart from one minor detail, the police have found Truffles in the park and returned her home to Mildred. She is annoyed that George has lost the dog, but when he triumphantly walks in with the replacement 'Truffles' under his arm, her expression changes to confusion. After Mildred undertakes a brief inspection of the new pet she confronts George about it's true identity. There is something on the dog that wasn't there when it left, something unmistakably male...

Chortle Rating: Classic punch line, and I particularly like the way the dogs get credited in the closing titles! 9/10

Recollections... The little bit in the park was somewhere in Teddington, it was filmed long before they did the studio recordings, and this was the first bit of *George and Mildred* to ever be recorded. Brian Murphy was telling me how Yootha didn't think the series would work, but it clearly wasn't the case, it was an incredibly successful show. - Bella Emberg

Guest Stars: Paul Angelis, Norman Mitchell, Anthony Heaton, Verne Morgan, Bella Emberg, Pussy Galore, James Bond

Best Foot Forward - Series 1, Episode 8
Broadcast: Monday October 25th 1976 at 20:00
Repeated on Thames: October 21st 1986 19:30
Viewing households - 9.4 Million
National television chart position - 1

After a dismal lunch at a toffee-nosed pub, The Genevieve, where there is gin and tonic on draught - The Ropers go home to spend the rest of the afternoon in front of the telly. When the set begins to flicker and Gordon Honeycomb starts bouncing about the screen, George climbs up to the roof so he can repair the aerial. Without a ladder of his own, Roper temporarily pinches the Fourmile's, but when Jeffrey finds out he is quick to reclaim his property. As he snatches the ladder away, George falls off the roof and breaks his leg on the way!

Jeffrey is now indebted to his neighbour, a position he detests being in. Faced with George's ongoing threat of taking legal action, Jeffrey is at his beck and call, even disrupting Tristram's birthday party by allowing him to watch the racing. In a final attempt of kindness, Fourmile pushes George in his wheelchair down to the newsagents to get some cigarettes, but when Jeffrey leaves his invalid unattended, George releases the brakes of his wheelchair and starts to roll away, causing havoc thundering down the hill, knocking over greengrocer's displays and startling several old ladies. What can possibly stop the runaway Roper?

Titbits... Careful inspection will reveal that a Brian Murphy stunt double is performing the runaway wheelchair scene. After knocking over the fruit stall, the chair turns and the double has to use his arm to shield his face from the camera. It is at this point that you can clearly see the join around his wig!

Chortle Rating: Brilliant. 9/10

Guest Stars: Sebastian Breaks, Ken Watson, Gail Lidstone, Mike Lewin, Ralph Ball, Maxine Horne, Pussy Galore

George and Mildred - Episode Guide

My Husband Next Door - Series 1, Episode 9

Broadcast: Monday November 1st 1976 at 20:00
Repeated on ITV: November 4th 1986 at 19:30
VTR: 13642

Mildred is occupying her spare time by taking an interest in interior design, reading an arty magazine that she pinched from the dentist's waiting room. After reading about how all the stars are having their houses refurbished, she decides her house is in need of a renovation. George is happy to have no part in such activities, but after the television blows up during *Wacky Races,* he finds himself being roped into revamping the house.

Next door, the Fourmiles are off on a fishing holiday to Scotland, Jeffrey basking in his own self-confidence in angling abilities but Ann not convinced. They hand over the house keys to Mildred so she can keep an eye on things, and start the long drive up north. With the Fourmiles gone, George uses the opportunity to retreat next door and watch their telly instead.

Sick to the back teeth of her husband's avoidance of refurbishing, Mildred has no choice but to call in professional decorators. They shortly arrive but mistakenly follow George into the Fourmiles' house where he is watching the television, leading them to assume that it's the property they have to renovate. When George is ordered back home for lunch, they bring in the equipment and start to rip out the Fourmiles' expensive wallpaper and replace everything with plain Magnolia!

George discovers the mistake he is responsible for and swiftly blames the decorators, causing them to walk off and leave the Ropers to sort out the damage. Phoning up the Fourmile's in Scotland, they manage to extract the name of the their wallpaper design, and set about putting the stripped out lounge back to normal. After wasting several rolls, they finally finish the job just in time for the return of Jeffrey, Ann and Tristram. All seems well when they get home, except for one thing Tristram notices...the walls appear to be upside down...

Chortle Rating: I can name a dozen sitcoms that have done 'the wallpaper routine', but *George and Mildred* is the finest example of such slapstick. 10/10

Guest Stars: Keith Smith, John Lyons, Raymond Farrell, Jenny Till

Family Planning - Series 1, Episode 10
Broadcast: Monday November 8th 1976 at 20:00
Repeated on ITV: October 7th 1986 at 19:30
VTR: 13643

Mildred's mother has paid a visit to the Ropers. Mildred is filled with glee and George with anguish, which is worsened when he has to cough up £6 for his mother-in-law's taxi fare from Dagenham. When Mildred suggests that her mother stays with them permanently, it pushes George to the edge of reason and he threatens to leave home.

With Mother becoming ever more senile, Mildred's relatives hold a family conference on who should get lumbered with her now that she is getting too old to live on her own. To keep Mother absent from the argument, George takes her down to the pub. As they discuss families, Mother lets slip that she is going to live with her son Arthur in New Zealand in a few weeks, meaning that she won't be occupying any space at the Roper's household.

George is delighted to hear the news, and is quick to get back to Peacock Crescent and tell everyone that Mother can stay with him and Mildred, bragging at their generosity but safe in the knowing that she will soon be going to the other side of the world. Only one small snag, Arthur died in 1950, and George has just agreed to a old lodger!

Chortle Rating: Interesting to see Mildred's full extended family. 8/10.

Guest Stars: Avril Elgar, Reginald Marsh, Gretchen Franklin, Jean Marlow, Pussy Galore

Jumble Pie - Series 2, Episode 1
Broadcast: Monday November 14th 1977 at 20:00
Repeated on ITV: November 11th 1986 at 19:30
VTR: 18059

When Mildred hears there is a jumble sale to be held at St. Butolph's church hall, she is all to happy to donate some items for the cause. She can use the opportunity to mingle with her peers and feel socially accepted for an hour or two, 'hobnobbing with the blue rinses' as George mocks. The hunt begins for some unwanted junk to send to the sale and Mildred is quick to get her clutches on a box of George's old gardening magazines, entirely ignorant of what lurks below the top layer of horticultural literature.

Whilst sorting through the Roper's donations, Jeffrey Fourmile soon finds what lies in the box and is disgusted at his discovery. Below the contributed gardening magazines are dozens of George's smutty top shelf magazines. When Mildred finds out what she has inadvertently donated, she is horrified and frog-marches George to the hall to reclaim his filth before the vicar finds it. They may be too late...

Chortle Rating: Excellent first episode for series two. 7/10

Guest Stars: Trevor Baxter

All Around the Clock - Series 2, Episode 2
Broadcast: Monday November 21st 1977 at 20:00
Repeated on ITV: November 18th 1986 at 19:30
VTR: 18060

It's George and Mildred's 24th wedding anniversary, and time for the mandatory exchange of presents. Mildred has bought George a pipe to try and lend him a dash of debonair (a waste of time), and in the knowledge that there would be pain if he didn't, George has purchased something for his wife, a gold carriage clock, bought off a bloke in a pub for a tenner.

Next door, the Fourmiles have returned from a golfing holiday in Scotland, only to find their house has been broken into with devastating results. Thieves have gained entry through the back door and have stolen some treasured items. Jeffrey is convinced that it's a working class break-in, no doubt undertaken by council estate yobs.

When Mildred hears that the Fourmiles have had a carriage clock stolen, she is quick to quiz George about the origins of her wedding anniversary present, probing for information about the vendor. The Fourmile's clock was stolen last week, George bought her's last week - it all adds up.

Worried they may be arrested for handling stolen goods, the Ropers start scheming as to how they can return the clock to the Fourmiles without them noticing. The resulting hatched plan being that they sneak it back onto their mantelpiece whilst consoling Jeffrey about the theft. George manages to subtly place the timepiece back where it belongs, but it is soon spotted by Jeffrey and the Ropers are rumbled. That is until Ann walks in clutching a box of their items. The police have caught two public schoolboys and returned most of the stolen wares, including a gold clock...

Recollections... I vividly remember this episode, it shocked me quite a lot. I was rehearsing a scene where I am talking with a little boy [Nicholas Owen] and at the end I completely unconsciously patted him on the head. The director came up to me in a most curious way and said 'when you pat his head, perhaps you shouldn't do that'. Even back then there was this fear that people can't physically reach out to each other, I remember that so vividly in my mind. - Robert Gillespie

Chortle Rating: Favourable twist. 9/10

Guest Stars: Richard Coleman, Robert Gillespie, Bill Rourke

The Travelling Man - Series 2, Episode 3

Broadcast: Monday November 28th 1977 at 20:00
Repeated on ITV: November 25th 1986 at 19:30
VTR: 18061

When destitution once again falls on the Ropers, George has the suggestion of taking in a lodger. Mildred disagrees, but her argument has little credence as George has already placed an advert in the local paper. She is furious, but when the suave Edward Rogers comes to her door to view the spare room, there is an instant change of heart.

In less than a week, Mildred has drawn close to her paying guest, making him special meals, sighing when she irons his underpants and seemingly favouring her lodger over her husband. George can see what's going on and becomes concerned that Rogers is winning his wife's affections. He consults Jeffrey for advice when his concerns grow further. Fortunately though, Edward will be leaving soon.

When Rogers' last day at the Roper's arrives, Mildred dishes up a special farewell meal for him, and with George away at a darts match, she utilises her last chance to make a move on the lodger, closing in on him with her man-hungry desires. Mildred is downtrodden when Rogers brushes off her advances, saying that he is gay. Mrs. Roper is appalled but takes it on the chin, however down at the pub that evening there is some evidence that she may have been deceived. Rogers is deep in intimate conversation with an attractive barmaid and Mildred is far from happy...

Titbits... This episode is one of the very few that harkens back to *Man About the House*, with George's suggestion of 'doing what we used to do' and taking in guests.

Chortle Rating: Great guest work from Derek Waring. 9/10

Guest Stars: Harry Littlewood, Catherine Kessler, Derek Waring

The Unkindest Cut of All - Series 2, Episode 4
Broadcast: Monday December 5th 1977 at 20:00
VTR: 18062
Individual viewers: 19.7 Million
National television chart position - 1

Ethel and Humphrey are coming round to the Roper's for dinner and George is being given a lecture on what not to do when in company, Mildred nagging him not to blow his nose on the napkins or take his teeth out. Mildred is taking care of every possible angle to avoid a problematic evening, and attempting to make an impression with fancy napkins and gunk-less bottles of ketchup.

There is one snag that she hasn't banked on. While Mildred is round borrowing some stuffing mixture from Ann, George gets a visit from the electricity board who cut off the power to the house, a result of him neglecting to pay the bills. When he thinks what Mildred will do to him when she can't use the oven, Roper is fearing for his life, so quickly arranges a plan to save the evening. With the Fourmiles just leaving to go to visit Jeffrey's mother, George creeps into their house and plugs in a very long extension cord.

When the Fourmiles arrive home early and discover their electricity is being diverted, Jeffrey is far from pleased and makes the second cut of the day. George and Mildred are now entirely power-less and dinner is ruined. Thankfully, Humphrey offers to take everyone out for dinner at a swanky restaurant, and telephones ahead to make a reservation. For some reason the Roper's telephone isn't working. It seems that George has failed to pay another bill...

Chortle Rating: The lamp moving along the lounge floor stands as one of my favourite examples of visual humour in the series. 10/10.

Guest Stars: Avril Elgar, Reginald Marsh, Norman Mitchell

The Right Way to Travel - Series 2, Episode 5
Broadcast: Monday December 12th 1977 at 20:00
Repeated on ITV: December 2nd 1986 at 19:30
VTR: 18063

Mildred is sick of going to Mrs. Muldoon's Blackpool boarding house for a holiday every year, badgering George to go somewhere more exotic, like Majorca. He doesn't like to break the tradition of their yearly ritual, and besides neither of them speak a word of Majorcan, but after heavy persuasion, George agrees to the Balearic islands. There is, however, one more hurdle in the way of a perfect holiday, and it lies with the association George has to join in order to qualify for the cheap package deal - the Conservatives!

Jeffrey is on the local committee, and when he sees that George has applied to become a 'Tory Twit', he is astonished. Convinced there must be an ulterior motive, he demands the Ropers attend an interview. Fourmile subjects them to an intense inquisition, and it emerges they are only joining to nab the cheap holiday. Their application is swiftly rejected. As it looks like Muldoon's may be the destination again, George phones up to book their room, but is shocked to learn the hotel is full. The reason? A local conference by the Labour party!

Chortle Rating: Enjoyable political stereotyping. 9/10

Guest Stars: Edward Evans, Zulema Dene

The Dorothy Letters - Series 2, Episode 6
Broadcast: Monday December 19th 1977 at 20:00
Repeated on ITV: December 9th 1986 at 19:30
VTR: 18064

George and Mildred are sorting through some old bits of junk; George's gasmask, his membership card to the Ovalteenies and a Dick Barton Annual. When George leaves to take the dog for a walk, Mildred makes a discovery of her own - several rather raunchy letters to a woman called Dorothy, all written in George's hand, and some of them quite recent. Could Roper really be having an affair?

On George's return, Mildred confronts him over the bundle of letters, but Roper refuses to be pressed on the matter. Desperate for some answers, Mildred drags him to a marriage guidance councillor. After a fruitless discussion, George finally comes clean about the mysterious Dorothy. They are drafts of fan mail letters. For Dorothy Lamour!

Titbits... Watch closely at the bottom left of the screen whilst the Ropers are at the marriage guidance councillor. A few moments after George says 'its shocking', and the camera pans backwards, the black hood of another camera can be seen creeping into shot.

Chortle Rating: Very funny. 9/10

Guest Stars: Pussy Galore, James Cosmo, Peggy Sinclair

No Business Like Show Business - Series 2, Episode 7
Alternate Title: Christmas with George and Mildred

Broadcast: Monday December 26th 1977 at 20:00
Repeated on ITV: December 23rd 1986 at 1930
Repeated on ITV: December 26th 1989 at 19:30
Repeated on FIVE: December 27th 2004 at 20:20
VTR: 18065

Jeffrey Fourmile is relishing the responsibility of directing and producing the Hampton Wick player's annual cantata, which this year is *Cinderella*. Short of an ugly sister, Mildred is cast into the production as Griselda, and for once George agrees that his wife has made the right choice - exclaiming how well she's been typecast.

Sadly when Mildred's big time comes, she is suffering with flu, brought on from travelling in George's motorcycle sidecar. With her chances of stardom reduced to tatters, George is faced with having to don a sparkly dress and wig to take her place and entertain the children. He naturally refuses, but when Humphrey and Ethel start him thinking about how worldwide success may come from his performance, George decides that the show must go on. Alas, a traffic accident on the way to the theatre means that George can't attend, and it falls to Jeffrey to step into Griselda's big shoes. Whoever heard of an ugly sister with a moustache?

Chortle Rating: Jeffrey is annoying when it comes to creativity. 7/10

Guest Stars: Reginald Marsh, Avril Elgar, Roy Barraclough, Sue Bond, Rosanne Wickes, Derek Deadman, Mike Lewin

Opportunity Knocks - Series 3, Episode 1
Broadcast: Thursday September 7th 1978 at 20.00
VTR: 18791

Mildred is saddened when her coffee morning fails miserably, with only Ann turning up of out forty invited guests - most of whom were local at local councillor's wife Mrs. Clifton-White's garden party.

Meanwhile, George is desperate for money to fund a large stake share in Jerry's Kentucky Fried Pigeon scheme, joining the other share holders, an Arab Consortium - Abdul and his missus from the sweet shop. The only way Roper can summon the cash is to put his house on the market behind Mildred's back, delighting a bewildered Jeffrey Fourmile at the thought his class-less neighbours may be moving.

A couple arrive from Potters Bar to view the Roper's Georgian town-house property, but their inventory is interrupted when Mildred returns home early from shopping. She is startled to learn how George has been opening the doors to strangers, showing them their bedroom and allowing them to scoff at the size of the living room and state of the ceiling.

When they leave, Mildred is speechless about what has just happened, disgusted at the way her home has been traipsed through with disregard. When Ann mentions that George has put the house on the market, the penny drops for Mildred and she confronts her sly husband, questioning how he wants his funeral arranged...

Chortle Rating: Roy Kinnear at his finest. 9/10

Guest Stars: Roy Kinnear, Robert Raglan, Patricia Kneale, Lesley Staples, Michael Wynne

And So To Bed - Series 3, Episode 2
Broadcast: Thursday September 14th 1978 at 20:00
VTR: 18792

When Mildred starts nagging about the quality of her home's furnishings, George performs a flying leap onto the bed to prove that the 'good solid pre-war British Workmanship' is still up to scratch. His efforts collapse it, and cause numerous springs to explode through the mattress.

The Roper's go and look for a replacement at the bed shop the next morning. Mildred has her eye on the luxury models, but George thinking on the cheap side. They eventually meet halfway, settling on a tacky shop-soiled vinyl model. It seems like they have got their new bed, until George reveals he is on a hired purchase blacklist.

Mildred is frustrated, but when she learns that George is very close to winning a bet on a three-way accumulator, she is adamant that if he wins, the money will go on a new bed. Incredibly, all the horses that he has backed cross the line first. George has won £160. Mildred is delighted to accompany him to the betting shop to claim his winnings, but unfortunately Roper has a few unpaid slates. When he is forced to pay up, it reduces his winnings to just 85p. It looks as if he will be sleeping on the sofa for a good few weeks to come...

Titbits... A keen observer will notice on the wall of the Fourmile's kitchen in this episode, a metal plate which says LNER 269664. This is just a standard prop department asset that was wheeled out to dress the set, but in reality is an identity plate that once belonged to a London North Eastern Railway 'Diagram 100' 20 ton HTO coal hopper built in 1944.

Titbits... It is also interesting to notice some continuity issues between episodes. Mildred can drive in this episode and is asked by Ann to take her and Tristram to the shops, but later in series five we see Mildred taking lessons!

Chortle Rating: Some excellent sleeping bag visual humour. 9/10

Guest Stars: Jimmy Thompson, John Lyons, Harry Littlewood

I Believe in Yesterday - Series 3, Episode 3

Broadcast: Thursday September 21st 1978 at 20:00
VTR: 18793
Individual viewers - 17.5 Million
National television chart position - 3

Mildred is surprised when her mother gives her a letter from America that was delivered to the wrong address. It is from an old friend of her's, Lee Kennedy, from the American airbase where Mildred used to work. Lee is coming over to England and would like to meet up with her, arranging a private room at the Dorchester Hotel. George is jealous, and decides that two can tango - phoning up an old friend of his own, Gloria Rumbold.

Mildred is desperately looking forward to her date, buying a new frock and going to the beauty parlour before the meeting, but her ambitions are deflated when she learns that Lee has also invited along twenty other girls from the airbase for the gathering. The night is a washout. George is also having a dismal evening waiting for Gloria. When he sees a lardy blond woman who works at a massage parlour strutting into the pub, he makes a quick retreat.

George and Mildred meet up back home after both having a rough time. They both soon realise that they have to make do with what life offers, however miserable it may be...

Titbits... Just before the commercial break, a keen eye will notice a stowaway on the set. When Yootha says the line, 'I'm Going!', there is a big fly walking around on her heavily lacquered hair.

Titbits... Sitcom fans will notice uncanny similarities in this programme to the *Rising Damp* episode 'Pink Carnations', which was made at roughly the same time in 1978. Very similar lines match both series together, with references to surgical appliances, flowers in buttonholes and private rooms. It's a wonder of who thought of the idea first!

Chortle Rating: A great bunch of support actors. 9/10

Guest Stars: Eunice Black, Claire Davenport, Lionel Murton, Gretchen Franklin, George Malpas, Peter Quince

George and Mildred - Episode Guide

The Four Letter Word - Series 3, Episode 4
Broadcast: Thursday September 28th 1978 at 20:00
VTR: 18794

George is relishing in his domestic situation; living off the dole and lazing at home on the sofa in his socks, reading saucy newspaper segments. Mildred is determined to get her bone idle husband back out to work, and the very opportunity arises when her sister and brother-in-law pay a visit.

Ethel and Humphrey have popped round to invite the Roper's to a 'showing off' party at their new house, and whilst they are conversing over tea and sponge fingers, the topic of conversation turns to careers. Humphrey suggests that George goes into business with him in the meat trade. Roper reluctantly goes along the next day to see exactly what 'the offal king of Oxshott' has on offer, but his natural nosiness gets in the way whilst waiting in the office and he finds two tickets for a holiday to Jersey for Humphrey and his secretary. George uses his newly found upper-hand to engage in a spot of blackmail, holding Humphrey to ransom that if he doesn't cancel the job offer to George, the beans will be spilled to Ethel.

That evening, the Roper's attend Ethel and Humphries dinner party. With the guests pre-occupied in the lounge, Ethel confronts Humphrey over something that has discovered whilst dusting his pockets - two tickets to Jersey. In a futile attempt to escape his predicament, Humphrey tells Ethel that he booked the holiday for George and Mildred to go instead.

Ethel is slightly confused, but delighted all the same to be openly charitable to her less wealthy sibling, presenting the first class tickets to Mildred whilst George is in the bathroom. Roper returns and is quick to deny ever seeing the tickets, adding that he doesn't want to go on holiday with Humphrey's secretary. Ethel soon twigs exactly what is going on and in a spate of angry ripping, the tickets are destroyed. Mildred is devastated, but George is plain confused...

Chortle Rating: Great scripts with classic outcome. 9/10

Recollections... The location of Ethel and Humphrey's house was a great big mansion in Burwood Park, Weybridge. When filming outside, the location director hadn't arranged a dressing room for the cast to change in, so we had to ask the owner of the house if Yootha could change in the master bedroom! - Kathleen Russell (Wardrobe Mistress)

Guest Stars: Avril Elgar, Reginald Marsh, Mimi De Braie, Jennifer Guy

The Delivery Man - Series 3, Episode 5
Broadcast: Thursday October 5th 1978 at 20:00

Ann's labour pains start a week early, taking her completely by surprise. Jeffrey is at a meeting in Birmingham for the day, and with Ann confined to bed to ease the discomfort, it falls to Mildred to make the arrangements for the baby's imminent arrival.

With all the minicab companies having hour long waiting lists, and unable to get Ann to the hospital on foot, George has to escort the expectant mother in his motorbike sidecar. When they arrive at the maternity unit, George is mistaken for Ann's husband and conscripted into the delivery room for the duration of the birth, an event he will remember for the rest of his life.

Jeffrey arrives at the hospital too late, missing the birth of baby Tarquin. His day is further ruined when Ann suggests that the new addition to the family be named after the man who got her to the maternity unit on time...

Chortle Rating: George's gormlessness in the hospital is hilarious. 10/10

Recollections... The sad truth is that I remember nothing about my few days on *George and Mildred*. I know I played a doctor, but no other details survive in my mind, alas. I don't recall how I was cast or how the other actors were. It was simply another job for me, a lot of water under the bridge since then. - Paul Meier

Guest Stars: Simon Lloyd, Gail Lidstone, Cass Allen, Michael Redfern, Paul Meier

Life with Father - Series 3, Episode 6
Broadcast: Thursday October 12th 1978 at 20:00
VTR: 18796

George's father is having his house pulled down by the council and has found new accommodation with the Twilight home for the elderly. It seems a pleasant enough place, but after being dropped off on George's bike, Roper senior is shortly back on his son's doorstep, complaining he has been thrown out. In actual fact, he has left on his own accord because the home refused to let him keep a pet ferret.

Mildred is disturbed to find the creature has been smuggled into her home in a wicker basket and she is eager to get shot of it, temporarily consigning it to the garage until George's dad can face parting with it. Thankfully a solution is at hand, in the form of Jeffrey's car thundering down the street and flattening the runaway pet. Roper senior is gutted, but George and Mildred are quietly delighted, now lacking the obstruction that is preventing dad going into the home. That is until Jeffrey buys a replacement...

Chortle Rating: An excellent cameo by Reg Lye. 8/10

Guest Stars: Reg Lye, Beatrix Mackey, Tim Barrett, Tom Hardy

Just the Job - Series 4, Episode 1
Broadcast: Thursday November 16th 1978 at 20:00

George is depressed when the job centre arrange for him to attend an interview for a traffic warden. Roper reluctantly goes along, making his usual impression by complaining how wardens make motoring a misery, and likening them all to 'little Hitlers'. His potential employers are far from happy, but being incredibly short-staffed, they take him on for the training scheme, making him a full time traffic warden in a matter of weeks.

Meanwhile back home, Ann is talking to Mildred about a forthcoming prize-giving ceremony at Tristram's school, explaining how the Mayor will be attending as celebrity guest. With a chance to hobnob with local dignitaries, Mildred jumps at the chance to go along too, dragging her significant other in on the act.

George makes a total nuisance of himself at the event, erupting with flatulence in the middle of headmaster's speech and complaining how having only boys at the school is likely to alter their preferences in partnerships. Embarrassed to the hilt, Mildred instantly despatches him home. When the event draws to a close, Mildred leaves with the Fourmiles. George, however, is still at work - issuing tickets to the cars outside, including the Mayor's!

Titbits... Tristram's school in this episode is called 'Morland House School', and by casting an eye at the close-up of the sign, the headmaster's name can be seen to be a certain 'J Peasmold'. Coincidentally, Peasmold was a favourite character from *Round the Horne* and appeared in several episodes of the Radio Comedy.

Chortle Rating: A Great Job for George! 10/10

Guest Stars: Simon Lloyd, Anthony Sharp, Michael Hawkins, Robert Raglan, Gerald Chase, Leonard Woodrow

Days of Beer and Rosie - Series 4, Episode 2
Broadcast: Thursday November 23rd 1978 at 20:00

George is startled when someone walks up to him in the pub claiming to be his long lost son. It all started on VE night in 1945 with Rosie Albright, a companion George found after ringing a telephone number scrawled on a bomb shelter. After a memorable night to celebrate the end of the war, passion took over George and Rosie, and nine months later came Bill Albright. Could Roper really be his father?

Mildred is adamant that he can't be, and in a pursuit of the truth, the Ropers go to see Ernie, a friend who was with George and Rosie on the memorable night. But when he remembers the gang going back to Rosie's house and George heading up to bed, Mildred accepts that she may be a step-mother after all and invites Bill round for a meeting.

George is savouring his suddenly extended family, but the next time he goes round to see his son, there is disappointing news. Bill has been to the solicitors and found that Rosie was paid child support by his real father for years, Ernie!

Recollections... Peter Frazer-Jones remembered me from *Man About the House* and asked me back for *George and Mildred*. I had to grow a moustache to look more like Brian's son. He was wonderful to work with, and he kept complaining how he was too young to have a son!. It was a lot of fun to be on the show, and Yootha was terrific. I saw this episode again recently and I thought it was wonderful. The scripting was hilarious and the show is timeless. - Jeremy Bulloch

Recollections... I only had one scene in this episode with Brian Murphy, but I do remember it was very enjoyable. He was very kind with the baby who played my child. I have subsequently worked with Norman Eshley who I got on very well with. - Jean Rogers

Chortle Rating: Excellent comedy. 9/10

Guest Stars: Jeremy Bulloch, Tony Melody, Jean Rogers, Richard Shaw, Robert Michaels, Ursula Granville

You Must Have Showers - Series 4, Episode 3
Broadcast: Thursday November 30th 1978 at 20:00

When Mildred pops next door to the Fourmiles to reclaim an exercise book she has lent to Ann, she is instantly taken by the family's bathroom. Jeffrey has installed a fitted shower and the finished product looks wonderfully inviting. It doesn't take Mildred long to come to the conclusion that she too would like a fitted shower in her bathroom...

George is despatched to get some quotes, but when he returns from the plumbers with expensive estimates, Mildred's dreams of vertical cleanliness evaporate in a cloud of steam. That is until a certain 'Trans World Intercontinental Plumbers' quotes a suspiciously cheap option. There has to be something dubious behind it, and there is - Jerry!

With great reluctance, Mildred allows Jerry to carry out the job, and the portly Jack of all trades starts work the next morning. After an extensive few days of ruining the property, Jerry proclaims that his efforts have concluded and that the shower will shortly be ready to use. However the water has to remain off until the chewing gum hardens.

Mildred doesn't have time to view Jerry's masterpiece. She has a few members of her exercise class coming round for light refreshments, and she is busy making sure everything is tidy. George is the first untidy object in her sights. Caked with cement dust and grout, he is ordered to have a bath, but with the water still turned off, he has to resort to war-time measures, and set up the old tin bath tub in the centre of the lounge. His bathing is interrupted when Mildred returns with her friends, and George has to swiftly duck underwater to keep out of their way. When he surfaces suddenly, Mildred's social life looks finished forever...

Recollections... The bathtub scene was a wonderful part of the episode. We had these screens put up and I hid behind them and stepped in the bath out of sight of the audience. I had to stay underwater for about a minute to build up to the big reveal, and then suddenly, you see the duck popping up to the top, which got a good laugh. Then I appeared and that brought the house down. I emerged from the old tin bath, made my excuses and backed off and it was a wonderful scene to play and a wonderful exit, the audience were in hysterics. It was a real highlight. - Brian Murphy

Chortle Rating: Hilarious visual comedy from Brian and Norman. 10/10

Guest Stars: Simon Lloyd, Roy Kinnear, Cass Allen, Peggyann Clifford

No Work No Pay - Series 4, Episode 4
Broadcast: Thursday December 7th 1978 at 20:00

George's job as a traffic warden is hanging by a thread. His constant rule breaking; booking police cars and giving tickets to the senior traffic warden's bicycle, has upset his boss Mr Higson and Roper is dragged into the office for a firm dressing down.

George doesn't listen to the ominous warnings, and is soon back to his old ways. This time, however, Higson is lying in wait and collars his idle employee talking to Jerry. After a heated exchange, and egged on by his fat friend, Roper resigns from his traffic warden duties there and then. It soon dawns on him what he has done, and he will now have to face the wrath of Mildred.

Roper spends the next week still in uniform and collecting his sandwiches, before leaving the house for fictional work. Mildred is unawares that her husband is, in reality, loitering around the park and reading the newspapers in the public library. His parade is rained on when Mildred receives an enlightening call from Mr Higson, and soon latches on to what George has been up to...

Chortle Rating: A firm guest appearance by Blake Butler. 8/10

Guest Stars: Roy Kinnear, Blake Butler, Dany Clare, Ted Burnett

Nappy Days - Series 4, Episode 5
Broadcast: Thursday December 14th 1978 at 20:00

Once again, Mildred is scaling the social ladder, attending night time art classes and reading about sculptures in magazines. George doesn't care much for high brow art, and is instead more concerned with the British Legion darts match. There is a chance for him to play on the team, but the other members aren't keen on Roper's inclusion.

Next door, the Fourmiles are in need of a capable baby sitter, as they are off to a funeral. With the majority of the family attending the memorial, Mildred is chosen for the job of child minding. She accepts with delight, and looks after baby Tarquin for the afternoon. However, when the clock strikes eight, she has to leave for art class and decides, rather unwillingly, to leave infant Tarquin in the care of George.

Just as she leaves, the Fourmiles ring up to explain they are stranded and their car has broken down. There will be a delay in collecting the baby. The significance of the comment is lost on Roper, until he receives a call from the British Legion. At last, George has been asked to play for the team. Can Roper really take a baby along to a dart's match?

Chortle Rating: Great stereotyping of farmers! 9/10

Guest Stars: Simon Lloyd, Norman Mitchell, Marjie Lawrence, Russell Waters, Billy Burden, Peggy Aitchinson

George and Mildred - Episode Guide

The Mating Game - Series 4, Episode 6
Broadcast: Thursday December 21st 1978 at 20:00
Individual viewers - 20.8
National television chart position - 2

The Roper's Yorkshire Terrier, Truffles, is currently in season and gaining a large amount of attention from randy Spaniels and horny Dalmatians who are forming a queue outside the front door. Mildred knows why, but George just can't grasp the mating game. He never could!

In search of a solution, the Ropers decide to get some advice on what they can do about their dog, and head along to the vets. When the suggestion arises that they could try breeding, Mildred thinks it's a wonderful idea. George, however, is of the opinion that one dog is enough. When he is told that he could sell pedigree pups for up to £40 each, he changes his mind.

It just so happens that Ethel and Humphrey have a pedigree dog. A Terrier stud called Pomeroy. Mildred invites them discuss the possible chance of breeding, and later that day the dogs are introduced. Some while later, it is confirmed by the vet that Truffles is expecting and the long tense wait until the big day commences.

Truffles nestles down in the airing cupboard in preparation for the arrival of the litter. The vet arrives to help out with the delivery, and the pups arrive safely. Ethel and Humphrey arrive to snaffle the pick of the litter for themselves, but annoyingly it seems that the black and white mongrel from down the road has got there first. Truffles has produced a worthless quartet of cross-bred pups. George's hopes for a £160 jackpot are dashed, but he has more pressing matters on his mind. Can there be money in breeding goldfish?

Chortle Rating: Comical viewing. 9/10

Guest Stars: Simon Lloyd, Reginald Marsh, Avril Elgar, Robert Gillespie, John Carlin, Aimee Delamann

On The Second Day of Christmas - Series 4, Episode 7
Broadcast: Thursday December 28th 1978 at 20:00
Repeated on Channel 5: December 26th 2005 at 20:25

The Roper's are having a dismal Christmas; with a turkey frozen solid, a blown up television and unlucky lucky charms from Christmas crackers. They have been stuck with each other's company all over the festive period, without even so much as a wayward visitor. The Fourmiles, however, have had a whale of a time with dozens of callers popping in and plenty of presents beneath the tree. When the mad rush finishes, Ann asks George and Mildred come round for a drink, Jeffrey's response being a distinct 'Bah Humbug'.

With Mildred preoccupied, casting envious glances at Ann's new blender, George challenges Tristram to a game of 'Telly Tennis', and wins all of his pocket money. Jeffrey is disgusted that Roper could stoop so low, and is quick to play against George, working him into debt with a run of 'double or quits' bets.

The Roper's time next door is interrupted by Ethel and Humphrey turning up at their house unexpectedly. They come bearing gifts, but as the Ropers assumed there would be no festive callers, they have scoffed their chocolates and drunk their brandy. When Ethel and Humphrey end up being presented with an improvised pair of oven gloves and a block of cheese, their facial expression is one of ingratitude.

Chortle Rating: Festive fun. 9/10

Guest Stars: Simon Lloyd, Avril Elgar, Reginald Marsh, Gretchen Franklin

George and Mildred - Episode Guide

Finders Keepers - Series 5, Episode 1
Broadcast: Wednesday October 24th 1979 at 20:30

When George presents Mildred with a fur coat as an anniversary present, she is naturally delighted, but exceptionally curious as to how her skinflint husband could have possibly afforded it. When Ann tells her that George found a credit card in the pub, Mildred is convinced that he used it fraudulently to purchase the gift.

Wanting no part of the stolen goods, Mildred takes the coat back to the shop where George bought it, Oxfam. In attempt to put things rights and get the money refunded onto the stolen credit card, she asks the counter assistant to cancel the charge and take back the coat.

Later that afternoon, a Mr MacDonald calls at Peacock Crescent asking after the credit card. Mildred is worried her husband will be arrested, however upon hearing that George has returned the credit card to the rightful owner and Mr MacDonald has come round to thank him, she is aghast, and races back to the shop to reclaim her coat. Sadly, she is too late. George isn't happy that Mildred has shunned his gift, but it still begs the question as to how George paid for it. The answer comes out under interrogation, he withdrew £30 from her post office savings account!

Chortle Rating: Enjoyable George Vs Mildred conflict. 9/10

Recollections... My agents called me up for *George and Mildred*. I only had a few lines so don't remember too much. Everyone was very professional and it went along without any hang-ups, I remember the Make-up girls all gossiping how I was Michael Robbins' wife - there were notes all over my chair! - Hal Dyer

Titbits... This episode was aired on the same night that the longest ever ITV strike came to an end. The EETPU and NATTKE unions sparked the walk-out on July 23rd 1979, and over the subsequent three months, regional stations were only intermittently operational. The bitter dispute ended on October 24th 1979.

Guest Stars: Derek Deadman, Hal Dyer, Trevor Baxter, Ivor Roberts, Roy Herrick, Ewan Roberts

In Sickness and In Health - Series 5, Episode 2
Broadcast: Wednesday October 30th 1979 at 20:30

Mildred is due to go into hospital to undergo an operation for a grumbling appendix, having to stay on the ward for three days. When Jerry finds out about her absence, it doesn't take him long to pressure George into allowing him to stay at his house whilst he sorts out a problem with his landlord. Being a pal, George agrees, but is startled when Jerry brings along his floozy...er...niece, as well!

Mildred undergoes countless tests at the hospital, and eventually receives some good news. The doctor has come to the conclusion that her appendix problem is actually just indigestion, and she can go home immediately. Mildred heads back to Peacock Crescent triumphantly, but when she discovers Jerry and his bit of fluff nesting under her roof, she is far from pleased and evicts the unwelcome guests instantly.

Meanwhile next door, Tristram is eager to camp outside in the garden to gain his woodcraft badge for the boy scouts. Jeffrey doesn't think it's a good idea, worried about what the neighbours would think, but after persistent requests he eventually relents. Tristram heads outside but is back in within seconds, he can't sleep in the tent. It's occupied - by a fat man and his niece!

Recollections... Johnnie didn't take much inspiration from domestic life for his writing, but one thing that I certainly recognise is in this episode when Jeffrey says; 'look what your son has done' and Ann rolls her eyes and says; 'My son!'. That was so much like mum and dad. - Roger Mortimer, Johnnie Mortimer's son.

Chortle Rating: Another favourite. 10/10

Guest Stars: Roy Kinnear, Sue Bond, Nina Baden-Semper, Aimee Delaman, Royston Tickner

George and Mildred - Episode Guide

The Last Straw - Series 5, Episode 3
Broadcast: Wednesday November 6th 1979 at 20:30
Individual viewers - 16.5 Million
National television chart position - 6

Mildred is depressed at not being invited to the top garden parties and soirees that the area has to offer. It gets her thinking that she and George may be out of their depth in the district ridden with the toffee-nosed snobs, so they consider their options of moving house.

The Ropers pay a visit to an old friend of George's in Lascar Street down the East End, but when they see how the once pleasant little row of houses has been since replaced by a concrete jungle, the area loses its appeal. There must be somewhere the Ropers will fit in. Perhaps a little further south... Like, say... Australia?

When Jeffrey Fourmile gets wind of his neighbours plans to relocate to the other side of the world, he is delighted at finally being shot of the working class couple. He does everything he can to speed up the process, arranging an appointment for them at Australia House and offering to chauffeur drive them there. But it appears that even Australia won't have the Ropers, turning them down after hearing of George's lack of skills. It looks like George and Mildred will be stuck in Hampton Wick for a few years to come. Jeffrey needs some consoling....

Chortle Rating: Superb double act from Michael and Queenie. 9/10

Guest Stars: Simon Lloyd, Michael Robbins, Queenie Watts, Frederic Abbott, Brian Godfrey, Bobby Collins, Tommy Barnett

A Driving Ambition - Series 5, Episode 4
Broadcast: Wednesday November 13th 1979 at 20:30

Mildred is taking driving lessons behind George's back, disguising her motoring activity by pretending to attend keep fit classes with Ann. If George learnt that his wife was learning to drive, he would insist on teaching her himself - the sort of tutoring that Mildred could do without.

But when George is down at the post box that afternoon, posting a cornflake competition entry, he sights his wife in a car with a man, and becomes convinced that she is having an affair. George turns to Jeffrey Fourmile for advice, who suggests that he tries to appreciate his wife more, buying flowers and having, dare he say it, early nights!

Roper takes his neighbour's counselling on board and takes Mildred out for a romantic dinner at the Fish 'n' Chip shop. She seems to be re-wooed, but the next day when a man arrives at the front door asking after her, George is after some answers...

Chortle Rating: Superb storyline with great innuendo humour. 9/10

Guest Stars: Simon Lloyd, Robert Raglan, Harry Littlewood

A Military Pickle - Series 5, Episode 5
Broadcast: Wednesday November 27th 1979 at 20:30

George is given a letter by his brother, Charlie, who is in town for a fleeting reunion. It arrived at his old house in 1949. Roper opens the envelope and is stunned to read the first line; 'Report to Caterick Barracks at 0800 hours!', they're his call up papers!

Virtually soiling himself at the fear of the police coming round and shooting him for being a deserter, George is quick to put together a new identity. He dons dark glasses, draws the curtains and retreats to the attic with a few tins in preparation for a siege. No disguise would be complete without a new name, and George takes inspiration from the tinned food to christen himself as John West.

Mildred thinks that her husband has finally flipped, but having put up with George's irregular behaviour for over twenty-five years, turns a blind eye. But when Roper turns away one of her visitors, Mildred is determined to uncover the truth behind his activities. She soon finds out, and frog-marches George around to the army recruitment office to face the music. The army sergeant tells the Roper's what they don't want to hear. The G. Roper addressed on the envelope is indeed a deserter. But it isn't George, its his sister Gloria!

Chortle Rating: Hilarious ending. 8/10

Recollections... I had worked with Thames for a little while, and I believe Peter Frazer-Jones saw my work and called my agent to see if I could do *George and Mildred*. I remember it was enjoyable to do, Yootha was a lot of fun. - David Neville.

Guest Stars: Peter Birrel, David Neville, Michael Maynard, Richard Shaw, Harry Littlewood, Mark Holms

Fishy Business - Series 5, Episode 6
Broadcast: Wednesday December 4th 1979 at 20:30

George is distraught when Mildred pulls the plug in the kitchen sink and sends Moby the goldfish to a watery grave, the aquatic pet having been waiting in the sink whilst his bowl was being cleaned. Roper is close to wearing a black armband for the rest of his life, when he realises how his fishy friend has departed this world for good. Still mourning, he takes a bag of gravel back to the pet shop for a refund, but is given a hard sell by the assistant and ends up with a replacement pet - a couple of racing pigeons!

When Jeffrey gets wind of his neighbours new animals, he is aghast at the thought of all the droppings that will land on his car and the vermin that will no doubt invade his garden. George doesn't care about his neighbour's gripes, concentrating more on the monetary value that may come from racing the birds.

The Ropers drive down to the park on the motorbike to release the pigeons for the inaugural flight, rushing home to meet the fowl but finding that the birds are nowhere in sight. Upon ringing the pet shop George receives some bad news, he released the pigeons too early and they will never return. Mildred can see her husband is disappointed, more with the loss of £15 than the loss of the birds. She instead gets him a condolences gift, a new fish - Moby 2. She was given it by the rag and bone man, in exchange for George's motorbike!

Chortle Rating: Nice work from Norman Mitchell. 9/10

Titbits... Notice how Moby II changes size between the studio shots and the location shots of Mildred holding the tank on the doorstep!

Guest Stars: Simon Lloyd, Norman Mitchell, Ted Burnett

George and Mildred - Episode Guide

I Gotta Horse - Series 5, Episode 7
Broadcast: Wednesday December 18th 1979 at 20:30

Mildred's sister, Ethel is taking her turn at looking after Mother, entertaining her with drives around the countryside in one of the many vehicles in Ethel's fleet, and dining with fine china in one of her many lounges. It's all going quite tediously for Ethel, until mother notices an article in *Country Life* magazine, stating how a certain china horse sold at auction for £10,000. There is only another one like it in the world, that will be the one that Mildred has!

Ethel is determined to get her greasy clutches on the horse and races round to Mildred's to stake her claim on it. Not quite the master of subtlety, Ethel's eagerness for the article instantly has Mildred suspicious, but nevertheless she promises to root out the china horse from the garage, asking Ethel to return the next day.

Whilst taking afternoon tea with Ann, the horse comes into question. Ann recognises it from somewhere. She too has seen the article. Mildred takes a look at the magazine item and is astounded. It's blatantly apparent that her devious sister has been after the £10,000 rather than a family heirloom, and she is resolute in the fact that Ethel won't be getting hold of this particular nag.

Mildred takes the horse to an antiques shop for valuation, but sadly it turns out that her statue is a cheap imitation and only worth around 30 Shillings. Several people have brought in their replicas in disbelief and the antiques shop is full of them. Mildred goes home and mulls over her misfortune when George triumphantly returns from the dole office. He has passed the antique shop on the way home and spotted several other valuable horses in the window and was quick to snaffle them up. The Ropers now own four, despite their only being two of them in the world.

Ethel is unawares as to what has been going on and is quickly on the doorstep to snaffle the china horse. She wants it so much that she splashes out hundreds of pounds to take it off Mildred's hands, and is soon in possession of the sacred animal. When Ethel drops it, she is distraught. But never mind, there happen to be several others tucked in the Roper's sideboard...

Chortle Rating: Excellent episode. Mimi De Braie is fantastic. 10/10

Guest Stars: Avril Elgar, Gretchen Franklin, John Carlin, Mimi De Braie

drama in the past, with scripts for *The Saint* and *General Hospital* under his belt, so the step for him to be solely responsible for screenplay of a comedy movie was an irregular one.

Nevertheless, an enjoyable, if not somewhat lacking, film was produced. Whereas the screenplay provided some especially enjoyable segments of dialogue, it missed out on the special formula that had provided four years of success with the television series, and the movie failed to draw in many people to the box office. The writing missed Cooke and Mortimer's flair and ingenuity. Should all three writers have contributed to the scripts, then the *George and Mildred* movie may have received significantly more critical acclaim.

Plot

The plot of the film was familiar. The picture once again revolves around Mildred's never-ending chase after a bit of love and attention from her ferrety husband. This time the action follows the days surrounding the Roper's wedding anniversary. Mildred is determined that it won't be another case of a miserable time in the local boozer, with all the crisps she can eat, and has her eyes set higher, a luxurious extended weekend at the exclusive London Hotel.

George has completely forgotten the event, as usual, and is blissfully unaware that there are secret plans afoot to part him from his money. It falls to Tristram to provide a gentle reminder to his neighbour that it's his anniversary, prompting George to quickly think up a cheap celebration of his own - choosing to take Mildred back to the restaurant that they went to on their first date. The eatery has changed a little since they first went there over twenty years ago, it's now a haunt for a hardened team of bikers noshing on hammer and nail sandwiches and 'coffee so strong the sugar bounces out'. George's stupidity leads him into a fight with Jacko, the leader of the gang, and he narrowly escapes with teeth in tact. Suffice to say, its an evening that Mildred would rather forget, so she remains determined to get her pound of flesh and eventually persuades George to go to the London Hotel.

The suite at the top floor of the hotel is presently occupied by gangster Harry Pinto (Stratford Johns) and his cronies, who are undertaking countless nefarious deeds from their hotel base. One of such activity is 'the removal of adversaries' and Pinto is expecting a hit-man to arrive any minute to be given the dossier on rival he has to dispose of. Pinto's gormless assistant, Elvis (David Barry), is sent down to meet the assassin. Unfortunately, the leader of a rival gang, Harvey (Kenneth Cope) has got to him first and left him for dead in his car. George Roper has just parked his Morris in the underground car park, conveniently right next to the real hit man's Rolls Royce, and after a significant bit of misunderstanding between him and Elvis, it is believed that Roper is the contract killer!

After a long farce of the delusional Elvis catering for Roper as if he is a hit-man, it is soon discovered that George is in fact a traffic warden. The gang are horrified and quickly set about trying to pry the dossier envelope off Roper. When they fail, they set about bumping him and Mildred off as well.

The film cumulates when the Ropers decide to leave the hotel early, just as the police turn up to investigate the spate of murders. George and Mildred drive off in their Morris and are followed by Pinto's mob, who are being tailed by Harvey and his boss (Garfield Morgan). A crazy car chase kicks off around London, the entourage causing havoc wherever it drives, with George and Mildred blissfully unaware that anything at all has happened.

The criminals are soon picked up by the police and George and Mildred arrive home safely and significantly alive. The Fourmile's are far from happy with the Roper's arriving back early but grit their teeth none the less.

Recollections... On set, much time was spent just hanging around. Neil McCarthy (the chauffeur) and Kenneth Cope and I spent much time playing games in the dressing room, mainly a game called 'Botticelli'. I got on very well with Stratford Johns. When on location for the car chase, I shared a caravan with him and he asked his driver to get a crate of beer out of the boot for us to share - it was Carlsberg Special Brew! - David Barry (Elvis)

Filming Locations
The 'London Hotel' that George and Mildred retreat to was actually the Copthorne Tara Hotel, in Scarsdale Place, Kensington, South London. The majority of the film was made here on location, with interiors being filmed at Elstree studios. The hotel today shares an exterior that is practically identical to the brutalism architecture witnessed in the 1980 film, with the front parking places remaining unchanged and even the lobby resembling the same features. The front revolving doors have been partially covered by an extension of glass awning, but little else has changed.

While the Cat's Away
George and Mildred on Stage

Yootha Joyce and Brian Murphy were an incredibly popular duo, and they were wanted everywhere. The only way around this problem was to take them to the masses. In 1977, Brian Cooke and Johnnie Mortimer did just that, a national theatre tour of *George and Mildred*. The show was a sell-out wherever it went.

'We encouraged Johnnie and Brian to write for the theatre', Brian Murphy explained. 'We asked them why they didn't do an adaptation of *George and Mildred*. Yootha and I knew about the theatre and we could help guide them, and they knew about writing. So between us, we all got on with it and we made a very funny farce. We had a few teething problems at first getting used to it, but afterwards it was fine'.

'We played a summer season in Bournemouth in 1977 which broke all records and played to capacity houses for over 16 weeks, twice nightly. It was the first time we had ever played in Bournemouth and we were mobbed all the way along the pier by fans and holiday makers wanting to shake our hands. It meant I had to set off a good hour earlier to get to the theatre on time!'

Whilst performing a national tour of *George and Mildred*, Brian and Yootha also appeared as the ugly sisters 'Mildred and Georgina' in *Cinderella*. 'We appeared at the London Palladium, the great Mecca of all theatres where we did the pantomime' elucidated Brian. 'Richard O'Sullivan played buttons, Fiona Fullerton was Cinderella and Yootha and myself played the sisters. It was a sell-out, a total sell-out, and we were doing that show for over four months'.

Cinderella was presented jointly by Louis Benjamin and Leslie Grade. The show also starred Robert Young, Richard (Mr. Pastry) Hearne and Roger de Courcey with Nookie the Bear. Albert J. Knight devised and produced the show. 'We went from *Cinderella*, to a summer season of the *George and Mildred* play and then back to the television versions of George and Mildred' says Brian. 'We went off to Jersey, toured the countryside and it was really the mega-time. It was all built around *George and Mildred*'.

The plot for the stage show, later renamed as *While the Cat's Away* after Yootha Joyce died, followed the story of Ethel taking Mildred on a trip to Paris, and Humphrey persuading George to have a bit of fun in the absence of their wives. The men invite round two young girls, Jennifer Frazer and Shirley, to occupy their time. Predictably, both Mildred and Ethel return early and catch them in the act!

While the Cat's Away - George and Mildred on Stage

The play toured the United Kingdom, and the cast varied accordingly to each theatre season. A run at the Edinburgh Kings Theatre saw Dilys Laye play Ethel, joined by Sue Bond and Katie Fawkes as the girls. The record-breaking stint in Bournemouth was performed with Vanda Godsell and Peter Hughes as Ethel and Humphrey, with Sue Bond and Rosanne Wickes (who had previously appeared together in the *George and Mildred* episode 'No Business Like Show Business'). Brian and Yootha completed the tour themselves, but on standby should anything go wrong were their understudies; Harry Littlewood and Susanna Pope.

Thomas Hardy was the stage manager for the Bournemouth stint, accompanied by his deputy, Betty Adey and assistant, Hilary Holden. A run at Edinburgh saw Terry Lee Dickson join the production as stage manager (it's no coincidence that Terry and Yootha Joyce were in a relationship at the time), and Michael Worsley was his deputy with Mary Cornford his assistant. Costumes were designed by Lyn Harvey, who had previously worked on the television series, and Derek Barnes worked as assistant to executive producer Mark Furness.

Each show on the tour was directed by Tony Clayton. The set design fell to Terry Parsons and the lighting was organised by Stuart Anderson.

The champagne used on stage was gratefully received courtesy of Moet & Chandon and the soda syphons were lent from BOC Ltd. The telephone equipment was supplied by the General Post Office, and Miss Joyce's wigs came from Wig Creations Ltd.

It wasn't just Britain where the stage play toured. 'We also took it off to New Zealand and Australia' Brian Murphy continued. 'It was incredible. There was no time for anything else. We were asked individually to do other types of plays, but we had to decline. We lived and breathed *George and Mildred*'.

'We were playing at different towns each week around Australia and it was very punishing. Yootha hated flying and she always used to sit next to me and dig her fingernails into my arm very deep during the take-off and landing. She was quite scared. I used to ask her if I could sit by the window, not to look at the view but to spare my left arm and let my right one get some punishment. I went around with these deep gouges in my arm for days afterwards!'

'When we got back to the UK we were asked to go back to Bournemouth but Yootha didn't want to, she wanted a break before the next series'.

The stage show finished it's tour in 1979, but has since become a popular choice for amateur productions.

Allnutt, Wendy
Various Characters in *Man About the House*

Born on may 1st 1946 in Lincoln, Allnutt studied at the Central School of Speech and Drama in 1963. Originally working in theatre before making a move to television, Allnutt performed in *Julius Caesar* in Nottingham's Playhouse Theatre with Alan Dossor in 1966.

Her first screen part came in 1968 when she took a small role in *The Avengers*. Further credits include; *Doctor in Charge, The Regiment, Napoleon and Love, Miss Jones and Son, Sorry* and *Robin's Nest*. Her most recent work was in *The Bill* in 1999, and Wendy is now Head of Movement at the Guildhall School of Music and Drama in London.

Allnutt was married to actor Colin McCormack until his death in 2004. They had two children together, Katherine and Andrew.

Angelis, Michael
Cafe Proprietor in the *George and Mildred* Movie

Born in Liverpool on January 18th 1952, Michael took early acting work in *Thirty-Minute Theatre* before starring in *The Gaffer, Robin's Nest, The Russ Abbot Show, The Jump* and *The Bill*. He is perhaps best known for narrating almost two-hundred-and-fifty episodes of T*homas the Tank Engine and Friends* over a sixteen year span until 2007. Angelis still acts to this day but works predominantly in voice-overs.

Angelis, Paul
Mick in *Man About the House* episode 'Colour Me Yellow'
Man in Pub in *George and Mildred* episode 'The Little Dog Laughed'

Born in Liverpool on January 18th 1943, Angelis is best known for being the voice of George and Ringo in the Beatles' film, *Yellow Submarine*.

Angelis took his first credited part in 1967 in *The Mini-Affair* and later worked on; *Robin's Nest, Runners, London's Burning* and *The Bill*.

Angelis retired in 2005, having taken his final work as an actor early that year in *The Baby War*. The Equity Journal reported his death on August 13th 2009.

Anwar, Rafiq
Doctor in *George and Mildred* episode 'Your Money or Your Life'

Anwar produced, directed and starred in *Ilzaam* in 1953, prior to taking on further roles in *Z Cars, It Ain't Half Hot Mum, The Changes, Red Letter Days*, and also a brief part as a doctor in *Steptoe and Son Rise Again*.

Anwar died in 1977.

Avon, Roger
Commissionaire in the *George and Mildred* Movie.

Born on November 23rd 1914, Avon became a prolific comedy actor in his time, working on scores sitcoms. Notable mentions include; *Steptoe and Son, The*

Complete A-Z of Support Cast

Likely Lads, Dad's Army, Bless This House and *Yus My Dear*. Avon died on December 21st 1988 aged 74.

B

Baden-Semper, Nina
Sister in *George and Mildred* episode 'In Sickness and In Health'
   Born in 1945, Baden-Semper shot to fame as Barbie in the Thames sitcom *Love thy Neighbour*. After a few lesser roles subsequently, she took a final credit with *Crossroads* in 2002.

Ball, Ralph
Various Characters in *George and Mildred*
   After making a debut on *A Man from the Sun* in 1956, Ball later worked on; *Dad's Army, The Avengers, Thriller, Z Cars* and *Happy Ever After*. He died in 2002.

Barraclough, Roy
Henry in *George and Mildred* episode 'No Business Like Show Business'
   Barraclough was born on July 12th 1935 in Preston. Originally working at an engineering factory, Barraclough followed his dream of performing by working as a holiday camp entertainer and dedicating his spare time to local drama groups.
   Barraclough later joined the Huddersfield repertory company and after several terms in theatre, worked his way into television, debuting with *The War of Darkie Pilbeam* and later working on *Castle Haven*. Further roles soon followed with notable mentions; *The Lovers, Sez Les, Pardon My Genie, Strangers* and *Mother's Ruin*. Roy Barraclough is perhaps best known for his long running role as Alec Gilroy in *Coronation Street*.
   In recent years, Barraclough has been awarded the MBE for his services to drama and still works as an actor in television and theatre. Roy appeared in *All the Small Things* in 2009.

Barrett, Tim
Doctor in *George and Mildred* episode 'Life With Father'
   Barrett has starred in; *The Avengers, Never Say Die, Keep It in the Family, Dad's Army, Are You Being Served, Terry and June* and *Minder*.
   Barrett died on August 20th 1990, his last role came the previous year in *Sob Sisters*.

Barry, David
Elvis in the *George and Mildred* Movie
   Born in Bangor on April 30th 1943, Barry trained at the Corona Academy in Chiswick before making a screen debut in *Lilith* in 1964. Four years later Barry

took on the part of Frankie Abbott in the popular series, *Please Sir*, later recurring the character in the spin-off, *The Fenn Street Gang* and the *Please Sir!* film. His work on the latter secured his casting for the *George and Mildred* film in 1980.

'I played Frankie Abbott in the film version of *Please, Sir!*, and the producer for that was the assistant producer for *George and Mildred* and he suggested me for the role of Elvis'.

In recent years Barry has stepped out of the acting business to concentrate on his autobiography, 'Flashback - An Actor's Life' in which he details his extensive career.

Baxter, Trevor
Various Characters in *George and Mildred*

Born on November 18th 1932, Baxter worked predominantly in theatre in his early years, with classical productions of *Hamlet* and *Richard III* under his belt as well as; *What the Butler Saw, The Doctor's Dilemma* and *School for Scandal*.

Baxter's move to television came in 1961 with a debut appearance in *Harper's West One*. Since then, he has appeared in *Adam Adamant Lives, Lorna Doone, Doctor Who, Ping Pong, Doctors* and *My Family*. Most recently, Baxter appeared in the film *Van Wilder 2*.

Trevor has also written plays for theatre, including *Edith Grove, Lies* and *The Undertaking*. Most recently, Baxter voiced a television advertisement for Whiskas cat food.

Birrel, Peter
George's brother, Charlie Roper

Birrel was born on July 19th 1935 and spent over thirty years as an actor, appearing in; *David, Target, Don't Drink the Water, Steptoe and Son* and as a Draconian Prince monster in four episodes of *Doctor Who* in 1973.

Peter died in Bath on June 23rd 2004, aged 68. He was married to Stephanie Cole, the actress behind Delphine Featherstone in *Open All Hours*.

Black, Eunice
Gladys in *George and Mildred* episode 'I Believe in Yesterday'

Born as Eunice Holden in 1915, Black took to the stage for the first time in 1937 at London's Unity Theatre before jobbing with repertory companies. Her first television role arrived in 1961 with *A Taste of Honey*, later works including *Sykes, HMS Paradise* and *Chitty Chitty Bang Bang*.

Black tended towards comedy roles, becoming one of Britain's finest female character actresses, working on; *Please Sir, On the Buses, Father Dear Father, The Benny Hill Show* and *Last of the Summer Wine*.

Eunice retired in 1990, after her final part on television, a cameo appearance in *Bullseye*. Black died seventeen years later on August 27th 2007.

Complete A-Z of Support Cast

Bond, Sue
Marlene in the *George and Mildred* Movie.
Various Characters in *George and Mildred*

Bond was born on May 9th 1945 and originally worked on under the counter films *Hot Teddy, Secrets of Sex* and *The Yes Girls* before becoming a more mainstream actress and appearing in; *The Fenn Street Gang, Casanova* and *Doctor in Charge*.

Bond frequently appeared on *The Benny Hill Show* in the early 1970's and later took work on *And Mother Makes Three, Love Thy Neighbour* and *Jack of Diamonds*. Her last known work as an actress was in 1986 with the revival of *Mind Your Language,* and Sue later became a cabaret singer.

Boyce, Eamonn
Paddy in *Man About the House* episode 'Colour Me Yellow'
Mechanic in *George and Mildred* episode 'Where My Caravan...'

After twenty years in a varied showbusiness career, Eamonn Boyce took a final credit as a detective constable in 1982's *The History Makers*.

Previous work includes: *Minder, Target, Steptoe and Son Ride Again, Budgie, Softly Softly* and *Road to Freedom*.

Boyle, Marc
Warrant Officer in *Man About the House* episode 'One for the Road'

Born on September 5th 1945, Marc Boyle began as an actor in *Rogues Gallery* in 1969, with later appearances in *Steptoe and Son, Get Some In* and *The Professionals*.

Braid, Hilda
Mrs Hollins in the *Man About the House* episode 'The Party's Over'

Braid was born in Northfleet on March 3rd 1929.
After training at RADA, Braid furthered her acting experience in local repertory and later the Royal Shakespeare Company.

Hilda made her television debut during 1961 in *ITV's Play of the Week,* later progressing to; *Softly Softly, Catweazle, Doctor on the Go, Robin's Nest* and *Citizen Smith*. In 1982, Braid was reunited with Brian Murphy in *L for Lester*, playing Mrs Davies.

In recent years Braid clocked up over two hundred appearances in *Eastenders* as Nana Moon, a role which ended in 2005 when Hilda was written out due to her own ill health. Braid died in Sussex County Hospital two years later on November 6th 2007. She was 78.

Breaks, Sebastian
Peter in *George and Mildred* episode 'Best Foot Forward'

After working in Theatre, with appearances including *Much Ado About Nothing* in 1963, Breaks moved into television, making a debut with *As You Like It*.

Breaks is perhaps best known for playing PC Tate over thirty episodes of *Z Cars*. His other television appearances include; *Justice, Number 10* and *Cold Warrior.*

Breaks' last known television part came in 1987 with *Intimate Contact.*

Brice, Bridget
Receptionist in the *George and Mildred* Movie.

After making a debut with *A Man for All Seasons* in 1966, Brice worked on; *Z Cars, Public Eye, Doctor at Sea, The Sweeney, Dick Turpin* and *The Professionals*. Her last acting work was in *Wilderness Edge* in 1992.

Briggs, Johnnie
Milkman in the *Man About the House* film.

Born in London on September 5th 1935, Briggs won a scholarship with the Italia Conti Academy Stage School in 1947, and after graduating, made his theatre debut in *Opera Company.*

Briggs made a screen debut the next year with the 1948 film *Quartet*. Later work included; *The Younger Generation, No Hiding Place, Bless This House, Au pair Girls, Crossroads, Yus Me Dear* and *Z Cars.*

Briggs is best known for his work on *Coronation Street*, on which he played the character of Mike Baldwin for an astonishing thirty-two years, finally retiring from the street when his character was killed off in 2007. Since then, he has appeared in *Holby City, Echo Beach* and most recently *Doctors*. He was awarded the MBE for his services to entertainment in 2007.

Bulloch, Jeremy
Derek in *Man About the House* episode 'Three of a Kind'.
Bill in *George and Mildred* episode 'Days of Beer and Rosie'

Bulloch was born in Market Harborough on February 16th 1945, and became an actor after his sporting ambitions failed to materialise.

'I was nearly twelve, and I was hoping to take on a sports scholarship. I took the 11 plus exam, but I failed, so it wasn't looking good for the scholarship. My godmother was a continuity girl at Ealing film studios and she and mum thought I should go into acting. Three months later, I was doing my first work which was a for a cereal commercial. I think it was shredded wheat. I had to promote a plastic toy frogman by playing about it with it. I later did a few films with the children's film society, including *Carry On Teacher* with Richard O'Sullivan. A few years later, I was in *Summer Holiday* with Cliff Richard'.

Jeremy Bulloch appeared in both *Man About the House* and *George and Mildred,* appearing firstly as trainee doctor and poker player, Derek. Bulloch's later work has included; *Crown Court, Hoffman, Thriller* and *Octopussy*, but Jeremy is remembered most fondly by fans for his portrayal of Boba Fett in the *Star Wars* saga - leading him to attend numerous worldwide conventions yearly.

'I've done an awful lot of Sci-fi. I did *Doctor Who* with William Hartnell which was fun, and then came Boba Fett in *Star Wars*. It was a tiny part, but it's taken over most of my spare time, the legacy is amazing.'

Bulloch still works as an actor today, and resides in London with his wife Maureen.

'I've been lucky enough to enjoy 99.9% of the things I've done. My favourite ever show was a play I did in the West End called *Dangerous Obsession,* it was a psychological thriller. There were only three people in it, but it was great, my name was in lights. I feel that you remain an actor all your life, the profession eventually retires you. I am still looking forward to each job I do, but when that feeling goes, it's time to give up'.

Burden, Billy
Farmer in *George and Mildred* episode 'Nappy Days'

Born on June 15th 1914, Burden made a debut in *A Present for Dickie* in 1969 before appearing in *George and Mildred* in 1978.

Since then, Burden has starred in *Hi-de-Hi, The Boys in Blue* and *Oh Happy Band*, before taking on a role he is best remembered for, playing Mr Moulterd in the *Are You Being Served?* spin-off *Grace and Favour.*

Burden died at his home in Dorset on June 3rd 1994, aged 79.

Burnett, Ted
Various Characters in *George and Mildred*

Born on November 8th 1926 in London, Burnett was 51 when he took his first credited work as an actor, in *Doctor on the Go* in 1977. Since then, he has been a prolific support artist, with parts in *Star Wars, Out, Lets get Laid, Fox* and *The Incredible Mr. Tanner.*

Ted made his last appearance in *Britannia Hospital* in 1982 and died on October 1st 2001.

Butler, Blake
Mr Higson in *George and Mildred* episode 'All Work and No Pay'

Born in Barrow-in-Furness on October 22nd 1924, Butler debuted with *Fact and Fiction* in 1960, before working on; *Compact, Dixon of Dock Green, Lock Up Your Daughters, Last of the Summer Wine* and *Mind Your Language.*

Blake's last work as an actor was in 1981 when he appeared in *The Incredible Mr Tanner.*

C

Carlin, John
Various characters in *Man About the House*.
Various characters in *George and Mildred,*
Casino Supervisor in the *George and Mildred* Movie.

Carlin schooled at the Royal Scottish Academy of Dramatic Art, later progressing to seasons at the Glasgow Citizens and Manchester Library theatres before joining as a permanent fixture at Birmingham repertory. After a move to London, John drifted into television and made a debut in a 1962 episode of *Dixon of Dock Green*.

Carlin went on to work with many of the big names in entertainment, including; Frankie Howerd, Sid James, Joan Sims and Barbara Windsor. He has also appeared in several films in the *Carry On* series, including: *Emmanuelle, England* and the TV series, *Carry on Laughing*.

John has proved a popular choice with the writing and casting crew from *Man About the House*, appearing also in *George and Mildred* and *Robin's Nest,* as well as Johnnie Mortimer's *Never the Twain* and Brian Cooke's *Keep It in the Family*.

Carlin's later work extended to *Rumpole of the Bailey, Taggart, She-Wolf of London* and *The Darling Buds of May*. After years of being a sought-after character actor, predominantly with Thames television, John made his last recognised screen role in a 1992 episode of *Agatha Christie's Poirot*.

Carlin is now retired and lives in Stroud, Gloucestershire, where he is the president of a local players association. It is apparent, however, that John has moved his career swiftly on from the days of *Man About the House,* and would rather forget them than mull on them - regrettably, Carlin explained how he 'has no interest in discussing these shows'.

Case, Gerald

Jones in *George and Mildred* episode 'Just the Job'

Born on January 26th 1905 in Horton, Case worked in local repertory theatre before moving to the screen, debuting with *Museum Mystery* in 1937.

Gerald later appeared in; *Landfall, The Fake, Barnacle Bill, Bernie, Two's Company* and *The Elephant Man*. Case made his last appearance in *For the Love of Egypt* in 1982.

He died on May 22nd 1985, aged 80.

Cellier, Peter

Morris Pluthero in the *Man About the House* film.

Born in 1928, Cellier made his acting debut at the Leatherhead theatre in 1958, before moving into television with early credits; *ITV Play of the Week* and *The Root of All Evil*.

Later work included *Doctor Who, Sorry!, Rumpole of the Bailey* and Sir Gordon, the permanent secretary of the treasury in *Yes, Prime Minister*. Cellier has also appeared as the Major in *Keeping Up Appearances*.

Peter still works today and has made recent appearances in *Casualty* and *The Thieving Headmistress*.

Chappell, Norman

Mr Morris in *Man About the House* episode 'Cuckoo in the Nest'

Complete A-Z of Support Cast

Chappell was born in 1929 in Lucknow, India and moved to the United Kingdom as a child.

Following early television appearances in *Quatermass and the Pit* and *Peticoat Pirates*, Chappell went on to co-write the 1964 *Comedy Workshop* Production, *Love and Maud Carver*, with Brian Murphy.

A familiar face in the *Carry On* film series, as well *The Avengers,* Chappell's main calling was comedy. Over his career he has worked on *Bless This House, Nearest and Dearest, The Likely Lads, Love Thy Neighbour, Sez Les* and *Some Mothers Do 'Ave 'Em.*

Norman died on July 21st 1983.

Chittell, Christopher
Alan in *Man About the House* episode 'Somebody Out There Likes Me'

Born in Aldershot on May 19th 1948, Chittell made his debut in *Knock on Any Door* in 1965, later appearing as Potter in *To Sir, With Love* in 1967.

Over his career he has starred in *Freewheelers, Doomwatch, The Intruders, Zulu Dawn* and *Tucker's Luck* before becoming renowned for his role in *Emmerdale* as Eric Pollard, a part he has been playing since 1987.

Chitty, Erik
Magistrate in *Man About the House* episode 'One for the Road'

Chitty was born in Dover on July 8th 1907. His earliest recognised work was in *James Simpson* in 1937, with further credits coming shortly after in pre-war productions of *Henry IV, Julius Caesar, The Day is Gone* and *Katherine and Petruchio*.

Chitty's acting career was put on hold during the second world war, resuming in 1946 with *Contraband*. Since then, Erik proved a tireless performer, appearing in; *John Weasly, Footsteps in the Fog, Dixon of Dock Green, Billy Liar, Crown Court, Dad's Army* and *A Bridge too Far*.

Chitty died on July 22nd 1977, aged 70.

Clare, Dany
Elsie Wainwright in *George and Mildred* episode 'Just the Job'

After debuting in *And Mother Makes Three*, Clare became a popular choice for casting by Peter Frazer-Jones, appearing in his productions of; *And Mother Makes Five, Robin's Nest, Miss Jones and Son* and *George and Mildred*. Clare's last credit was in 1978.

Clifford, Peggyann
Miss Ware in *George and Mildred* episode 'You Must Have Showers'
Mrs James in *Man About the House* episode 'I Won't Dance...'

Born in Bournemouth on March 23rd 1921, Clifford started in repertory theatre before moving into television with a debut in *Forbidden* in 1948. Further parts soon followed including; *Lost, Heavens Above, Father Dear Father, Born and Bred, Are You Being Served?* and *'Allo 'Allo*.

Peggyann died in 1984 at the age of 64. She was married to Peking-born actor George Fenneman and had three children.

Colclough, John
Various Characters in *Man About the House*
After taking several small roles on television, Colclough was cast the *Man About the House* episode 'I Won't Dance, Don't Ask Me'.

'I was good friends with Susie Shields who was PA to Peter Frazer-Jones. She set up a meeting and I was cast as Nigel. I was in my late twenties and still considered myself to be a young actor trying to make a living. I do recall rehearsals only lasting the morning and then everyone went to the bar. The regulars seemed to get through an awful lot of wine, but I rarely stayed. I was trying to save money to buy my first flat!'

'I just felt privileged to be working with such well known people. I was just a jobbing actor and not really part of the gang, but it was still a wonderful period in my life. I was doing shows like; *Playschool, Onedin Line, Z Cars* and *My Wife Next Door*. I still occasionally get repeat fees from overseas transmissions!'

Colclough made a final on-screen appearance in *Just Good Friends* in 1983. Since then he has turned to working for himself, launching his own independent over-the-phone consultancy for actors and actresses, taking over from the discontinued service offered by 'The Spotlight'.

Coleman, Richard
Charles Newman in *George and Mildred* episode 'All Around the Clock'
Born on January 20th 1930, Coleman trained at RADA and worked in theatre before taking an early part as an uncredited officer in *The Dam Busters* in 1955. Later work followed with; *Redcap, 10 Rillington Place, And Mother Makes Three, Robins Nest, Freddie and Max* and *Virtual Murder*.

Richard retired from the business in 1996, his final part falling earlier that year in *Down Rusty Down*. Coleman moved to France with his wife, actress Peggy Sinclair. Coleman died of cancer on December 16th 2008.

Collins, Bobby
Shane in *George and Mildred* episode 'The Last Straw'
Beginning as an actor at a young age, Collins secured early parts in *Ace of Wands* in 1972 and *The Sweeney* in 1975. He also appeared in two episodes of *Grange Hill*.

Cooper, Mark
Desmond in *Man About the House* episode 'Love and Let Love'
Cooper made his debut in *Man About the House,* later playing a robot in four episodes of *Doctor Who* in 1977, and taking a small role in *The Upchat Connection* in 1978. Cooper's last role was in *Hawk the Slayer* in 1980.

Complete A-Z of Support Cast

Cope, Kenneth
Harvey in the *George and Mildred* Movie.
   Born on June 14th 1931 in Liverpool, Cope made a debut in 1954 with *Impulse*, before working on *Kipps, Naked Fury, Carry on Jack* and most famously alongside Mike Pratt in the cult series *Randall and Hopkirk Deceased*. Cope worked on two further *Carry On* films (*Matron* and *Convenience*), as well as *Minder, Last of the Summer Wine* and *Hustle*. Most recently, he has reprised his role as Jed Stone in the popular soap *Coronation Street*.

Cornish, Berry
PA in the *Man About the House* film.
   Cornish had previously worked on *Love thy Neighbour* and *Can Merkin Forget*. She also appeared occasionally on *The Benny Hill Show*.

Cosmo, James
Keith in *George and Mildred* episode 'The Dorothy Letters'
   Cosmo was born on May 24th 1948 and attended the Royal Scottish Academy of Music and Dramatic art before making an early television appearance in *St Ives* in 1967. Cosmo made later appearances in; *Thundercloud, Warship, The Professionals, Saracen, Between the Lines, The Bill, Free Jimmy, Merlin, The Clan* and *Hotel Caledonia*.

D

Davenport, Claire
Various Characters in *George and Mildred*
   Born on April 24th 1933, Davenport entered television in 1963, debuting with an episode of *The Rag Trade*, before later working on *Doctor Who, ITV Playhouse, Crossplot* and *Queenie's Castle*.
   Davenport made a nude appearance as 'Sycorax' in the 1979 film adaptation of *The Tempest*, before turning back to comedy with *Mind Your Language, Frankie Howerd* and *Not the Nine O'clock News*.
   Claire took her final credit on *The Smell of Reeves and Mortimer* in 1993. She retired later that year and died on March 4th 2002 from renal failure, aged 68.

Davidson, Lawrence
Waiter in *Man About the House* episode 'Mum Always Liked You...'
   Lawrence was born on April 7th 1927 and made his first television appearance at the age of twenty-four in an episode of *Pride and Prejudice*. Since then he has been seen in *The Saint, Doctor Who, Spearhead, Lytton's Diary* and *The Curse of the Pink Panther*, before making a final appearance in *The Young Indiana Jones Chronicles*.

Davidson retired in 1993 and died on October 14th 2000, aged 73.

Deadman, Derek
Various Characters in *George and Mildred*
Deadman's first television role came in 1972 with *The Darwin Adventure* and since then he has appeared in scores of productions with notable credits including; *The Fenn Street Gang, Doctor In Charge, Get Some In, The Sweeney, Porridge, Super Gran* and *The Benny Hill Show*. Deadman is best known for his long running part as Ringo in Johnnie Mortimer's *Never the Twain*.
Deadman's last work came in a 2002 episode of *Doctors*, and he now lives in France.

DeBraie, Mimi
1st Cleaning Lady in the *George and Mildred* Movie
Ethel's Housekeeper in *George and Mildred*
Usually credited as Muguette DeBraie, Mimi previously appeared in *Sykes (also as an Italian housekeeper), Father Dear Father* and *Don't Drink the Water*. After a minor role in a 1980 episode of *The Professionals* she ceased acting.

D'Union, Sheila
Chrissy's Sister, Susan
D'Union made her debut in 1970 with *Twinky*, before appearing in *Special Branch, Frankenstein* and *The Monster from Hell*. Her last credited role was in *Man About the House*.

Delamain, Aimee
Various Characters in *George and Mildred*
Delamain was born on April 21st 1906 in Sheffield and made a film debut with *The Secret* in 1955, before being cast in; *Z Cars, Six, The Saint, Menace, Shoestring, The Bill* and *You Rang M'Lord?*
Delamain took her final role in *Memento Mori* in 1992. She died seven years later on June 18th 1999 aged 93.

Dene, Zulema
Penelope Fordman in *George and Mildred* episode 'The Right Way...'
Dene made a television debut with ATV on a 1957 episode of *Emergency Ward 10*, later working alongside Sid James and Peggy Mount in *George and the Dragon*.
Following parts in *The Avengers, Bowler, Doctor in Charge, Crown Court, Yes Minister, Coronation Street* and *Anna Lee*, Dene made her most recent appearance on *The Queen's Nose* in 2002. She still acts today, but dedicates most of her time to theatre work.

Complete A-Z of Support Cast

Doran, Veronica
Myra in *Man About the House* episode 'Love and Let Love'

Born on May 17th 1948, Doran attended St Patrick's School in Carlisle and later moved to Blackpool where she joined a local dance troupe.

'I trained as a dancer and I was in a children's show in Blackpool where I lived. I spent a few years there but sadly I was too big to be in the line, so I thought instead how I really wanted to become a comedienne. We had a local rep which I got into as an ASM at about seventeen, after a couple of years there I got into radio and then television. I think my first appearance was in *It's Dark Outside*, which would have been in 1964'.

After a few further television roles, Doran starred in the Michael Armstrong directed horror film, *Haunted House of Horror* in 1969, a film also starring Richard O'Sullivan.

'I had a great time on that film, Richard was smashing and I had a great respect for him. We both have Irish blood and a similar sense of humour, so we were asked to ad-lib together in one of the scenes. We went on for ages as we both wanted to get the last line, I had to give up in the end and let Richard have it!'.

Then *Man About the House* came along and Veronica made a guest appearance as Myra, one of Larry's girlfriend's. 'My agent called me up and asked me in for the show. I had a very happy week there and everyone was so kind. I met up with Robbie Stewart from *Bless this House* who was in *Haunted House* with me and Michael Armstrong came along to watch the show as well. It was a fantastic reunion for me to meet everyone again, I had a wonderful time. I later did some work on *Coronation Street* as Eddie Yate's wife which was a fantastic part of my career. I was in it for about two years and wouldn't have missed it for the world. Geoffrey Hughes was hilarious'.

Veronica took further work in *Lady Killers, Jubilee, Funny Man, Precious Bane* and *The Brittas Empire*. Her most recent work came in 2000 with *City Central*.

'I had to stop acting after a spell of ill health, but I'm hoping to make a return very soon. I'd just love to get back to work'.

Dowdeswell, Caroline
Angie in *Man About the House* episode 'Come Into My Parlour'

Born in 1945 in Oldham, Dowdeswell made her acting debut in 1964 on *The Villains* and later took work on five episodes of *Dad's Army* as Janet King. Dowdeswell has also appeared on *Ours is a Nice House* and *Mutiny On the Buses*. Caroline took her last role in an episode of *Miss Jones and Son*.

Draisey, Veida
Jill in *George and Mildred* episode 'Baby Talk'

After a short stint on *Crossroads* in 1966, Draisey appeared in *George and Mildred*, her last credited role.

Drzewicki, Janine

Sheila in the *Man About the House* episode 'And Then There Were Two.'

Relatively unknown when she appeared in *Man About the House*, Janine Drzewicki is now one of Britain's most familiar character actresses, making scores of appearances as Jacqueline Stewart in *Benidorm*, as well as Victor Meldrew's neighbour in *One Foot in the Grave*.

Dyer, Hal

Mrs Peasley in *George and Mildred* episode 'Finders Keepers'

Hal Dyer made an early appearance with *Fact and Fiction* in 1960 with later credits including; *Doctor at large, On the Buses, Robin's Nest, Butterflies* and *Just William*. Dyer's most recent appearance came in 1993 with *The Bill*.

'My parents were all in variety theatre, my grandmother was a male impersonator. I got into the business on their shoulders, I was a Pantomime babe to begin with and I then went to dancing school and did three years at Drama school in Birmingham'.

'I still do acting these days, but the majority is in theatre. I run a small company called 'The Green Room Theatre Company', and we have a few shows at Hever Castle and other National Trust properties, and at a lovely old theatre in Tonbridge Wells, where I met Linda and Brian Murphy at one of the shows. I used to run a little coffee shop in Lingfields and we used the room above to put on productions'.

E

Edwards, Glynn

Chrissy's Father in *Man About the House*

Born on February 2nd 1931 in Malaya, Edwards moved to the United Kingdom but failed to make it as an actor in his younger years, deciding instead to put on and star in his own theatrical productions. While auditioning girls for one of his shows, Glynn was impressed with the talents of Yootha Joyce, and decided to engage her - in both senses of the word - Yootha got the job and the pair later married.

Glynn made his debut in 1957 on *The Heart Within* and later worked on *Sparrows Can't Sing, Zulu, Get Carter, The Saint, Man Hunt* and *The Main Chance*. Edwards' most notable role was as Dave Harris, the barman of the Winchester pub in *Minder*. Edwards worked with the show until 1994 when he retired.

These days, Glynn has left the public spotlight to live a quiet life, alternating between homes in Scotland and Spain. He is married to Valerie, his third wife and has a son, Tom, from a previous partnership with Christine Pilgrim.

Complete A-Z of Support Cast

Elgar, Avril
Mildred's sister, Ethel, in *George and Mildred.*

Avril Elgar was born in Halifax, West Yorkshire on April 1st 1932.

Son of a British Army officer, Albert Elgar, Avril trained at London's Old Vic theatre school and after working on radio, made a television debut in 1958, as Louise in *BBC Sunday Night Theatre.* Later credits included; *Probation officer, Armchair Mystery Theatre, Kraft Mystery Theatre, Comedy Playhouse, Callan, Z Cars, Carrie's War* and *Middlemen* before Elgar was cast in *George and Mildred.*

When *George and Mildred* came to an end in 1979, Elgar continued acting on both screen and stage; performing in *Half-Life* in 1978 at London's Duke of York Theatre, and with Kathy Burke in a production of *Amongst Barbarians* at Manchester's Royal Exchange theatre in the late 1980's. Elgar's television appearances run to particular highlights as *Tales of the Unexpected, Minder* and *A Taste of Death.*

Elgar still works as an actress to this day; most recently appearing in hospital drama *Doctors* in 2008. She works predominantly in theatre, appearing regularly at Bristol's Old Vic Theatre and in productions put on by The Tobacco Factory Shakespeare Theatre. Avril was married to actor James Maxwell until his death in 1995.

Emberg, Bella
Podge's Mother in *Man About the House* episode 'Two Foot Two, Eyes...'
Traffic Warden in *Man About the House* series four opening titles
Woman in Park in *George and Mildred* episode 'The Little Dog Laughed.'

Born in Brighton on September 16th 1937, Emberg has since become a much sought-after actress, but originally fancied quite a different career.

'I had wanted to work on the ships at first, but in those days women couldn't really do that. So instead, I went to a theatre when I was about eleven, and I got hooked from there. I think my first television work came when I was about twenty-two'.

Bella is perhaps best known for her work alongside comic geniuses, Benny Hill and Russ Abbot. 'Director David Bell phoned me up one day, and asked me about working with Benny. I was happy to take the job, and Ben certainly fostered my talent, he taught me everything he knew. David Bell went on to become controller at LWT, and he introduced me to Russ Abbott for the first time'.

Emberg worked with Russ Abbot and Les Dennis throughout the 1980's and early 1990's, taking on different characters for *Russ Abbot's Madhouse.* Out of all of these, the hilarious action hero sidekick 'Blunderwoman' is the most notable, but sadly, Bella has decided it is time to hang up her cape for the last time. 'Blunderwoman was wonderful, I had so much fun doing that, but I'm not doing it anymore. I still have the costume, and I got in it about five years ago for a pantomime, but it looks fairly awful these days, like mutton dressed as lamb!'.

Bella Emberg still acts to this day, appearing most recently in children's sitcom *Bear Behaving Badly.* 'I love this show, its a wonderful part, because I can just play myself. The two things I had always wanted to be was a zombie and a mummy, and in this series I've done both!'.

Bella's one remaining acting ambition is to be a monster in *Doctor Who*. 'I was in *Doctor Who* with Jon Pertwee, and we were filming in Guildford. There were so many people in the production team that I had to stay in the wardrobe trailer, they put a bed in there for me. This was, of course, where they kept all the monster costumes and outfits, and I had a bit of fun when nobody was looking, clumping about in these great big monster feet, so that may be the closest I get to my ambition!'.

Evans, Edward
Bernard West in *George and Mildred* episode 'The Right Way to Travel'

Evans was born on June 4th 1914 and made an early appearance on *The Small Voice* in 1948, later working on *London Belongs to Me* and *Hindle Wakes*. Edwards since appeared in; *Dad's Army, 10 Rillington Place, Dixon of Dock Green, Father Brown, Doctor Who, Lifeforce* and *The Bill*. Evans retired from television in 1987, a farewell role preceding him in *Heart of the Country*. After a lifetime on screen, Edwards Evans died on December 20th 2001, aged 87.

Evans, Mostyn
Sandra's Dad in *Man About the House* episode 'Never Give Your Real...'

Evans started his career in showbusiness with a part in *Espionage* in 1964. He later made several appearances in *Doctor Who* in the early 1970's, as well as a few minor roles in *Killers, And Mother Makes Five, The Citadel* and *Grange Hill*. He died on November 23rd 1990.

F

Farrell, Raymond
Bank clerk in the *Man About the House* episode 'It's Only money'
Decorator in the *George and Mildred* episode 'My Husband Next Door'

Farrell made his television debut in 1967 in *Adam Adamant Lives*. A later appearance in *And Mother Makes Three* led to a role in *Man About the House*, as well as a later episode of *George and Mildred*.

After a final appearance in 1978 as the Schoolmaster in *Tycoon*, Farrell retired from acting.

Farrier, Jeannette
Typist in Jeffrey Fourmile's estate agency in *George and Mildred*.

Making her debut in television with *George and Mildred*, Farrier took her only other acting role in an episode of *ITV Playhouse* in 1977.

Since then, she took a short stint as a costume designer in television, and Far-

Complete A-Z of Support Cast

rier currently works as an independent, and highly acclaimed, fabric designer. She spends much of her time in India, working with locals who assist in the production of her Kantha cloth.

Flanagan, John
James in *Man About the House* episode 'One More for the Pot'
   Flanagan was born in Ripley on April 30th 1947 and made his first credited television appearance in *ITV Saturday Night Theatre*, before honing his acting skills in; *Parkin's Patch, The Lovers, Secret Army, Casualty, Heartbeat* and *The Bill*.
   Flanagan still acts, with a recent credit in The Royal Today in 2008

Four, Ambrose Quilby
The band in *Man About the House* episode 'I Won't Dance, Don't...'
   No other credited works on television.

Fowler, Harry
Fisher in the *George and Mildred* Movie.
Cafe Owner in the *George and Mildred* episode 'A Driving Ambition'.
   Born in London on December 10th 1926, Fowler served in the RAF before moving into acting. He made several uncredited appearances in films in the early 1950's, before moving on to television, with; *Landfall, Hue and Cry, The Vise, Z Cars* and also an episode of *The Flockton Flyer*.
   Fowler also made a brief appearance in the *George and Mildred* Film. He still acts to this day, with a recent part in *The Impressionable Jon Culshaw*. Fowler was married to film star Joan Dowling, until her death in 1954.

Franklin, Gretchen
Mildred's Mother
   The dotty old mother of Ethel and Mildred was played by the supreme Gretchen Franklin, an actress with a career spanning over eighty years.
   Born in Covent Garden, London on July 7th 1911, Gretchen followed her family's theatrical footsteps and entered show business during her school years at Bournemouth theatres and clubs as a pantomime chorus girl. After taking dance lessons at the Theatre Girls club in Soho during the late 1920's, Franklin started to perform as a tap dancer, becoming a renowned entertainer and founding member the Four Brilliant Blondes quartet.
   After continued stage work, Gretchen made the gradual move into film and television, with a debut arriving in *The Passing Show* in 1951. Franklin later took roles in the Richard Lester directed films *How I Won the War* and the Beatles film - *Help!* - both also starring Roy Kinnear. After working on *George and Mildred*, Franklin made further television appearances, most notably in *Eastenders* where she played Ethel Skinner. Franklin became one of the favourite cast members in the soap.
   After a lifetime in the entertainment industry, Franklin died at her home in Barnes on July 11th 2005 - just four days before her 94th birthday.

Fraser, Helen
Gabrielle in *Man About the House* episode 'Three's A Crowd'.
 Fraser was born in Oldham in 1942 and took the stage for the first time at the age of fifteen. Helen trained at RADA and local repertory theatre before moving on to television and film. Her first notable part came in 1965 when she starred alongside Tom Courtney in the critically acclaimed *Billy Liar*. Helen later worked with Richard O'Sullivan in *Doctor in Charge*, in which she married his character, Dr. Lawrence Bingham.
 In recent years, Fraser has played the long running part of Sylvia Hollamby in almost one hundred episodes of *Bad Girls*. Her most recent screen credit was for the 2008 Christmas special of BBC's *The Royale Family*.

Fraser, Richard
Simon Randall in *Man About the House* episode 'Two Foot Two...'
 Fraser began his showbiz career in 1972 in *Bless This House*, later making appearances in *My Name is Harry Worth* and his last role *The Many Wives of Patrick*, in 1976.

Frith, Linda
Angela in the *George and Mildred* Movie
 Later works included *Who, Sir? Me, Sir?* and *Press Gang* in 1990.

G

Galore, Pussy
Truffles the Dog in *George and Mildred*
 Born sometime in the early 1970's, Pussy Galore was reared by Dorothy Stephens, who used to train dogs for work in film and television, and was also responsible for providing the St. Bernard 'HG Wells' in *Father Dear Father*.
 Snuffles, the other Yorkshire Terrier dog who appears later in the sitcom, is credited as James Bond, so it is very likely to be from the same source as Galore. After thirty-five years, both dogs are now undoubtedly dead.

Gardiner, Jeffrey
Maurice in *Man About the House* episode 'While the Cat's Away'
 Jeffrey started in drama school before moving on to repertory theatre and winning his first credited role, in a 1961 television episode of *ITV Play of the Week*. He has also starred in *Are You Being Served?*, *Dad's Army*, *My Wife Next Door* and *Please Sir*, among others, making a final screen appearance in a 1993 episode of *You Rang M'Lord?*
 In recent years, Gardiner has devoted much of his talent to theatre.

Complete A-Z of Support Cast

Gardner, Caron
Bishop's 1st Lady in the *George and Mildred* Movie
   Born in London on January 9th 1941, Gardner made her film debut in 1961's *The Hellfire Club,* prior to working as an uncredited pilot in Pussy Galore's flying circus in the film *Goldfinger.* Following parts in *The Saint, Monty Python's Flying Circus* and *Three Piece Suite,* Caron took her most recent credit in *Second Thoughts* in 1992.

Garrity, Jo
Vera in *Man About the House* episode 'All in the Game'
   Garrity's acting career was brief, beginning in 1972 with *Comedy Playhouse* and cumulating just five years later with her final appearance in *Mr. Big.* In between came appearances in *Poldark* and *Angels* as well as an episode of *Miss Jones and Son.*

Gillespie, Robert
Various Characters in *George and Mildred*
   Robert Gillespie was born in Lille, France on November 9th 1933.
   After moving to the United Kingdom as a child, he joined RADA and later extended his training at London's Old Vic Theatre School. After making a television debut in *The Black Brigade* in 1956, he found his niche playing the 'deadpan policeman' in situation comedies.
   'My first role as a copper was in *Hugh and I Spy*, I played a Moroccan policeman and I was cast from then onwards. Johnnie and Brian picked me up on it and put me in *George and Mildred*. I really enjoyed playing the deadpan policeman, the best version I feel was in an episode of *Whatever Happened to The Likely Lads*'.
   'After *George and Mildred,* I was also in a few episodes of *Robin's Nest.* One of these involved an identity parade and it was a really good episode. Tony Britton had to walk along this line of people who each had a crazy line to say and it was hilariously funny, but poor Tony never got through without breaking up and laughing!'
   In 1986, Robert Gillespie was cast as lead character Dudley Rush in Brian Cooke's sitcom *Keep it in the Family.* The popular character had been written especially for Robert, with the sitcom itself based on Cooke's own experience as a cartoonist.
   'Brian dug into my persona and made me a cartoonist, he told me how; "It's you - I made him a manic depressive!", but it was an excellent series. I had someone call me up and say how they were watching in bed and laughed so much they fell out. In fact I got the biggest laugh of my career in that sitcom, it was in the court room scene in the episode 'All Through the Night'. Dudley Rush was my all time favourite character'.
   In recent years, Gillespie has drifted from the main screen to work on his own theatre plays.

'Once I was cast in a starring role, people stopped casting me as a support actor. I did a lot of commercials in the 1970's but they dried up too. I don't really want to do any more background roles - I could never face playing a sad old man in a hospital. These days I write my own plays, and I direct as well. Theatre is affordable unlike movies. I came up with my own theatre company, Jane Nightwork Productions, named after a little known Shakespearean character in Henry IV. I always loved the name!'.

Godfrey, Brian
Reporter in *George and Mildred* episode 'The Last Straw'
Brian had several small roles in Cooke and Mortimer's *Father Dear Father*, leading to repeat casting in *George and Mildred*. He later appeared in *Hi-de-Hi*, *Love and Let Love* and *The Kenny Everett Show*.
Most recently, Godfrey has become a theatre director. His latest credit was the 2009 tour of Arne Sultan and Ray Cooney's stage farce *Wife Begins at Forty* starring Trevor Bannister and Vicki Michelle.

Granville, Ursula
Office Clerk in *George and Mildred* episode 'Day's Of Beer and Rosie'
Granville started touring with repertory theatre in the early 1950's, working on the stage show *Personal Enemy* initially, prior to starring in numerous theatrical productions, usually in Northern England. Granville made the jump to the television screen with *ITV Play of the Week* in 1965, having previously made a film debut with *The Three Weird Sisters* in 1948.
Ursula later appeared in; *Upstairs Downstairs, Six Days of Justice, Miss Jones and Son* and *Sentimental Education*. She made her last appearance in *George and Mildred*.
Granville died in 1992, she is survived by her son Edward who now resides in Tasmania.

Greene, Peter
Neil in *Man About the House* episode 'The Last Picture Show'
Making his first appearance on television hidden behind a mask, as a Cyberman in a 1967 four part special of *Doctor Who*, Greene made a transition to comedy roles. Credits include; *Sykes, Doctor in Charge, Some Mothers Do 'Ave 'Em, Are You Being Served* and *The Young Ones*. His last role was in *The Waiter* in 1993 and Greene is now believed to work for a market research company.

Grundy, Bill
Interviewer in the *Man About the House* film.
Born in Manchester on February 20th 1923, Grundy became a television presenter after an audition with Granada in 1956. Best known for his work on Thames' *The Today Show*, Grundy has also presented *A Better Read, What the*

Complete A-Z of Support Cast

Papers Say, Sweet and Sour and *The Lancashire Lads*.

Grundy died following a heart attack on February 9th 1993, he was 69.

Guy, Jennifer
Maggie in the *George and Mildred* episode 'The Four Letter Word'

Guy was born in Carshalton and has been a common face in comedy over the years, appearing in; *Sykes, On the Buses, Are You Being Served?* and *Birds of a Feather*.

In recent times, Jennifer has appeared in children's drama *Cavegirl* and has recently taken work on *Harry and Cosh* and *Nelson's Trafalgar*. Guy also makes regular appearances in theatre as a member of the Kent repertory group.

H

Hanley, Jenny
Liz, Robin's Girlfriend in the *Man About the House*.

Hanley was born on August 15th 1947 in Gerrards Cross, Buckinghamshire. After some early work as a child model, Hanley made her screen debut in the film *Joanna* in 1968, appearing in the James Bond film *On Her Majesty's Secret Service* the next year.

After several television credits, including *The Two Ronnies* and *Morecambe and Wise*, Hanley made her last credited appearance in 1983 in *West Country Tales*, but is still registered as an actress with Equity. She is best known for her work on *Magpie* from 1974 to 1980.

Jenny's brother was Sir Jeremy Hanley, Foreign Secretary in John Major's conservative government. Hanley's mother was the actress Dinah Sheridan who worked alongside Sally Thomsett in *The Railway Children*.

Hardy, Tom
Barman in *George and Mildred* episode 'Life With Father'

Hardy's only credited appearance on television was in this episode of *George and Mildred*.

Harrison, Sally
Denise in *Man About the House* episode 'I Won't Dance, Don't Ask Me'

Debuting in *Theatre 625* in 1968, Harrison later starred in *Confessions of a Pop Performer, Thriller, Blake's 7, The Professionals* and *I'm Not Feeling Myself Tonight*.

Sally now owns Axarquia Properties, a Malaga based estate agency.

Harvey, John
Doctor in *Man About the House* episode 'Mum Always Liked You Best'

Charles in *George and Mildred* episode 'The Bad Penny'

Born in London on September 27th 1911, Harvey was a prolific actor in a career spanning over thirty years. His first notable performance was in the 1948 film *The Gunman Has Escaped*, with later credits including *Noose, Stage Fright, Castle in the Air* and *Lady Godiva Rides Again*.

On television, Harvey appeared in; *The Vice, Invisible Man, Our Man at Saint Mark's* and *Sykes*.

John Harvey retired in 1979 after a final appearance in *The Dick Francis Thriller*. He died in Oxfordshire on July 19th 1982.

Hawkins, Michael
Mayor in *George and Mildred* episode 'Just the Job'

Hawkins was born on November 26th 1928 and took an early role in *The Hound of the Baskervilles* in 1959. Later work included; *The Avengers, The Brothers, Doctor Who, Secret Army* and *Everyday Maths*.

Hawkins' last work as an actor was in *A Family Affair* in 1979.

Hayes, Annie
Rita in *Man About the House* episode 'Of Mice and Women'

Man About the House was only the second television role for Hayes, who was born on April 17th 1946 in Birmingham.

After numerous dramatic parts in shows like; *Play For Today, Shoestring* and *Casualty*, Annie gained her last credit in a 1997 episode of *The Bill*. She died later that year on April 2nd 1997, aged 50.

Hayes, Melvyn
Nigel in the *Man About the House* film.

Born in London on January 11th 1935, Hayes began his career in entertainment with the *Comedy Theatre* in 1950, prior to making a film debut in *Adventures in the Hopfields* in 1954.

Over his lengthy career, Hayes has also appeared in; *Bottoms Up, The Young Ones, Go for a Take, Love thy Neighbour, Carry on England* and *Robin Hood*. Hayes is perhaps most fondly remembered for being Gloria Beaumont in the popular war-time sitcom *It Ain't Half Hot Mum,* in which he starred for seven years.

Hayes is still an active performer, and recently appeared in *Sleeping Beauty* at Worthing's Connaught Theatre.

Heaton, Anthony
Policeman in *George and Mildred* episode 'The Little Dog Laughed'

Born in 1947, Heaton made a television debut in *The Beast in the Cellar* in 1970, with later roles coming with *The Sweeney, Target, Dick Barton, Minder* and *Widows*.

Complete A-Z of Support Cast

Hennessy, Emmett
Policeman in *Man About the House* episode 'No Children, No Dogs'
   Hennessy's part as a policeman in the pub scene of this episode was not credited in the closing titles. Previous roles for him included; *Upstairs Downstairs, Softly Softly* and *Z Cars*.
   Hennessy made one more appearance after *Man About the House,* appearing in an episode of *Some Mothers Do 'Ave 'Em* in 1973, before fading out of acting.
   He currently lives in Trinidad with his wife, Allyson.

Herrick, Roy
Nigel in *George and Mildred* episode 'Finders Keepers'
   Making a debut in *Festival* in 1963, Herrick has appeared in dozens of productions in British television and film, most notably: *Callan, The Regiment, Doctor Who, Robin's Nest, Bernie, Never the Twain* and *Howard's Way.* Herrick took his last part in *Macbeth* in 1988. He died later that year on October 1st 1988.

Hewlett, Arthur
Elderly man in the *Man About the House* film.
   Born on March 12th 1907 in Southampton, Arthur Reginald Hewlett made his film debut on *Jonah* in 1950, prior to appearing in; *The Third Alibi, Hugh and I, Benny Hill, Doctor Who, James and the Giant Peach, Crown Court, The Love Child* and *Moondial.*
   Hewlett was married to actress Margaret Denyer until his death in February 1997.

Hobbs, Cecily
Muriel in *Man About the House* episode 'Fire Down Below'
   Hobbs made her television debut on *Man About the House,* before later working on *White City, Grange Hill, Ruth Rendell Mysteries* and *One Foot in the Grave.* Hobbs is still in the business, and appeared most recently in *Happy Birthday Shakespeare* in 2000.

Horne, Maxine
Joanne in *George and Mildred* episode 'Best Foot Forward'
   This episode of *George and Mildred* was Horne's only recognised appearance on television.

Holms, Marks
Sid in George and Mildred episode 'A Military Pickle'
   Playing the part of a duty sergeant was an early credit for Holms in *Law and Order* in 1978. He later went on to appear in; *Lillie, Cowboys, Time Bandits* and *Funny Man.* His last work as an actor was on *Monty Python's Meaning of Life.*

Howard, Arthur
Vicar in *George and Mildred* episode 'And Women Must Weep'

Born on January 18th 1910, Howard took an early screen appearance in the 1933 film *The Private Life of Henry VIII* and later *The Lady is Willing*. Following a career break over the second world war, Howard returned to film in 1947 with *Freda*.

Later appearances included; *Passport to Pimlico, The Avengers, Ladies Who Do, Grand Prix, Steptoe and Son, Moonraker, Never the Twain* and *The Russ Abbot Show*.

Howard died on June 18th 1995, aged 85.

Howman, Karl
Phillip in *Man About the House* episode 'Two Foot Two, Eyes of Blue'

Born in Woolwich on December 13th 1952, Howman made a debut in 1972, later building on his career with appearances in *Warship, Softly Softly, Brush Strokes, Marked Personal, Get Some In* and *The Bill*.

He still acts to this day, and recently turned his hand to writing and directing, with the 2009 film *Fathers of Girls* being his most recent project. Howman will also be familiar to many for his work on the 'Flash' detergent commercials.

Hughes, Alison
Various Characters in *Man About the House*

Hughes took early acting work on *The Mind of Mr J G Reeder*, before being cast in her most notable work, the cult 1973 film *The Wicker Man,* with Edward Woodward and Christopher Lee.

Following further parts in; *Crown Court, Village Hall* and *Marked Personal*, Hughes appeared as Maddie in *Man About the House*, later appearing as a new character, Robin's girlfriend, Linda.

Hughes' last credited role as an actress was in 1982 with *County Hall*.

J

Jackson, Michael J.
Barry in *Man About the House* episode 'Match of the Day'

Michael J. Jackson made his television debut in *Man About the House* and has since starred in numerous productions, including; *Doctors, Judge John Deed* and *Casualty*.

Jackson won an Evening Standard Award for Most Promising Newcomer in 1979 and most recently has appeared as Max Hill in *The Royal Today* in 2008.

Jeater, Frances
Marjorie in *Man About the House* episode 'I Won't Dance, Don't...'

Complete A-Z of Support Cast

Jeater trained as an actress whilst in repertory in Scarborough, and later became a member of the Birmingham Repertory Company.

Making her television debut in 1967, Jeater has appeared in: *Wycliffe, The Bill, Casualty, Bad Girls* and *Doctors*. She remains an active performer, and as well as spell in radio work, has recently appeared in *Holby City*.

Johns, Stratford

Harry Pinto in the *George and Mildred* Movie.

Born on September 22nd 1925 in Pietermaritzburg, South Africa, Johns served with the Navy before working as an accountant. He took up acting after joining local repertory theatre, and at the age of twenty-two, moved to the United Kingdom to settle in Southend-on-Sea, where he continued his work with repertory. Stratford made a screen debut in the 1955 film *The Night My Number Came Up*.

Johns is best remembered for his work as Detective Chief Inspector Barlow in *Z Cars*. Later notable career mentions include; *Softly Softly, Barlow at Large, Return of the Saint, Doctor Who, Brond* and *Minder*. Johns retired in 1998 when ill health forced him out of the business.

Johns died on January 22nd 2002, aged 74.

Johnson, Gareth

Stuart in *Man About the House* episode 'I Won't Dance, Don't Ask Me'

Johnson took early work in an episode of *Trial* in 1971, and later *And Mother Makes Five*. Following his appearance in *Man About the House*, Johnson took his last credit on *Buccaneer* in 1980.

'Gareth Johnson, son of Noel Johnson, who played Dick Barton on the radio, played opposite me at the dining table in this episode' recalls actor John Colclough. 'Noel came to see Gareth one lunch and I said to him that every time I passed his house in St. Margaret's, I thought to myself, "Dick Barton lives there" - He was amazingly flattered, I was delighted to meet another schoolboy hero'.

Jones, Peter

Mr Morris in *Man About the House* episode 'A Little Knowledge'

Born in Shropshire on June 12th 1920, Jones started his career in entertainment after attending repertory theatre, making a West End debut in *The Doctor's Dilemma* in 1942.

Jones turned his talents to radio, in particular the popular *In All Directions*, prior to concentrating on screen-based roles, most notably as Mr Fenner in Ronald Wolfe and Ronald Chesney's sitcom, *The Rag Trade*.

Further television work followed in; *Mr Digby Darling, Love thy Neighbour, Q5, I Thought You'd Gone, The Mixer, The Bill* and *Midsomer Murders*.

Jones died on April 10th 2000 at the age of 79.

Jordan, Frankie

Deidre in *Man About the House* episode 'Fire Down Below'

Playing an Office Girl in *Z Cars* in 1973 was an early television performance for

Jordan, who later appeared in *Marked Personal, Rosie, Dangerfield, Doctors* and *Heartbeat*.

'Acting was always my career path, there was no alternative. I went to A level at the Bristol Old Vic Theatre School, which was quite difficult to get into, and I tremendously enjoyed my time there. I can't recall how I was cast in *Man About the House* but it is most likely that I was called back by the director for it, at the time I had been in a lot of stuff with Thames'.

In recent times, Jordan has stepped out of television to work as a professional storyteller. She also became the focus of local press following her purchase of the Tom Thumb Theatre in Cliftonville. With seating for just 60 patrons, it is reportedly the smallest theatre in the world.

'The theatre came up for sale at auction and our family bought it. It's certainly the smallest stage in the world, only a few feet either way, but we still manage to do a lot of shows there, such as a brand new pantomime which is coming up soon'.

'It did occur to me that perhaps I should go back into television, but a few years ago I began to realise that it was losing its enjoyment value to work on. Rehearsals hardly ever happen these days and besides they don't write quality stuff for middle aged women any more. I was considering going back, mainly because I need the money for the theatre!'

I

No surnames beginning with this letter

K

Kendall, Jo
Podge Randall in *Man About the House* episode 'Two Foot Two...'

After studying at Cambridge University with a galaxy of future stars including; Bill Oddie, Graeme Garden, John Cleese and Tim Brooke-Taylor, Kendall started out in theatre with the show *Cambridge Circus*. The production, directed by Humphrey Barclay, toured as far as the United States and New Zealand.

Following radio work in popular series *The Burkiss Way*, Jo moved into television, an early credit coming from her roles in *Broaden Your Mind,* again with Garden and Brooke-Taylor.

Following a long stint in *Emmerdale Farm,* Kendall starred in *Scum, The New Avengers, The Goodies, Fortunes of War, The Bill* and *Bridge of Dragons*. She currently resides in Suffolk.

Complete A-Z of Support Cast

Kessler, Catherine
Brenda in *George and Mildred* episode 'The Travelling Man'

Following early parts in the late 1960's with *Love Story, Armchair Theatre* and *The Expert*, Kessler began to expand her work as an actress, appearing in *On the Buses, Z Cars* and *The Fenn Street Gang*.

Kessler later worked on *Crown Court, Miss Jones and Son, Within These Walls* and *Murder by Decree*. Her last role came with an appearance on *The Latchkey Children* in 1980.

King, Diana
Margaret in *George and Mildred* episode 'The Bad Penny'

Born on August 2nd 1918, King made her acting debut in the 1939 film *Little Ladyship*, before starring in; *A Farewell to Arms, Offbeat* and *Jango*.

King later dedicated her acting talents to sitcom work, and her filmography in this genre is extensive. Comedy appearances include; *Some Mothers Do 'Ave 'Em, Are you Being Served, Terry and June, Rising Damp, Come Back Mrs Noah, Doctor on the Go, Yus Me Dear, And Mother Makes Five, The Fenn Street Gang, Fawlty Towers, Romany Jones, Love Thy Neighbour, Bless This House, Dad's Army, The Liver Birds, Father Dear Father* and *Please Sir*.

King died on July 31st 1986.

Kinnear, Roy
George's friend, Jerry

Roy Mitchell Kinnear was born on January 8th 1934 in Wigan, Lancashire, the son of Anne Smith and Rugby player Roy Muir Kinnear. He was educated at George Herriot's school in Edinburgh, and upon leaving, enrolled in RADA to train as an actor, however Kinnear was conscripted for national service, putting a temporary halt to his theatrical studies.

In 1959, Roy joined up with the prestigious Joan Littlewood Theatre School at Theatre Royal Stratford East. His first film role was in the workshop adapted play, *Sparrow's Can't Sing,* where he starred alongside his future co-workers, Yootha Joyce and Brian Murphy.

'Roy Kinnear joined the theatre workshop a good while later than me', remembers Brian Murphy. 'He was a great bubble of fun and he was very easy to get on with, very funny. He made me laugh both on stage and off. The trouble laughing at him on stage, was that Joan was a great disciplinarian. Sometimes I had so much trouble with Roy I had to march him down off the stage and tell him to stay there until I had finished what I had to say. He was a great character, and became a great dear friend.'

In the early 1960's, Kinnear continued his work for stage and radio, making his first major television appearance, *That Was the Week That Was* in 1962. After scores of further screen appearances, including a part opposite Christopher Lee in *Dracula,* and also in the Beatles' film *Help!,* Kinnear was cast as Jerry in *Man about the House,* later reprising the character in *George and Mildred*.

During his career, Roy has also turned his talents to voice-overs, narrating several characters in the animated film *Watership Down,* as well as character of Bulk in *SuperTed*. He also reunited with Brian Murphy in *The Incredible Mr. Tanner* and worked again with Richard O'Sullivan as an occasional background character in *Dick Turpin*.

Kinnear's last work came in 1988 with *The Return of the Musketeers,* as Roy died during the film's production in Toledo, Spain. Following a fall from his horse, he was admitted to Madrid hospital with a broken pelvis, but after complications in his recovery, suffered a heart attack and died on September 20th 1988. He was survived by his wife, *Eastenders* star Carmel Cryan and their children, who have since founded the Roy Kinnear trust in his memory, a charity established to aid youngsters born with cerebral palsy.

Carmel explained how Roy's work continues to interest generations of new fans. 'My son was at a wedding last week and was approached by a couple enthusing about Roy's work', she recalled. 'In particular their love of the 1970s British sitcom. The legacy goes on...'

Kitts, Doris
Shop Assistant in *George and Mildred* episode 'And Women Must...'

Kitts took an early credit on *Play for Today* in 1975 and after appearing in *George and Mildred*, took her final role in *Tales of the Unexpected* in 1983.

Kneale, Patricia
Mrs Clifton-White in *George and Mildred* episode 'Opportunity Knocks'

Kneale was born on October 17th 1925 in Torquay.

Originally working as a typist with Vogue magazine, Kneale later trained at RADA, where she was awarded the Bancroft Medal.

After taking early stage work at Regent's Park Open Air Theatre in the late 1940's, with Shakespearean plays such as *Twelfth Night* and *A Midsummer Nights Dream*, Patricia moved into television and her first role; *The Adventures of Sir Lancelot* in 1957. Kneale later starred in *Crane, A for Andromeda, Thriller* and *Rosie*, before accepting her final role in *Potter* in 1983.

Kneale died on December 27th 2008.

Kriseman, Hilda
Various Characters in *Man About the House*

Krisemen's early career credits included *Theatre 625* in 1966 and later *The Guardians* and *BBC Play of the Month*

She also appeared under direction of Peter Frazer-Jones in *And Mother Makes Five*, making her a suitable choice for Robin's mum in *Man About the House*. Kriseman also played a shop assistant in one episode.

Hilda's last work was on *Butterflies* in 1980.

Complete A-Z of Support Cast

L

Lacey, Margaret
Woman at Door in *George and Mildred* episode 'Moving On'
   Born in 1910, Lacey made her debut in *Brothers in Law* in 1957. She later appeared alongside Ian Carmichael in *I'm Alright Jack,* and subsequently; *Suspect, Nearest and Dearest, Black Beauty* and *Billy Liar*. Lacey is perhaps most noted for her brief appearance in *Diamonds Are Forever,* the drowned Mrs Whistler who is found in the Amsterdam canals. After retiring from acting in 1985, Lacey died three years later on October 4th 1988.

Lamont, Duncan
Dr Macleod in *Man About the House*
   Duncan Lamont was born in Lisbon, Portugal in 1918. He made his debut in the 1950 film, *Waterfront* and has since made almost one hundred screen appearances, with *Man About the House* coming fairly late in his career.
   Lamont also popped up in two episodes of *Robin's Nest*, before his death in December 1978 at his home in Tunbridge Wells.

Lavender, Ian
Mark in *Man About the House* episode 'While the Cat's Away'
   Lavender trained at the Bristol Old Vic theatre school before joining local repertory, making a television debut in *Half Hour Story*. His most memorable part to date arrived shortly afterwards. In 1968, Lavender took on the role of the 'stupid boy' Private Pike in *Dad's Army*.
   Since then he has starred in numerous sitcoms, including; *Come Back Mrs. Noah, Yes Minister, Keeping Up Appearances* and *Goodnight Sweetheart*. Lavender still acts and recently appeared in *31 North 62 East*.

Lawrence, Andria
Miss Bird in the *Man About the House film.*
   Hardy ever off the screens during the 1970's, Lawrence made her debut in *An Arabian Night* in 1960, before further roles in; *Londoners, The Wednesday Play, On the Buses, Doctor at Large, The Fenn Street Gang, The Goodies* and *Love thy Neighbour*.
   Andria's last television work came in 1976 with *I'm Not Feeling Myself Tonight*.

Lawrence, Marjie
Ada in *George and Mildred* episode 'Nappy Days'
   Born in 1935, Lawrence took early television parts in *Round at the Redways, Without Love* and *Tales from Dickens* in the late 1950's, before progressing her career with later credits; *Gideon's Way, The Dustbinmen, Out of the Trees* and *Danger UXB*.

- 175 -

Prior to working on *George and Mildred*, Lawrence had previously played Brian Murphy's on-screen wife in the 1976 sex comedy, *I'm Not Feeling Myself Tonight*. Marjie's later works includes; *Screen One, Large, Shiner* and her last known credit, a 2007 episode of *Doctors*.

Leake, Annie
Tweedy lady in the *Man About the House* film

Leake debuted in *Hancock* in 1961. She later appeared on; *Sykes, Love thy Neighbour, Clayhanger, Beryl's Lot, Born and Bred* and *The Bill*. Her last work was on the 1985 feature-length episode of *Only Fools and Horses*, 'To Hull and Back'.

Lester, Frank
Clerk of the Court in *Man About the House* episode 'One for the Road'

After making his first television appearance on *Jackanory* in 1971, Lester focused mainly on comedy roles over the rest of his career. He has starred in; *The Two Ronnies, And Mother Makes Four, The Liver Birds, Monty Python* and *The Good Life*.

Lester's last credit came in 1984 with *Airwolf*.

Lewin, Mike
Ambulance Man in *George and Mildred* episode 'Best Foot Forward'

Lewin started acting on television in the early 1950's, with *The Philco Television Playhouse* proving to be his earliest recognised role. Since then he has appeared on *The Avengers, Freewheelers, The Sweeney, And Mother Makes Five, Grange Hill* and *Sorry*. Lewin's last credited part came in 1988 with *Jack the Ripper*.

Lidstone, Gail
Various Characters in *George and Mildred*

Lidstone's debut came in *The Beast in the Cellar* in 1970.

After appearing in *Miss Jones and Son*, Lidstone worked on *George and Mildred*, which was her last credited television role.

Littlewood, Harry
Various Characters in *Man About the House*
Various Characters in *George and Mildred*

Born in Manchester in 1921, Littlewood was fundamentally a character actor for over thirty years, making his debut in 1959 with *The Budds of Paragon Row*. Since then, Littlewood has appeared in: *Suspense, The Plane Makers, No Hiding Place, Dr Finlay's Casebook, The Saint, Z Cars, Bottle Boys* and *Howard's Way*. Littlewood also wrote and starred in *Ours is a Nice House* with Thora Hird.

His work with Johnnie Mortimer and Brian Cooke includes; *Alcock and Gander, George and Mildred*, The *George and Mildred* film, *Robin's Nest* and Johnnie Mortimer's *Never The Twain*. Littlewood also starred in *L for Lester* with Brian Murphy and was Murphy's understudy for the *George and Mildred* stage show.

Complete A-Z of Support Cast

His last credit came in 1991, with Harry retiring later the same year.

Littlewood died on Boxing day, 2003 at his Chelsea home aged 81.

Lloyd, Simon
Tarquin Fourmile in *George and Mildred*

The Fourmile's second son, baby Tarquin, was played by Simon Lloyd, with *George and Mildred* being his only credited on screen work as an actor. Lloyd was only six months old at the time of filming, but was still chauffeur driven to the studios in a limo!

Lowe, Arthur
Spiros in the *Man About the House* film.

Born in Derbyshire on September 22nd 1915, Lowe worked on his harboured ambitions of entertaining by organising army shows during world war two, and later joined the Manchester repertory theatre upon demobilisation.

After making numerous theatre appearances, Lowe moved into television, with early credits including; *One Way Out, Inside Story, All Aboard* and *The Long Way Home*. Lowe is best remembered, however, for his work as Captain Mainwaring in the exceptionally popular comedy, *Dad's Army*.

Arthur Lowe collapsed in his dressing room from a stroke, prior to going on stage in *Home at Seven* in Birmingham. He was rushed to hospital where he died on April 15th 1982, aged 66.

Lye, Reg
George's Father

Reginald Lye was born in Sydney, Australia in 1912, and drew upon his theatrical training to enter film and television in 1953. Since then he has been seen in over a hundred film and television productions, including many popular ITC shows like *The Saint* and *The Professionals*.

Lye won the 1975 Honourable Mention Award for his work on *Sunday Too Far Away*. His last credited performance was in *Joe Wilson* in 1988, he died later that year at the age of 76.

Lyons, John
Dustman in *Man About the House* episode 'How Does Your Garden Grow'
Various characters in *George and Mildred*

Born on September 14th 1943, Lyon's earliest television work was in 1964 with *Catch Hand,* later appearing in; *United, Z Cars, The Liver Birds, UFO, On the Buses, Mind Your Language* and *Doctors*. In recent times, John achieved a greater exposure for his role as DS Toolan in *A Touch of Frost* with David Jason, before his character was killed off in 2010.

'I ended up being cast in *Man About the House* after the director, Peter Frazer-Jones, saw me in a few other TV Sitcoms and asked me back for an audition. It was just like old times working on the series, I had worked with both Brian and Yootha before at the Theatre Workshop Stratford East. I still keep in touch with Brian and some of the other members of the workshop, we meet for dinner about four times a year'.

M

MacDonald, Aimi
Hazel Lovett in the *Man About the House* film.

Born in Glasgow on February 27th 1942, MacDonald took to the stage in her early teens, originally as a dancer, before making a move into television and rising to fame in *At Last the 1948 Show*, where she gained the stage name 'The Lovely Aimi MacDonald'.

Further credits include; *The Saint, The Avengers, Shirley's World, Man at the Top, Vampira, Rentaghost, Get Real* and *Baddiel's Syndrome*. Aimi is still an active performer today, appearing most recently in *Doctors*.

Mackey, Beatrix
Matron in *George and Mildred* episode 'Life with Father'

Following early work in *Stranger on the Shore, Silas Marner* and *No Hiding Place*, Mackey made later appearances on; *Miss Jones and Son, Sink or Swim* and *Robin's Nest*.

Her last known part was in 1983 on an episode of Juliet Bravo.

Malpas, George
Marvin Shumaker in *George and Mildred* episode 'I Believe in Yesterday'

Not exactly the most American person around, Malpas was actually born in Warrington in 1926. He made his first televised appearance as an actor in *Crossroads* in 1964 before working on; *Last of the Summer Wine, Nearest and Dearest, Terry and June, Boon, Peak Practise* and *The Missing Postman*.

George retired in 1998, with a final role preceding in *Bramwell*. Malpas died three years later on February 26th 2001 in Bradford.

Marlow, Jean
Mildred's sister, Hilda, in *George and Mildred*

Marlow debuted in 1957 on *Armchair Theatre*, later building on her career with appearances in *Hancock, Suspense, Miss Jones and Son, Your Only Young Twice, Potter, The Bill, Mary Barton* and *Blackmail*.

Jean is still active, recently appearing in the 2006 film *On the Other Hand*. Marlow was good friends with Yootha Joyce, paying tribute to the actress on *The Unforgettable Yootha Joyce* in 2001.

Complete A-Z of Support Cast

Marsh, Reginald
Mildred's brother-in-law, Humphrey.

Reginald Marsh was born on September 17th 1926 in London, but spent the majority of his childhood on the south coast town of Worthing. Upon leaving school he worked at as a clerk at a local bank - but after realising he truly wanted to be an actor, spoke to his father who introduced him to a retired actress. It was through her that Reginald found his first theatrical agent, and gained his first stage role at the age of sixteen, in J.B. Priestley's *Eden End*.

Marsh progressed to local repertory theatre, taking a job in television in 1958 when he worked backstage with Granada. Reginald soon made the transition to the front of the camera, with his screen debut coming in *ITV Television Playhouse*. After several television roles Marsh branched into films including *Young Winston*, but the majority of his work was on the small screen.

Having starred in scores of television programmes, including; *The Stone Tape, Emmerdale Farm, Bless this House* and *The Sweeney*, Reginald Marsh appeared in *The Good Life* as Jerry's boss, as well as Terry's boss in *Terry and June*. Marsh progressed to further sitcoms roles; including; *Only When I Laugh* and *Home to Roost*.

Marsh made his last appearance on television in 1997 on *Galton and Simpson's* before he retired from the acting business. Marsh lived on the Isle of Wight with his wife, actress Rosemary Murray. An active supporter of MENCAP, Marsh frequently appeared at charity fund-raising events on the island.

Reginald Marsh died in the town of Ryde on February 9th 2001.

Martin, Louisa
Nurse in *Man About the House* episode 'Three of a Kind'

After playing Phyllis in *Cider with Rosie* in 1971, Martin subsequently appeared in: *Colditz, Emmerdale Farm, Wind at my Back* and *The City*. Her most recent credit was the 2001 television production, *Jackie, Ethel, Joan: The Women of Camelot*.

Maynard, Bill
Kitchen chef in the *Man About the House* film.

Born on October 8th 1928, Maynard worked originally as a variety performer, before making a transition to the screen, a debut being *Great Scott, It's Maynard* in 1955 with Terry Scott. Further work included; *Till Death Us Do Part, Up Pompeii, Carry on Loving, Sykes, Steptoe and Son Ride Again, Carry on Dick, Oh No It's Selwyn Froggitt* and *The Royal*.

Maynard is still an active performer, most recently appearing on stage during 'The Pride of Bridlington Awards' in 2009, following an abrupt end to his radio work with BBC Leicester.

Maynard, Michael
Sergeant Regan in *George and Mildred* episode 'A Military Pickle'

Maynard made his acting debut in *Blake's 7* in 1979, and subsequently worked on; *Guinness - Magic, Armchair Thriller, The Professionals, Father's Day, English File* and *Black Silk*. Maynard took his last credit in 1988 on *Dramarama*.

McCarthy, Neil
Eddie in the *George and Mildred* Movie
Born in Lincoln on July 26th 1933, McCarthy has been a solid face of British television and cinema for years, with an impressive filmography including the smash Richard Burton and Clint Eastwood blockbuster *Where Eagles Dare* and the acclaimed 1964 film *Zulu*.

McCarthy later dedicated his acting talents to television sitcoms, with appearances in *Some Mothers Do 'Ave 'Em, Sykes, Steptoe and Son Ride Again* and *Keep it in the Family*. McCarthy died on February 6th 1985 from motor neurone disease, aged 51.

McCormack, Colin
Various characters in *Man About the House*
Various characters in *George and Mildred*
Born on December 2nd 1941, the son of a Cardiff railway worker, McCormack trained at the Central School of Speech and Drama, where he met future wife, actress Wendy Allnutt, who also appeared in *Man About the House*.

After a long career in television sitcoms, with credits including; *Terry and June, Yes Minister* and *The Good Life*, Colin McCormack died on June 19th 2004 after developing cancer.

Meier, Paul
Doctor in *George and Mildred* episode 'The Delivery Man'
Meier's work as an actor began in 1977 with *Marie Curie* and later included; *Cross of Fire* and *The Painting*.

Meier now works as a dialect coach for actors, helping behind the scenes on *Ride with the Devil, Caught in the Act* and *What's Wrong with Virginia*. He has also taught at RADA and most recently at the University of Kansas. Paul also works as a voice-over artist and has narrated commercials for; Ford, Coca-Cola, Bayer and the Wal-Mart character 'smiley'.

Melody, Tony
Ernest Groves in *George and Mildred* episode 'Days of Beer and Rosie'
Melody was born in London on December 18th 1922. After doing his national service with the RAF, Tony started out in local radio, taking part in the popular radio series *The Clitheroe Kid*, and later taking early television work with the on-screen adaptation entitled *Just Jimmy*.

He later made appearances in; *Steptoe and Son, Z Cars, Bless this House, The Nesbits are Coming, The Incredible Mr Tanner, Coronation Street* and *Last of the Summer Wine*.

Complete A-Z of Support Cast

Melody retired in 2003 to live at his Blackpool home with wife Margaret and his four children. He died on June 26th 2008, aged 85.

Michaels, Robert
Boy in Pub in *George and Mildred* episode 'Days of Beer and Rosie'
After making a television debut in 1977 with *Get Some In,* Michaels appeared in; *Miss Jones and Son, Funny Man, Blame it on the Night* and *Death Chase*. His last credit was for *Cybernator* in 1991.

Michelle, Vicki
Bishop's 2nd Lady in the *George and Mildred* Movie.
Long before Vicki donned a lace apron and a corny French accent in the hugely popular *'Allo 'Allo*, the Chigwell born actress appeared in a very brief cameo playing the Bishop's 2nd lady in the *George and Mildred* film.
Born on December 14th 1950, Michelle trained at the Aida Foster Theatre School before making an early television appearance in *Virgin Watch*, before progressing to *The Goodies, Are You Being Served* and *All In the Game*. Vicki still acts, and most recently appeared in *Emmerdale*.

Milligan, Spike
Appeared as himself in the *Man About the House* film.
Born in India on April 16th 1918, Milligan grew up in Poona and was educated at local Roman Catholic schools before moving to England, where he joined Lewisham Polytechnic.
After serving with the army during the second world war, and working as a jazz musician, Milligan gained his television break as a comic in 1951 on *Let's Go Crazy*, having previously made his name on the legendary radio programme *The Goon Show*.
Milligan gained great esteem for his career in comedy, with highlights including; *The Telegoons, Curry and Chips, Till Death Us Do Part* and *Q5*. After a lifetime in entertainment, Spike Milligan died on February 27th 2002, aged 83.

Minster, Hilary
Hell's Angel in *Man About the House* episode 'Home and Away'
Minster was born on March 21st 1944.
Best known for his portrayal of General Erich Von Klinkerhoffen in *'Allo 'Allo*, Minster made his television debut in *Crossroads* in 1964, and has appeared in scores of productions over the years, including the epic feature film *A Bridge Too Far*.
Hilary died in 1999 at the age of 55.

Mitchell, Norman
Doorman in the *Man About the House* film.
Various characters in *George and Mildred*.

Possibly one of Britain's most experienced actors, with an estimated two-thousand television and five-hundred radio appearances, Norman Mitchell was highly sought after for his talent, and became widely known as the hardest working actor in the business.

Born in Sheffield in August 20th 1918 as Norman Mitchell Driver, he was the son of a Mining engineer and his mother was a concert hall performer. Mitchell schooled at Carterknowle Grammar school before being accepted into the University of Sheffield. At the age of eighteen, he walked to London to follow his dreams of becoming an actor, later joining the Royal Shakespeare Company.

Mitchell appeared in four episodes of *George and Mildred* in various guises, including 'Pet shop owner' and 'Electric Man', he was the first choice of the casting directors when a support actor was called for. 'Jimmy Liggatt was the casting director for *George and Mildred*' explained Norman's old theatrical agent at St James Management. 'He used to ring me up and say "I'm sure Norman's doing three other jobs this week but he can fit this in!".

Mitchell has gone into great detail about his life and work as an actor in his autobiography, 'An actor's life for me'. On March 19th 2001, Norman died at his home in Downham Market, Norfolk. One of his last roles came a few months previously in the film *Room 36* directed by Jim Groves and also starring Brian Murphy.

Montague, Bruce
Spanish Businessman in the *George and Mildred* Movie
Born in Deal on March 24th 1939, Montague has worked in scores of productions over the last forty years, with worthy mentions including; *Crane, Lillie, Butterflies, Keeping Up Appearances, Doctors* and most recently, *The Afternoon Play*.

Moore, Suzanne
Sandra in *Man About the House* episode 'Never Give Your Real Name'
Moore's first appearance on television came in 1974 with *And Mother Makes Five*. After working on *Man About the House* the following year, she received her final credit with *Fox* in 1980.

Morray, Stella
Kate in *George and Mildred* episode 'Your Money or Your Life'
Born on July 29th 1923, Moray started a career in entertainment with ENSA, before making a screen debut in the 1951 television programme *The Passing Show*. Stella took further parts in *The Lovers, Mr Aitch, Z Cars, Love Thy Neighbour, The Benny Hill Show, Robin's Nest, Doctors* and *The Last Detective*. Moray died on August 6th 2006.

Morgan, Charles
Teacher in *Man About the House* episode 'How Does Your Garden Grow'
Launching his career with *Train of Events* in 1949, Morgan's extensive acting

Complete A-Z of Support Cast

credits include: *Robin's Nest, Miss Jones and Son, Softly Softly, Z Cars, Bless This House, Doctor Who* and *Never the Twain*.

After retiring in 1989, Morgan died in 2000.

Morgan, Garfield
Bridges in the *George and Mildred* Movie
Born in Birmingham on April 19th 1931, Morgan took his first acting work as an uncredited foreman in *Two Letter Alibi* in 1962.

After taking on further small parts, Morgan rose to fame as Frank Haskins in *The Sweeney* in 1975. Later works included; *Shelley, Minder, The Nineteenth Hole, Alas Smith and Jones, Bad Girls* and *The Bill*. After a long battle with cancer, Morgan died on December 5th 2009.

Morgan, Verne
Traffic Warden in *George and Mildred* episode 'The Little Dog Laughed'
Born in Kent on December 19th 1900, Morgan made his film debut in *The Limping Man* in 1953. Morgan made further film appearances in; *The Blazing Caravan, Blonde Bait* and *The Ugly Duckling*, before moving into television - appearing first in *Police Surgeon* in 1960.

Morgan's sitcom work is extensive, with credited roles including; *The Benny Hill Show, And Mother Makes Five, That's Your Funeral, Dad's Army* and *Robins Nest*.

Verne's final role came in Johnnie Mortimer and Brian Cooke's *Let There Be Love* in 1982. Morgan died two years later on April 23rd 1984, aged 83.

Morris, Aubrey
Lecturer in the *Man About the House* film.
Born in Hampshire in 1926, Morris began his long relationship with acting in the theatre, making the move from treading the boards to the front of the camera in the late 1950's.

Early screen work includes; *Oliver Twist, Not at All* and *Armchair Theatre,* with his later appearances following more mainstream drama and comedy. Morris has been an inexhaustible actor, taking credits in, among many others; *The Rag Trade, The Avengers, The Champions, Go for a Take, The Squirrels, Outlaws, The Others* and *Knee High Private Eye*.

Morris is still an active performer today, with his most recent work arriving in 2008 with *Visioneers*. Morris currently lives in Los Angelis.

Murton, Lionel
Lee Kennedy in *George and Mildred* episode 'I Believe in Yesterday'
Murton was born in London on June 2nd 1915, but spent the majority of his early life in Canada, making early film appearances in the late 1940's with; *Meet the Navy, Brass Money* and *Badger's Green*.

Murton found a late niche in comedy, appearing in *Doctor in Clover, Carry on*

Cowboy, Yanks Go Home and *Confessions of a Window Cleaner.*

Lionel appeared in one final role after *George and Mildred,* starring alongside Brian Murphy in *The Incredible Mr Tanner* in 1981. Murton retired that year. He died at his Basingstoke home on September 26th 2006.

N

Neville, David
Rowland in *George and Mildred* episode 'A Military Pickle'

A sought after character actor, usually cast for his upper-class characteristics, Neville made his television debut in *Affairs of the Heart* in 1974, later appearing in; *Barlow at Large, Fawlty Towers, Keep It in the Family, Auf Wiedersehen Pet* and *Boon*.

'I got into acting via drama school. I went to the East 15 school, which was an off-shoot to Joan Littlewood's Theatre Workshop. I'm not blessed with the most neutral accent, so I tended to end up playing the upper-class person on television. Whereas this niche was in my favour, it was also quite limiting on what I could do, and I started to tire of the typecasting and thought about a different career path'.

David Neville took his last television work on *Topsy-Turvy* in 1999. He has since left the profession to become a psychotherapist.

'I had some therapy myself in the 1970's and I always remembered it as something rather challenging and interesting. I took a three-year course and started to get a few clients and I found it a very rewarding job. I've been asked back to acting a few times, and I do miss the camaraderie of it all, but I find that this new career path gives me the most job satisfaction'.

Newell, Patrick
Sir Edmund Weir in the *Man About the House* film

Born on March 27th 1932, Newell made a television debut in 1955 with *Dial 999*, before appearing in *Probation Officer* and *Web*.

Out of all his extensive career works, Newell is perhaps best remembered for his work as 'Mother' in *The Avengers*, in which he starred for four years. Subsequent television work included; *Never Say Die, Casanova, Alcock and Gander, Robin's Nest, Call Me Mister* and *Casualty*. His last work came in 1988 in *Consuming Passions*.

Newell died from a heart attack on July 22nd 1988.

Nicholson, Audrey
Mrs Cross in *Man About the House* episode 'In Praise of Older Men'

Making her credited debut in 1955's *ITV Play of the Week,* Nicholson has worked on numerous shows, including; *St Ives, Vanity Fair* and *Garry Halliday*.

Complete A-Z of Support Cast

She has also provided support to Frankie Howerd on several occasions. Her last major appearance on television came in a 1981 episode of *Doctor's Daughters*.

O

Orchard, Julian
Producer in *Man About the House* film.
   Born on March 3rd 1930, Julian Dean Orchard trained at the Guildhall School of Music and Drama and worked in theatre, prior to making a television debut in *A Tale of Two Cities* in 1957.
   Later work followed with; *Benny Hill, Carry On Don't Lose Your Head, Carry On Doctor, Futtock's End, Carry On Henry, The Goodies, Odd Man Out* and *Happy Ever After*. Orchard's last work was on *Disneyland* in 1979.
   Orchard died on June 21st 1979, aged 49.

Owens, Suzanne
Croupier in the *George and Mildred* Movie
   Owens' last recognised work as an actress was with the *George and Mildred* film. She had previously starred in; *The Dirty Dozen, Theatre of Death, The Man Outside* and *No Hiding Place*.

Oxenford, Daphne
Chrissy's mother in *Man About the House*.
   Born in London in 1919, Oxenford started a long relationship with theatre after being signed up with ENSA during the second world war and touring Germany, understudying for Nellie Wallace. Upon return to England, Oxenford attended auditions for parts in West End theatre productions, and won a part in a revue with Joyce Grenfell and Max Wallace.
   Following numerous subsequent stage roles, Oxenford found her niche in radio, becoming world famous for providing the soothing voice 'Are you sitting comfortably?' on BBC's *Listen with Mother*.
   Daphne Oxenford made her television debut in the early 1960's, appearing initially in *Saki* and subsequently *It's a Woman's World*. Later credits include; *Coronation Street, Yanks Go Home, To the Manor Born, Never the Twain, Casualty, Heartbeat* and *The Royal*.
   Oxenford is still an active performer, most recently appearing in *Midsomer Murders* in 2008. She also recorded scenes for *Doctor Who*, but her offerings ended up on the cutting room floor. Daphne was married to David Marshall for 52 years, until his death in 2003. She currently lives in Cheshire.

P

Parkinson, Robin
Receptionist in the *George and Mildred* Movie.
　　Parkinson made a debut on *Hilda Lessways* in 1959.
Later work includes; *Billy Liar, On the Buses, The Liver Birds, Moody and Pegg, Rising Damp, The Many Wives of Patrick, Terry and June, Hi-de-Hi* and *Fresh Fields*.
　　Parkinson took over the role of Ernest Leclerc in *'Allo 'Allo*, following the death of Derek Royle, and still acts to this day, most recently appearing on a 2007 episode of *The Peter Serafinowicz Show*.

Patterson, Steve
David in the *Man About the House* episode 'Some Enchanted Evening'.
　　Patterson had a very short acting career, with only seven credited performances to his name, his debut being a 1968 episode of *The Sex Game*.
　　Patterson later worked on; *Doomwatch, Au Pair Girls, Sex Farm, Secrets of a Door to Door Salesman* as well as *And Mother Makes Five*. His appearance as David in *Man About the House* proved to be Patterson's last credited work as an actor.

Payne, Sandra
Penelope in the *George and Mildred* episode 'The Twenty Six Year Itch'
　　Born in Royston on September 24th 1944, Payne attended Selhurst Grammar School, and after several terms at the Italia Conti Academy, made an early appearance in *The Plane Makers* in 1963, with later notable credits including: *Z Cars, The Sweeney, Man At the Top, Only Fools and Horses, Never the Twain* and *Jack the Ripper*.
　　Payne retired from acting in 1996, taking her last role in *Roger Roger*.

Pearl, Pauline
Secretary in the *Man About the House* film.
　　After making a debut in *Suburban Wives* in 1971, Pearl appeared as Gloria in *Carry On Girls*, and later *The Satanic Rites of Dracula, Galton and Simpson's* and *Cuba*. Her most recent work was in 1994 with *Concrete Garden*.

Pertwee, Bill
Postman in the *Man About the House* film.
　　Born on July 21st 1926, Pertwee began his entertainment career in radio, working most notably on *Round the Horne*.
One of Pertwee's earliest, and best remembered roles on television, was as the miserable jobs-worth Warden Hodges in *Dads Army*. Pertwee had the interesting esteem of driving a Brough Superior motorcycle in the series, registration ATO 675 - the exact same bike that Brian Murphy used in *George and Mildred*!
　　Pertwee took subsequent parts in the *Dad's Army* spin-off, *It Stick's Out Half*

Complete A-Z of Support Cast

a Mile, and later took to working on; *Hi-de-Hi, Chance in a Million, Bernie, You Rang M'Lord* and *Woof*. Pertwee's most recent credit came on *Noel's House Party* in 1997, but he is still registered as an actor to this day. He was awarded the MBE in 2007 for his services to charity.

Peters, Irene
Uncredited Student in series one Opening Titles of *Man About the House*

Trained at the Italia Conti stage school, Irene was a frequent face on television in the 1970's, turning up in scores of sitcoms, from a couple of sketches in the *Dick Emery Show*, to evergreen classics like *Dad's Army* and *Some Mothers Do 'Ave 'Em*.

'My agent booked me for *Man About the House*' explained Peters. 'I have great memories of this show. Richard O'Sullivan was an absolute darling, and I still keep in contact with Sally'.

Peters, also known as Melinda Tracey, is married to musician Alan Jackson and the pair live in London. Her last credited television performance was in 1984 in *Knee's-Up*.

Plytas, Steve
Restaurant Manager in *Man About the House* episode 'Mum Always...'

Plytas was born in Istanbul on January 9th 1913 and made a cinema debut with *The Schirmer Inheritance* in 1957. Since then, Plytas has appeared in over one hundred productions, including a memorable performance in *Fawlty Towers* as Kurt, the drunken chef.

Career credits include: *Crane, Doctor Who, Sex Play, Carry on Emmanuelle* and *Superman IV*.

Plytas retired in 1990 and died four years later in December 1994.

Q

Quince, Peter
Barman in *George and Mildred* episode 'I Believe in Yesterday'

Debuting in *Carry on England* in 1976, Quince has appeared in; *Target, Van Der Valk, Robin's Nest, Minder* and *Happy Birthday Shakespeare*. His most recent work came in 2001 on *The Bill*.

R

Raglan, Robert
Various characters in *George and Mildred*

Raglan was born in 1906 in Surrey and made an early television appearance in 1946 with *Morning Departure*. Raglan moved on to appear in; *Circus Boy, The Yellow Robe, The Blakes, Ivanhoe* and *High Jump*.

In the 1970's, Raglan started to dedicate the majority of his time to sitcom roles, appearing in most of the classics; *Are You Being Served?, Dads Army, Bless This House, Love Thy Neighbour* and *Robin's Nest*.

Following an appearance in *Never the Twain* and *The Citadel*, Robert took his final part in *Shelley* in 1983 before his death two years later.

Ramsden, Dennis
Bishop in the *George and Mildred* Movie
Registrar in the *Man About the House* episode 'Another Bride, Another...'
Employment Clerk in *George and Mildred* episode 'And Women Must...'

Born in Leeds on November 7th 1918, Ramsden served with the RAF during World War II, later attending the Dundee repertory company in 1946. Dennis took parts theatrical roles in the West End in notable works including; *The Happiest Days of Your Life* with Margaret Rutherford and later the Brian Rix Theatre of Comedy. After appearing in *Starched Aprons* at the Embassy Theatre in 1953 alongside Alfie Bass and Miriam Karlin, Ramsden made his screen debut in a 1960 episode of *The Long Way Home*.

Dennis has appeared in countless comedies, as well as writing the scripts for them - penning episodes of; *Z Cars, A Roof Over My head, Terry and June* and *Hi-de-Hi*.

Ramsden took retirement from television in 1993 and concentrated on theatre work shortly afterwards. His most recent acting work was in the 2005 production of *Separate Tables* in Reading.

Redfern, Michael
Various characters in *Man About the House*
Various characters in *George and Mildred*

Born in March, 1943, Michael Redfern has been a familiar face in television sitcoms over the years, making appearances in *Some Mothers Do 'Ave 'Em, Bless This House, Porridge* and *Open All Hours*. Redfern is also known for his commercials, most notably as Lynda Bellingham's husband in the Oxo advertisements.

He made three appearances in *Man About the House,* his casting a result of an appearance in Brian Cooke and Johnnie Mortimer's *Alcock and Gander*. Redfern also took a couple of parts in *Robins Nest*.

Michael retired from acting in 2005 and now lives in Spain.

Riding, Catherine
Diana in *Man About the House* episode 'The Last Picture Show'

After playing Linda in the Michael Mills directed TV Short *The Last of the Best Men* in 1975, Riding built on her career with *The Rough and the Smooth* and *Within These Walls*.

Her last role was in an episode of *The Professionals* in 1980.

Complete A-Z of Support Cast

Ripper, Michael
Uncle Fred in *George and Mildred* episode 'Your Money or Your Life'
　Perhaps known best for his work on the *Hammer Horror* films, Ripper has made over two hundred screen appearances, the earliest back in 1936.
　After a long and fruitful life in the acting business, despite having a thyroid issue that significantly quietened his voice, Michael Ripper retired in 1992, and died in London on June 28th 2000.

Robbins, Michael
Second doorman in the *Man About the House* film
Alf in the *George and Mildred* episode 'The Last Straw'
　Born on November 14th 1930, Robbins left grammar school and followed his father's line of business to work as a bank clerk at his home in Hitchin. He swiftly left the job after drenching the bank manager with a fire extinguisher, and turned to drama, making a stage debut at the Gateway Theatre in Chester. After joining repertory, Robbins made his television debut shortly afterwards with Hilda Baker in *Be Soon* and has appeared in scores of productions including: *The Avengers, The Sweeney, The Pink Panther Strikes Again, Devenish, Hi-de-Hi* and *The Bill*. He is perhaps best known for his portrayal of Arthur Butler in *On the Buses*.
　'I met Michael whilst in theatre at Birmingham' explained Michael's widow, the actress Hal Dyer. 'We were doing a Christmas production of *The Silver Curlew* with Barry Jackson and we both played fairies, I had to teach him how to dance. I was later in *Holiday On the Buses* with him as well, me and Henry McGee were just cast to be a posh husband and wife - all the regular gang said that I wasn't common enough to be in the show more often. Michael kept being cast as the 'Cor Blimey' types over his career, but he was quite the opposite in real life. He had done a few plays in the past with Yootha and Brian so he knew them quite well'.
　Robbins died from cancer on December 11th 1992, aged of 62.

Roberts, Ewan
Mr. MacDonald in *George and Mildred* episode 'Finders Keepers'
　Born in Edinburgh on April 29th 1914, Roberts' first appearance came at the age of thirty-four as an uncredited policeman in *London Belongs to Me*. Further parts run to *The Titfield Thunderbolt, Sir Francis Drake, The Avengers, Baffled* and *Z Cars*.
　After a final appearance on *The Agatha Christie Hour* in 1982, Roberts died on January 10th 1983 at the age of 69.

Roberts, Ivor
Police Sergeant in *George and Mildred* episode 'Finders Keepers'
　Roberts was born on July 19th 1925 in Nottingham and originally worked backstage in television as an announcer with Television Wales and West, before making the move to stand in front of the cameras as an actor; Roberts' first part

coming in 1971 in *Ace of Wands*.

His career included worthy parts in; *Sam, Thriller, Porridge, My Brother's Keeper, Z Cars, Crossroads, The Nineteenth Hole* and *Boon*.

Ivor Roberts' last role came on *Peak Practice* in 1999. He died only days after the recording on September 5th 1999.

Rogers, Jean
Jenny in *George and Mildred* episode 'Day's of Beer and Rosie'

Born in Perivale on February 2nd 1942, Rogers worked on *Callan* in 1972, before appearing on *Crossroads, Emmerdale Farm, Last of the Summer Wine* and *Law and Disorder*.

'My agent put me up for the job, but I had worked with Peter Frazer-Jones before, so perhaps he remembered my work and chose to use me again. I used to love watching the show, but I haven't seen the episode I was in since it first went out'.

Rogers's most recent television appearance was in 2004 with *The Lazarus Child*. Since then, she has dedicated most of her time to stage work. Jean is a founding member of the Royal National Theatre and appeared in pantomime in Leeds in 2009.

Rogers, Mark
Boy scout in the *Man About the House* film.

Rogers made an acting debut in 1971, playing Cuthbert in *Tom Brown's Schooldays*. Later appearances included; *Z Cars, And Mother Makes Five, Romeo and Juliet* and *Jubilee*.

Mark's last work as an actor came in 1980, with an episode of *BBC2 Playhouse*.

Rourke, Bill
Dt. Cons. Mills in *George and Mildred* episode 'All Around the Clock'

After taking early parts in 1975 with *Churchill's People* and *Poldark*, Rourke made later appearances in; *Danger UXB, Minder, A Touch of Frost, The Bill* and *Waking the Dead*. Most recently, Bill has appeared in a 2005 episode of *Casualty*.

Rowlands, Patsy
Beryl in the *George and Mildred* episode 'The Twenty Six Year Itch'

Born in Palmers Green on January 19th 1934, Rowlands was only fifteen when she began a career in acting, winning a scholarship with the Guildhall School of Music and Drama. She is most fondly remembered for her part in nine films in the *Carry On* series.

After a life on screen, with notable past roles including; *Robin's Nest, Tess, Bless This House, Not on your Nellie* and *The Basil Brush Show*, Rowlands died on January 22nd 2005 from breast cancer.

Complete A-Z of Support Cast

S

Saks, Hessel
Colin in *Man About the House* episode 'All in the Game'
   Hessel Saks' first role was with *BBC Play of the Month* in 1969. An appearance in *Z Cars* five years later was followed by his final work in *Target* in 1977.

Sands, Leslie
Robin's Father
   Born in Bradford, Yorkshire on May 19th 1921, Leslie Sands made his professional debut at Sheffield's Lyceum Theatre in the 1941 production of *Do you Remember?* After several more theatrical productions, Sands made his way into television, making an early appearance in 1960 in *Counter-Attack*. Further roles beckoned soon after, and Sands was rarely off our screens.
   He was also an accomplished television writer, scripting episodes of the popular *Van Der Valk* in 1977 as well as *Z Cars*, *The Gold Robbers* and *The Plane Makers*.
   After retiring from the business in 1991, Leslie Sands died at the age of 79 on May 9th 2001, in Chepstow. He is survived by wife Pauline.

Savage, Mike
Various characters in *Man About the House*
   Savage was born in Ireland on May 20th 1943.
   'My parents were both in the medical professions and decided to come to England as doctors and nurses were in short supply. They eventually moved to Dorset. I initially got into acting after a term with the now closed Hampshire School of Speech and Drama in my hometown of Bournemouth. I then spent a number of years working in regional repertory, tours and west end shows. I got into television and TV commercials and became quite well known in the industry for what I did best, and I was cast on those attributes. As I worked on various Thames TV Comedies and entertainment shows, I got to know the producers and directors very well, most of them were in house personnel under contract from Thames'.
   'Unfortunately, I remember very little of my brief stint on *Man About the House,* but I do remember it was great fun to do, as were all the Thames sitcoms and comedy shows. There was a great buzz on Sunday when an audience of five hundred would arrived to watch some sort of sitcom or a Tommy Cooper, Benny Hill or Frankie Howerd comedy hour show. When Thames and its terrific film making arm, Euston Films, were ousted by the British establishment, it disappeared with on of the very best TV comedy and light entertainment departments in British Television'
   Recently, Savage has taken a back seat with his acting career and dedicates most of his time to the company XED Film and Television, which he co-founded with documentary maker Allan Beardsley.

Sawyer, Bill
Chauffeur in the *Man About the House* film.

Sawyer had previously worked on *Adventure Girl, Popular Pieces, The Safe, Never Take Sweets from a Stranger, Crossroads to Crime* and *Twins of Evil*.

Seaton, Derek
Various characters in *Man About the House*

Making a debut in *Troilus and Cressida* in 1966, Seaton appeared in several subsequent programmes, including *Dombey and Son* and *Marked Personal,* prior to taking two different parts in *Man About the House*. Seaton later appeared in *Robin's Nest, People Like Us, Shoestring* and *Escape*. His last role was as a journalist in the *ITV Playhouse* episode, *Only a Game*.

Derek was married to Paula Wilcox until his death in 1979. Seaton had previously starred alongside her in *Miss Jones and Son*.

Segal, Michael
Jim, Landlord of the Mucky Duck

Michael Segal made several appearances in early episodes of *Man About the House* as Jim the landlord of the Mucky Duck Pub.

Making his debut in *Return to the Lost Planet* in 1955, Segal expanded his acting career with appearances in *The Prisoner, Suspense* and *The Borderers* before accepting the part of Ian Smythe in four episodes of Cooke and Mortimer's *Father Dear Father*. Segal also appeared in three episodes of *And Mother Makes Three* directed by Peter Frazer-Jones.

Segal appeared in a minor role in *Robin's Nest* in 1976. He later appeared in *Reginald Perrin, That's my Boy*, and *Rumpole of the Bailey*. Segal died in 1996, having retired from acting a decade earlier.

Sinclair, Peggy
Mrs Eastham in *George and Mildred* episode 'The Dorothy Letters'

Sinclair took an early part in *Armchair Theatre* in 1964, and later built upon her career starring in; *Haunted, Z Cars, And Mother Makes Three, Let There Be Love* and *Hammer House of Horror*. Her last credited screen role came in 1996 with *Accused*.

Sinclair was married to *George and Mildred* star Richard Coleman until his death in 2008

Sharp, Anthony
Mr Matthews in *Man About the House* episode 'My Son, My Son'
Mr Trubshaw in *George and Mildred* episode 'And Women Must Weep'

Sharp was born on June 16th 1915 and originally worked with an insurance company, before joining the London Academy of Music and Dramatic Art. Sharp made a film debut in the 1946 production of *Teheran*.

Further parts followed with; *On Trial, Comedy Playhouse, Frankie Howerd,*

Complete A-Z of Support Cast

Crossplot, Nearest and Dearest, Steptoe and Son, Bernie, The Young Ones and *The Far Pavilions*. After taking a final role in *Affairs of the Heart*, Sharp died in London on July 23rd 1984, aged 69.

Sharp, Ian
Various characters in *Man About the House*
    Sharp debuted in a 1960 episode of *Play of the Week*, appearing briefly as a paper boy. Since then, he has appeared in *Softly Softly, The Lovers, Rating Notman, Snapshots* and *Screen 2: Honest Decent and True*.
    Sharp's last credited work as an actor came in 1991, as a fisherman on *Inspector Morse*.

Shaw, Richard
Various characters in *George and Mildred*
    Richard made a film debut in 1946 in *Johnny Comes Flying Home* and later worked on *Three Little Girls in Blue*. Shaw has had an extensive acting career spanning almost fifty years, with notable credits including; *Steptoe and Son, The Vise, Carry On Don't Lose Your Head, Freewheelers, Doctor Who* and *Robin's Nest*.
    Shaw's last credit came courtesy of *Matlock* in 1987.

Skinner-Carter, Corinne
Housewife in the *Man About the House* film.
    Corinne Skinner-Carter was born in Trinidad in 1931.
    Early television work included; *BBC Sunday Night Theatre* and *Boyd QC*, before Skinner progressed to work on; *Up Pompeii, Spyder's Web, Love thy Neighbour, Empire Road, Jury, Rides, Lovejoy, Eastenders* and *Doctors*.

Smethurst, Jack
Appeared as himself in the *Man About the House* film.
    Born in Manchester on April 9th 1932, Smethurst trained at the London Academy of Music and Dramatic Art, before making a screen debut in *Carry On Sergeant* in 1958 and achieving fame playing the bigoted Eddie Booth in *Love Thy Neighbour* from 1972.
    Further credits include; *Last of the Summer Wine, The Dustbinmen, Cluff, The Plane Makers* and most recently, *Coronation Street* and *Casualty*. His latest work was in a 2007 episode of *Doctors*.

Smith, Keith
TV Repairman in *George and Mildred* episode 'My Husband Next Door'
    Born on February 24th 1926, Smith has been a familiar face on television since the early 1950's, predominantly working on comedy programmes. Smith has worked alongside comic legends; Eric Sykes, Spike Milligan, Marty Feldman and Peter Sellers.
    Other credits include; *The Rag Trade, Bernie, Q5, Z Cars, My Wife Next Door,*

The Army Game, Andy Capp and *Last of the Summer Wine*. Smith retired in 1999.

Staples, Lesley
Mrs Williams in *George and Mildred* episode 'Opportunity Knocks'
    Staples took her first recognised television credit in *George and Mildred*, before making appearances on *Into the Fire, The Liver Birds* and *Last of the Summer Wine*. In recent years, Lesley has appeared in *Calendar Girls, Royal Face Off* and *Phoenix Falling*.
    Staples still acts today, and most recently took work in the 2010 film *Tortoise in Love*.

Sutton, Dudley
Jacko in the *George and Mildred* Movie.
    Born on April 6th 1933, Sutton took his national service with the RAF before attending RADA and also a term at Joan Littlewood's Theatre Workshop with Brian Murphy and Yootha Joyce.
    Sutton appeared in scores of television productions over his career including; *Z Cars, The House, Moses, The Goodbye Plane* and *Killing Time*. Sutton still works today, most recently starring in *The Shouting Men* in 2009.

Swales, Robert
Peter in *Man About the House* episode 'I Won't Dance, Don't Ask Me'
    Beginning his career with the National Youth Theatre, in the 1967 production of *Romeo and Juliet* at the Adeline Genee Theatre in East Grinstead, Swales made the step into television, debuting in ITV's *Within These Walls* in 1974.
    Later credits include: *1990, Van Der Valk, The Fourth Arm, Crossbow* and *Birds of a Feather*. Swales' last job was in the 1997 television comedy *Does China Exist?*

T

Thorns, Tricia
Barmaid in *George and Mildred* episode 'The Twenty Six Year Itch'
    Debuting in *The Rivals of Sherlock Holmes* in 1971, Thorns has since starred in several comedies including; *Robins Nest, Keeping up Appearances* and *The Nineteenth Hole*.

Thompson, Jimmy
Bed Salesman in *George and Mildred* episode 'And so to Bed'
    Thompson was born in Halifax, Yorkshire on October 30th 1925.
    After taking early work in theatre, Thompson moved into television and film, with his first part coming in 1952 with a small role in *The Pickwick Papers*. Later credits included *London playhouse, Pinky and Perky* and *The Whole Truth*.

Complete A-Z of Support Cast

Following a final television role in 1978 with *Bernie,* Thompson returned to the theatre and eventually retired in 1991. He died on April 21st 2005 at his home in York.

Tickner, Royston
Doctor in *George and Mildred* episode 'In Sickness and In Health'
   Born in Leicester on September 8th 1922, Tickner trained at the Scarborough Repertory Theatre before service with the Royal Navy during the second world war. After completing his national service, Tickner took on several jobs including a lighthouse keeper, before making a return to acting, initially in theatrical productions.
   In 1960 he took his first television role in *Armchair Mystery Theatre*, later appearing in; *The Plane Makers, Gideon's Way, Theatre 625, Porridge* and *The Secret Army.* Later parts include *Just Good Friends*, and Royston's last role, *Hitler's SS: Portrait of Evil.* Tickner retired in 1985 and died on July 7th 1997.

Till, Jenny
Receptionist in *George and Mildred* episode 'My Husband Next Door.'
   Till made an early appearance as an uncredited female dancer in T*he Masque of the Red Death,* before furthering her career working on; *Help!, Freewheelers, Softly Softly, The Rough with the Smooth* and *The First Great Train Robbery.* Till took her last role in 1980 with *The Good Old Days.*

Townsend, Chet
Waiter in *Man About the House* episode 'Mum Always Liked You Best'
   Making his acting debut as the French waiter in this episode of *Man About the House,* Townsend's stay as an actor was short lived. He took his final recognised role in 1977's *Premier.*

U

No surnames beginning with this letter.

V

Van, Stan
Removal Man in *George and Mildred* episode 'The Bad Penny'
   Van debuted in *And Mother Makes Five,* before being cast in *George and Mildred,* his only other credited work. Van has, however, made several non-speaking appearances as an extra, most notably as the confused milkman in the *Man*

About the House episode 'Of Mice and Women'

W

Wade, Johnny
Porter in *George and Mildred* Film
Removal man in *George and Mildred* Episode 'The Bad Penny'

Wade debuted in *Crossroads* in 1964, before expanding on his career with appearances in; *Carry On Again Doctor, Bless This House, Porridge, The Two Ronnies, Miss Jones and Son* and *You're Only Young Twice.* Wade also appeared in the *George and Mildred* film.

Later work included; *Never the Twain* and *Terry and June.* Wade received his most recent credit in 2000 with *Sunburn,* and is still registered as an actor with Equity.

Walker, Rudolph
Appeared as himself in the *Man About the House* film.

Born on September 28th 1939 in Trinidad, Walker migrated to England at the age of twenty to follow a career in acting. He subsequently made a television debut in *The Wednesday Play* in 1965, before joining Jack Smethurst in the sitcom *Love Thy Neighbour.*

Most recently, Rudolph Walker has appeared as Patrick Truman in *Eastenders*, starring in over five hundred episodes from 2001, and at one stage reuniting with his *Love thy Neighbour* co-star Kate Williams. Previous appearances include; *Maybury, Rules of Engagement, A Perfect State, The Crouches* and *Hit for Six.*

Walker was awarded the O.B.E. in 2006 for his services to drama.

Walters, Hugh
Waiter in the *George and Mildred* Movie

Born in Mexborough, on March 2nd 1939, Walters attended Worksop College before debuting in *Catch Us If You Can* in 1965.

Later work includes; *Never Say Die, Here Come the Double Deckers, Jason King, The Fenn Street Gang, Z Cars* and *Doctor Who.* Walters still acts and his most recent television work came in an episode of *Sold* in 2007.

Ward, Michael
Mr Gideon in the *Man About the House* film.

Born in Cornwall on April 9th 1909, Ward trained at the Central School of Speech and Drama prior to making his screen debut, in the 1947 film *An Ideal Husband.* Career highlights run to; *The Benny Hill Show, Morecambe and Wise, Carry On Cleo, The Avengers, Rising Damp, Sykes* and *The Golden Shot.* Ward died on November 8th 1997, aged 88.

Complete A-Z of Support Cast

Ware, Joan
2nd Cleaning Lady in the *George and Mildred* Movie
Ware's only other recognised on-screen work came in the 1982 television series *Made in Britain*.

Waring, Derek
Edward Rogers in the *George and Mildred* episode 'The Travelling Man'
Born on April 26th 1927, Waring trained at RADA, choosing the dramatic academy over a place at Oxford's St Edmund Hall. Upon graduating, Derek worked in local repertory around his Surrey home, before taking early roles on television in the late 1950's, including *Call Back Yesterday* and *No Hiding Place*. He is best known for his work as Neil Goss in *Z Cars*.

Derek's brother, Richard Waring was a television writer and scripted several shows directed by Peter Frazer-Jones, including the popular *Miss Jones and Son*. It was through his brother that Derek became known by Frazer-Jones, and was subsequently cast in several of his shows including; *Robin's Nest, And Mother Makes Five* and *Never the Twain*. Waring later appeared in *Partners, Angels, Indian Summer* and *Law and Disorder*. Derek's last role was in the 1995 seaside special of *Keeping Up Appearances*, with his television retirement coming shortly afterwards.

Derek died on February 20th 2007 aged 79. He was survived by his two children, both of whom are also actors. Waring's wife, Dame Dorothy Tutin, died in August 2001.

It is partially thanks to the Waring family that television exists in the first place. Derek's father, Wing Commander H J Barton-Chapple, an electrical engineer, worked on the development of the concept of television with John Logie Baird. He used to use Derek's wooden toys to simulate a person in front of the camera!

Waterman, Dennis
Franz Wasserman in *Man About the House* episode 'Did you Ever Meet...'
Waterman was born on 24th February 1948, and made his first stage appearance at the age of thirteen in *The Music Man*. In 1962, he made his television debut playing the juvenile lead in *William*, based on the books by Richmal Crompton. Dennis trained as an actor at the Corona stage academy and was good friends with Richard O'Sullivan, which led to his casting in *Man About the House*.

Waterman's career received a dramatic boost when he took on the part of George Carter in the 1970's crime-busting series; *The Sweeney*. Other notable roles included *Scars of Dracula, Minder, On the Up, Stay Lucky, The Knock* and *The Sextet*.

Waters, Russell
Fred in *George and Mildred* episode 'Nappy Days'
Waters was born in Glasgow on June 10th 1908, and took his first role in the 1934 film *And So To Work*. Further parts in the late 1930's followed with; *Tell Me*

If It Hurts, Laugh With Me and *Wooing of Anne Hathaway*, before Waters was conscripted for military service during the second world war.

Russell continued to act on his return, making a comeback appearance in *The Woman in the Hall* and later; *Time Bomb, The Vise, The Avengers, The Borderers, Robin's Nest* and *And Mother Makes Five*. Waters made a final appearance in *Never The Twain* in 1981. He died the following year aged 74.

Watling, Pamela
Mrs Morecambe in *George and Mildred* episode 'Where My Caravan...'

Watling made a debut in *George and Mildred*, before progressing to; *Miss Jones and Son, Let There Be Love, Fresh Fields* and *Never the Twain,* all under direction of Peter Frazer-Jones.

Watson, Ken
Various characters in *Man About the House*
Various characters in *George and Mildred*

Kenneth Watson trained as an actor with RADA before making a debut in *The First Lady* in 1969. After parts in *Follyfoot, Whodunit* and *Funny Ha-Ha,* Watson appeared in *Man About the House*. Credited with three parts in different episodes, mainly playing a police officer, Kenneth also had a part in *George and Mildred.*

After a further role in *Headmaster* and one-off part in *The Professionals* in 1980, Watson took his last acting credit in *Wycliffe* in 1994. The development of Pancreatic Cancer forced him out of the profession and led to his death on July 21st 1998.

Watts, Quennie
Gladys in *George and Mildred* episode 'The Last Straw'

Born in London on July 21st 1926, Watts was another student gaining experience at Joan Littlewood's theatre school, leading to her first role in the 1963 film produced by the company, *Sparrows Can't Sing.*

Perhaps best remembered for her work opposite Arthur Mullard, in sitcoms; *Yus me Dear, Romany Jones* and also the film *Holiday On the Buses*, Watts took on mainly comedy roles over her career in the business. Queenie has appeared in *Steptoe and Son, Dad's Army, The Goodies,* as well as *Sykes*.

George and Mildred was her penultimate television role, as Queenie Watts died the next year on January 25th 1980, ironically at the same age and in the same year as her friend and frequent co-star, Yootha Joyce.

Wickes, Rosanne
Gwen in *George and Mildred* episode 'No Business Like Show Business'

Wickes' first credited work as an actress was in this episode of *George and Mildred*, and she later appeared in *Edward and Mrs Simpson, Keep it in the Family* and *Dick Turpin*. Wickes' most recent role was in 1980 on *Rings on Their Fin-*

Complete A-Z of Support Cast

gers. She also appeared on stage in the *George and Mildred* tour.

Williamson, Alister
Police Sergeant in *Man About the House* episode 'One for the Road'
Breakers Man in *George and Mildred* episode 'Where My Caravan Has...'
   Williamson was born in Sydney, Australia in 1918 and made his acting debut in *The Flying Doctor* in 1959. Since then he has made numerous film and television appearances, including; *Ghost Squad, No Hiding Place, The Beverly Hillbillies, Funny Man* and *Potter*. Williamson retired in 1986, making a final appearance in *That's My Boy* before his death on May 19th 1999.

Wood, Drew
Hell's Angel in *Man About the House* episode 'Home and Away'
   After an introduction in *Dr. Finlay's Casebook*, Wood later participated in; *Assassin, Hawkeye, Marked Personal* and *Doctor Who*. His final role came in 1976 with *I'm Not Felling Myself Tonight*.

Wynne, Michael
Mr Williams in *George and Mildred* episode 'Opportunity Knocks'
   Born in 1936, Wynne took early credits in *The Crime of the Century, Rag Doll* and *The Men From Room 13* in the late 1950's, prior to later works on *Z Cars, Secret Army, The Bill, Minder* and *After the War*.
   Wynne still works as an actor, with his most recent role falling in a 2007 episode of *Doc Martin*.

Woodrow, Leonard
Smith in *George and Mildred* episode 'Just the Job'
   Making a debut in 1965 with *ITV Play of the Week*, Woodrow later worked on; *Doctor at Sea, Confessions for a Holiday Camp, Spearhead, Accident* and *Killers*. His last work came with this episode of *George and Mildred*.
   Leonard now lives in retirement in Spain.

Y

No Surnames beginning with this letter.

Z

No Surnames beginning with this letter.

Going Places - Transportation Used...

Cars and other vehicles feature largely in *Man About the House* and *George and Mildred*. Whether to support a story line, whereby an excursion is written off due to a breakdown, be used as an over-sized prop, or simply to provide a target for Roy Kinnear to drop a piano on to. Of all the motors used in the series, here are a few notable examples, and details of exactly what happened to them after filming.

Austin 7
The vintage black Austin 7 seen in the opening titles of the third and fourth series of *Man About the House,* is a 1925 model, registration number EU2657.

This exact same car, first registered on August 15th 1925, was also used in a few episodes of *Dad's Army*, and it is now a fully restored vehicle, registered with the Austin Owners Club.

Robin's Motorbike
The bike that Robin rides in the opening titles of the first two *Man About the House* series is a Honda 50, a popular model in the early 1970's. The bike holds the registration number CLC 654. With no current records relating to this cycle, it is more than likely it has since been scrapped.

Larry's Beetle
Seen in the *Man About the House* film, Larry owns a yellow Volkswagen Beetle, registration TMK 675M. This car, first registered on March 7th 1974, still exists and remains a registered and fully taxed vehicle. It has a 1200CC petrol engine.

George's Morris 1000
In early episodes of *Man About the House*, George is driving a Morris 1000 with the registration number TOC 746. The Morris 1000 is a car that George is clearly keen on, as in later years a new vehicle appears with the registration JMB 630C. This second Morris was destroyed on-screen in the episode 'Right Said George', by having a piano dropped onto it by a crane hoist.

Another Morris car appears in the episode 'Home and Away', registration number 9480MP. None of these vehicles survived past the

Going Places - Transportation Used...

1980's, and all are have since been scrapped.

In *George and Mildred*, Roper has yet another Morris 1000, this time a 1964 Convertible, registration CMS 990. The car is used as several episodes as well as the film, but like its predecessors, no longer exists.

George's Motorbike Combination
George Roper's infamously unreliable motorcycle combination in *George and Mildred* was a Brough Superior 1150 model, registration ATO 574. This model was first produced by Brough in 1930.

The exact same bike used in *George and Mildred* had been previously used as Warden Hodge's bike in the *Dad's Army* episode, 'Battle of the Giants'. It is now in storage with the London Motorcycle Museum.

Kensington and Hampton Wick Good Pub Guide

A handy guide to the watering holes surrounding South Kensington and Hampton Wick, featuring all the fictional bars the area can boast. George will have a brown ale, Mildred's is a Gin and Tonic, and Robin and the girls are skint, so better stick with a half...

Pub: The Mucky Duck
Landlord: Jim
Location: South Kensington

Just around the corner from Myddleton Terrace, The Mucky Duck is smoky saloon with a friendly Jim behind the bar, who is always happy to stick a pint on the slate, or recommend a dead-cert at Exeter. Cheese and Lettuce sandwiches are a speciality.

Pub: The White Swan
Landlord: Percival 'Jock' Strap
Location: South Kensington

In 1975, The 'Mucky Duck' clearly must have had a wash, as it suddenly becomes a white swan. The pub has apparently been taken over by Percy Strap and renamed as 'The White Swan'. Not a lot of changes come with the transferal between landlords, the price of half a pint is still a mere 15p, but watch out for an over-keen barman who may ruin your architectural sketches when he wipes the table!

Pub: The Feathers
Landlord: Unknown
Location: South Kensington

Heard, but never seen, the Feathers is another South Kensington pub learnt of in *Man About the House*. It is first heard when the big bruiser mentions the tavern in the episode 'Colour Me Yellow'. He tries to rat-

Kensington and Hampton Wick Good Pub Guide

tle Jim at the Mucky Duck by explaining how he nearly destroyed The Feathers. 'It was due for refurbishment' he scoffs, 'I just started it for him!'.

Pub: The Anchor
Landlord: Unknown
Location: South Kensington

Mentioned only once by Chrissy when she looks at Robin's underpants, which feature pub signs. She sees the Anchor and remarks how 'they do nice cheese sandwiches in there!'.

Pub: The Gay Gordon
Landlord: Unknown
Location: Hampton Wick

Mentioned only once in *George and Mildred*, 'The Gay Gordon' is a local tavern in Hampton Wick. Mildred telephones the establishment to speak to George and explain that his father has gone missing in the episode 'Life With Father'.

Pub: The British Legion
Landlord: Various
Location: Branches in both South Kensington and Hampton Wick

George's watering hole in both *Man About the House* and *George and Mildred.* He often attends to play darts, on one occasion even taking baby Tarquin along for the evening, and is spurred into making his own beer when the price of a pint at the legion gets increased by a penny. The Hampton branch has the friendly Ada behind the bar.

Pub: The Ship and Shovel
Landlord: Sid
Location: Hampton Wick

George and Gloria Rumbold's old stamping ground, where they used to meet up before a night out. The perfect setting for a romantic blind date, but watch out for the wilted tulips abandoned in the empty glasses of disenchanted patrons!

Pub: The Genevieve
Landlord: Peter
Barman: Sid
Location: Hampton Wick

The 'toffee-nosed' pub with Gin and Tonic on draught. Mildred and George go for lunch here and bump into Jeffrey Fourmile in the episode 'Best Foot Forward'

Pub: The Pig and Wellie
Landlord: --
Location: Hampton Wick

George doesn't like The Genevieve. He bemoans the fact that he would rather be frequenting the Pig and Wellie!

Robin's Nest

Summary

Robin's Nest was the second spin-off from *Man about the House,* in which Richard O'Sullivan continued his character of Robin Tripp joined by Tessa Wyatt and Tony Britton. Irish actor David Kelly starred as the one-armed kitchen porter, Albert Riddle.

Robin's Nest followed the plot line of Robin living with girlfriend Vicky above a Chinese takeaway in Fulham. They learn that the landlords have done a runner with unpaid bills, leaving the building in a dangerous state of possible repossession. To keep their home, they decide to take over the business downstairs - using Robin's culinary skills to turn it into a bistro restaurant. In order to gain funds to take the venture on, Robin takes on Vicky's father as business partner - resulting in an invitation for numerous comical capers with the mismatched duo.

Food was the main focus of the sitcom, with the chef from the Thames Television Canteen being given the responsibility of cooking the meals for the restaurant scenes. Issued with the menus a week in advance, he was able to prepare and dish up everything up fresh during the recording. This meant that *Robin's Nest* was a very popular choice for production crew to work on, as at the end of the day, they could enjoy the left-overs!

Main star Richard O'Sullivan was responsible for writing the title theme music, devising the early-techno piece with Brian Bennett arranging and performing it.

Whereas the majority of episodes were written by the original scribe duo Brian Cooke and Johnnie Mortimer, several programmes in latter series were penned by guest writers, when Johnnie and Brian set off to Hollywood to assist with the American version's of their shows. George Layton, of *Doctor in the House* fame, scripted thirteen episodes, with several other writers including Adele Rose and David Norton also given the task of penning various programmes.

As with *Man About the House,* some viewers objected to the way *Robin's Nest* contained references to casual out-of-marriage sex, and the show was transmitted amidst ripples of controversy. 'John and Brian needed to get advance permission from higher authority to air some scenes', explained Johnnie Mortimer's widow, Jytte. 'They needed clearance from the IBA to show scenes with Richard and Tessa in bed together, it was quite a ground-breaking show'. Despite this, *Robin's Nest* had strong viewing figures, with 14 Million individuals tuning in to watch in February 1977.

In recent years, *Robin's Nest* appears to have lessened in popularity. Unlike it's sitcom siblings, the second *Man About the House* spin-off has ranked consistently low in audited polls, and in comparison to the DVD sales of it's counterparts. Whereas the plots and acting maintains a highly enjoyable comedy, it appears that Johnnie Mortimer and Brian Cooke's absence from writing several episodes may have had an impact on the consistency in story-lines, and the overall popularity of *Robin's Nest*.

Robin's Nest Episode List:

Series 1: Sleeping Partners, The Bistro Kids, A Little Competition, The Maternal Triangle, Piggy In the Middle, A Matter of Note, Oh Happy Day

Series 2: As Long as He Needs Me, The Seven Pound Fiddle, Ups and Downs, Three Times Table, Great Expectations, Love & Marriage

Series 3: You Need Hands, The Candidate, Just Desserts, Away From All What?, England Expects, Once Two Is Three, Dinner Date, Everything You Wish Yourself, Be It Ever So Humble, Day Trippers, The Long Distance Runner, At Harm's Length, The Happy Hen

Series 4: Should Auld Acquaintance, Person Friday Required, Lost Weekend, Too Many Waiters Spoil The Bistro, September Song, Sorry Partner, Albert's Ball, Christmas at Robin's Nest

Series 5: Pastures New, A Man Of Property, If You Pass 'Go' Collect £200, Never Look a Gift Horse..., Just An Old-Fashioned Girl, Great Expectations, No Room at the Inn

Series 6: Move Over Darling, The Homecoming, No Smoke Without Fire, When Irish Eyes Are Smiling, Anniversary Waltz, Wish You Weren't Here, The Head-hunters of SW6

Transatlantic Tributes - Sitcoms Overseas

The brilliant British sitcoms produced in the 'Golden Age' of television, were so good that the writing could be translated into any language, and still achieve a large guffaw. This is truly evident by looking at the number of foreign versions of *Man About the House, George and Mildred* and *Robin's Nest* that were produced overseas.

The first show to be rejuvenated was *Man About the House,* which was remade by the Americans in 1977 and turned into a hugely successful series entitled *Three's Company,* which ran to an astonishing 172 episodes over eight seasons until it's end in 1984. The first episode of *Three's Company* aired on 15th March 1977 on ABC, and starred seasoned Hollywood actor, John Ritter in the part of Jack Tripper. Flatmates Janet Wood (Joyce DeWitt) and Chrissy Snow (Suzanne Somers) completed the trio, with Stanley and Helen Roper as their landlords (played by Norman Fell and Audra Lindley).

Television distributor Don Taffner saw the potential for an American remake of *Man About the House*, and with the assistance of Ted Bergman, pitched to all the major US broadcasters; ABC, NBC and PBS. At first, it seemed that the idea was far too risqué for America, and all stations initially refused, until Fred Silverman at ABC had a change of heart and allowed a pilot to be made. It cost $500,000 to make a single pilot for the sitcom, and ABC decided to make three of them, just to make sure they got it exactly the way they wanted. Out of the 250 actresses who auditioned to play the girls, the producers decided to trial several of them in the part, before settling on Joyce DeWitt and Suzanne Somers.

6 Myddleton Terrace transmogrified into Apartment 201, Santa Monica, California, and the classic British wit was copied practically verbatim in places. Scores of writers penned episodes over the run of the show, most just using the sole basis of Brian Cooke and Johnnie Mortimer's writing with gentle adaptation, a formula which led to Thames television being prized with the Queen's award for export. George Burditt and Martin Rips were responsible for the majority of the additional writing, and the show was usually directed by Dave Powers.

Man About the House was also reworked in several European countries. The Netherlands came up with *Sam Sam* in 1994, Sweden thought up *En Fyra For Tre* in 1996, Norway decided on *Tre pa toppen* in 1997 and Poland invented *Lokatorzy* in 2000.

George and Mildred has also found itself gaining laughs in a different guise. In 1979, American channel ABC made a spin-off from their version of *Man About the House* and called it *The Ropers*. It starred the ever popular Norman Fell and Audra Lindley back as Stan and Helen Roper, this new show seeing them move to 46, Peacock Drive in the Cheviot Hills. The setting and plot followed social-climbing Helen trying to fit in with her new surroundings, again, a formula lifted straight from the British version.

To complete the ensemble, *Robin's Nest* was also remade in America in 1984, entitled *Three's A Crowd*, spinning off from *Three's Company*. John Ritter was back as Jack Tripper, joined by Mary Cadorette who simulated his partner, Vicky Bradford.

Overlooking the mass remodelling that was amok on ABC at the time, it's congratulatory to the popularity of the British sitcom, that it's fame stretches thousands of miles away. The irreplaceable English tea-drinking wit creating laughter on the other side of the world surely is testament, that British is best.

In recent times, the original British versions of *Man About the House* and *George and Mildred* have been broadcast in Europe. Badly dubbed into the native language, *Man About the House* became; *'Ein Mann im Haus'* (Austria), *'Man over de vloer'* (Holland), *'Um hombre en casa'* (Spain) and *'Un uomo in casa'* (Italy).

George and Mildred enjoyed an airing in Italy and a popular run in Spain, turning it in to *Los Ropers*, and quite a cult series. It was first aired between 1979 and 1981, originally airing only the first four series. The fifth series was aired from February 1981 onwards, replacing the Spanish runs of *Fawlty Towers*.

Man About the House has also aired in Spain and has become increasingly successful. As with *George and Mildred*, the original British recordings had to be over-dubbed in a new language. Madrid born actor Luis Varela dubbed Richard O'Sullivan with Maipa Castro providing the voice of Paula Wilcox. Marisa Marco dubbed Sally Thomsett, with Rafael de Penagos as Brian Murphy, and Maria Romero as Yootha Joyce. Doug Fisher and Norman Eshley's appearances also got dubbed, and the responsible voice artists for their characters were Jose Moratalla and Manolo Garcia.

Thinking About Sitcoms

There was something about the situation comedies of the 60's, 70's and 80's. Something very unique and difficult to narrow down to a single reason. This period in time saw the birth of dozens of the very best comedies ever seen on British Television, making fun out of virtually every occupation; minister, bus driver, hotel manager, shop assistant; and driving millions of people to hysterics every week.

A few decades later and the sterling comedies have all but fizzled out. Television has been through major changes to suit the ever altering wants of its audiences. The average viewer these days is subjected to comedy riddled with excessive amounts of swearing. Is it all really necessary?

Brian Murphy doesn't think so. 'What I don't like about comedy today is the swearing' he explains. 'They call it hard-edge but I cant see how that comes to be'.

'If you call it hard edge, and it's funny that way, that is a total insult to my idols; Morecambe and Wise, Les Dawson, Tommy Cooper and so on. They didn't have to swear. They may have had their moments in private, I know Bob Monkhouse and Max Millar did some 'blue gigs' for nightclubs and stag parties, but generally speaking to a family audience which television was made to, there was no need to swear, they were funny people.'

'You felt warm in the company of these people' Brian continued. 'When they came on, you smiled. Comedy today misses that. There are too many inexperienced people in charge of the business today. It used to be called show-business, now it's just business. They are all qualified on paper, coming from university and college, but they lack the experience. You have to learn in order to gain experience. You don't pour on hot water overnight and suddenly become an experienced person. Comedy misses that today and it's a great shame'.

Actor Robert Gillespie concurs. 'That who era was amazing for television, they were turning out really classy stuff' he explained. 'These days, there is a lot of unfunny comedy on the radio and television. We have a lot of university students producing material which is just 'sub-sub-goonery', the sitcoms I worked on were universal, it reached out to everybody then, but not anymore'.

What does comedienne Bella Emberg think of sitcoms today?

'I don't', Bella said bluntly. 'There is no comedy on television these days, not like the great old shows we used to have back in the day. They call Benny Hill sexist. Rubbish. Most of the times in his shows, the girls were chasing him, rather than him chasing after them. It's total unfounded rubbish. I just wish we could see some of these classic shows back on television, but it doesn't look like that will happen any time soon'.

It does feel that the magic spark of brilliance is missing from our television screens today. When the causes for this are analysed, the most prominent reason stands out to be that we have socially progressed, and the things we could once lightheartedly laugh at about each other are now frowned upon and deemed politically incorrect. If a modern day Mr. Lucas was trying to grab hold of his co-worker's knockers, he would be arrested for sexual harassment.

The saying that 'It wouldn't be allowed today' never seemed more prominent.

Test Your Knowledge - A Quiz for the Bog...

Whether you were already a hardy fan of *Man About the House* and *George and Mildred,* or have learnt about it from this book, here is a fun brainteaser to while some time away in the smallest room... or as George Roper would say... 'A quiz for the bog!'

So have a go and see how much you know.
No prizes - just self satisfaction!

1. Norman Eshley played which relation of Robin in *Man About the House,* prior to playing Jeffrey Fourmile in *George and Mildred*?

2. Richard O'Sullivan was cast as Robin Tripp based on his memorable performance in which 1972 series written by Johnnie Mortimer and Brian Cooke?

3. Which *Man About the House* support actor was married to Paula Wilcox?

4. Which car does George drive in the *George and Mildred* Film?

5. What is the name of the nursing home George's father stays at in the *George and Mildred* episode 'Life with Father'?

6. How many full-length episodes of *Man About the House* were made?

7. What Short-lived Driving Instructor series starred Brian Murphy?

8. Where was Peacock Crescent really located?

9. What was the American *George and Mildred* spin-off called?

10. What name is written inside Chrissy's shoe when she loses it getting on the bus in the first series opening titles?

11. Who played Muriel in the *Man About the House* episode 'Fire Down Below'?

12. What charity did Yootha Joyce actively support?

13. Who ran the Theatre Workshop at Stratford East?

14. What month was the final *Man About the House* episode transmitted in?

15. Which *Minder* actor was married to Yootha Joyce?

16. In the *Man About the House* episode 'How Does Your Garden Grow', what was Mildred's flower arrangement called?

17. What is the local newspaper called in *Man About the House*?

18. What is Mildred's star sign?

19. What is the Roper's telephone number in *George and Mildred*?

20. How much money is George stated to have in his life savings?

21. What did George's father do to make money during the war?

22. What is Jerry's cousin called?

23. In the opening titles of series four of *Man About the House*, what time is displayed on the Big Ben clock?

24. In the *Man About the House* film, what telephone number is displayed on the Spiros advertising boards?

25. What hairdressers did Sally Thomsett go to have her hair lightened?

26. What was the American version of *Robin's Nest* called?

27. What film did Richard O'Sullivan appear in as Robin Stephens?

28. Who occupied the attic room of the Roper's house in *Man About the House*?

Test Your Knowledge... A Quiz for the Bog!

29. What was George's goldfish called?

30. What is Chrissy's sister's name?

Answers:
1. Robin's Brother
2. Alcock and Gander
3. Derek Seaton
4. Morris 1000 Convertible
5. Twilights Nursing Home
6. 39
7. L for Lester
8. Manor Road, Teddington
9. The Ropers
10. Sacha
11. Cecily Hobbs
12. The Canine Defence League
13. Joan Littlewood
14. April
15. Glynn Edwards
16. Poem of the Hedgerow
17. Kensington Herald
18. Virgo
19. Hampton 171 2325
20. £10.76
21. Forge clothing coupons
22. Kevin
23. The time is 3:56
24. 01953 1600
25. Daniel Galvin
26. Three's A Crowd
27. Carry On Teacher
28. Larry
29. Moby
30. Susan

1970's Phrase Dictionary

The English language evolves constantly, rendering many phrases from the last forty years positively antique. Should you be watching an episode of *Man About the House* or *George and Mildred* and hearken upon an unfamiliar term - have a look in this handy 1970's phrase dictionary!

Mike Yarwood - (Noun) - A popular impressionist entertainer. Mike had his own series on both BBC and ITV over the late 1970's and early 1980's, and is known best for his impersonations of Harold Wilson, Ken Dodd and Frankie Howerd. Referenced several times in *George and Mildred* in relation to the quality of George's impressions.

Gannex - (Noun) - A company that produced raincoats, worn famously by former prime minister Harold Wilson. The Gannex Mill still stands in Elland, Yorkshire but ceased making raincoats in the late 1980's. Gannex is referenced several times in *George and Mildred* in relation to Margaret Thatcher's 'lack of Gannex'.

Permissive Society - (Adj) - Phrase used to describe freedom of activity and behaviour in ways that may be deemed unacceptable by others. Used particularly in reference to sexual relationships, and often mentioned to describe Robin's activities.

Platonic - (Adj) - Term used to describe a relationship or friendship that, contrary to portrayal or obvious depiction, does not involve sexual engagement. Used a few times in *Man About the House,* once by Mildred to describe her relationship to George!

Strewth/Struth - (Interj) - An exclamation of shock and disbelief. A word derived from Australian slang but worked into British culture. 'Strewth' is used frequently by George Roper in both *Man About the House* and *George and Mildred* to express his irritation and surprise.

Avocado Suite - (Noun) - A delightfully decorative suite of matching bathroom fittings; Toilet, Sink, Bath and sometimes Bidet, all in a foul Avocado colour. The height of fashion in the 1970's, they were very

1970's Phrase Dictionary

common in newly redecorated houses and could be seen in the Roper's and Fourmile's houses in Peacock Crescent.

Bob - (Noun) - Slang for a British shilling, a former subunit of pre-decimal currency. The shilling vanished in 1971, but was still referenced for a long time afterwards.

Digs - (Noun) - Virtually defunct slang for a lodging or somewhere to stay. Common with students, a 'dig' tended to be a room in somebody's house that was let out.

Percy Thrower - (Noun) - A well known gardener and horticulturist.

Bog - (Noun) - Informal slang for a toilet.

Brothel Creepers - (Noun) - Men's suede shoes with thick rubber soles, popular around the time of the 1950's, so named because they were quiet to walk in. Reminisced by George when he recalls his relationship with Gloria Rumbold.

Knockers - (Noun) - Slang for a woman's breasts. Used frequently in practically every period sitcom, usually by randy blokes and Chauvinist Pigs.

Chauvinist Pigs - (Noun) - Insult coined in the 1960's to refer to men who believe they have superiority over women, or hold prejudice beliefs against the opposite sex. Used a couple of times by Chrissy to describe Robin.

Egon Ronay - (Noun) - A well-known food critic.

Gordon Honeycombe - (Noun) - Popular ITN newsreader throughout the 1970's.

Pong - (Noun) - One of the first ever video games, Pong or 'telly tennis' was an American invention that involved a small box being plugged into a television set's aerial socket, converting the picture to a basic interactive game of Ping Pong. Two handheld controls are used to move paddles up and down each side of the screen, and hit balls back to the opponent. George and Jeffrey play a game in the *George and Mildred* episode, 'The Second Day of Christmas'

Common Market - (Noun) - The original basis of what later became the European Union.

Clunk Click - (Noun) - Jimmy Saville's catchphrase from a long-running road safety commercial of the 1970's, encouraging the use of seatbelts more in car travel. The phrase 'clunk click' referred to the clunking of the door closing, and the clicking of the seatbelt in to the lock. Clunk click every trip!

Amy Turtle - (Noun) - Character in British Soap *Crossroads* played by Ann George intermittently between 1965 and 1988. Turtle was the local gossip who worked as a cleaner at the Crossroads Motel.

Sherry - (Noun) - Still a fairly popular aperitif these days, but drunk abundantly in the 1970's when the middle classes served it like water. Sherry is a fortified Mediterranean wine, it's made more potent with the addition of Brandy. It ranges in sweetness and aridity.

Green Shield Stamps - (Noun) - Issued by several stores and petrol stations as part of a customer loyalty scheme, Green Stamps were then redeemable against many household goods in the Green Shield Gift Catalogue.

Acknowledgments

Firstly, I'd like to thank Brian Cooke for being kind enough to give his blessings to this project, and Johnnie Mortimer's widow, Jytte, and son, Roger, for assisting so much in the biographies and working credits of these iconic scribes. I also have Jytte to thank for the majority of the images in this book, many of which haven't been printed before. Thanks also to Gordon Dickerson for putting me in touch in the first place.

My gratitude is never-ending towards Brian Murphy, the big cheese, George Roper himself, the very epitome of both these classic sitcoms, for offering his very valuable time. Thanks also to Paula Wilcox and Sally Thomsett, for taking time out to answer some questions for me.

Thanks also to: Robert Gillespie, Nicholas Owen, Frankie Jordan, Kay Russell, Hal Dyer, Jackie Mitchell, Jane Christie, John Colclough, Mike Savage, Veronica Doran, Bella Emberg, David Neville, Jeremy Bulloch, David Barry, George Layton, Carmel Kinnear, Paul Meier, Audrey Nicholson, John Lyons, Simon Lloyd, Sally Harrison, Wendy Allnutt, Jean Rogers, and everybody else who has assisted with their memories and thoughts.

As well as the theatrical agents of all those people listed above, for passing on my emails, letters, and telephone calls. My thanks also to former Thames directors, Anthony Parker and Stuart Allen, for the confirmed information on Peter Frazer-Jones.

Thanks to the BFI database for being a useful source of information relating to artist's television credits. Further thanks can be extended to the National Media Museum and Bradford Central Library, for allowing my sticky fingers to rummage through their extensive collection of TV Times magazines.

I'd like to pass on a 'Ta very much' to the gang at Deck Chair Press for seeing the merit in this book. Thanks to James Barratt for his help, and thanks to Geoff and Darren who were a great assistance.

Finally, I am grateful for the assistance and motivation provided by the fans of these classic shows, without whom this book would not be worthy of publication. Extended thanks to Phil, Mark and Elaine, and the rest of the gang at the Yahoo! M.A.T.H. fan group for their support.

Additional thanks to ITV3 for putting these series back on the telly in decent slots for new fans to enjoy.

Mildred...

Do you fancy an early night?